Conquest

Massimo Livi Bacci

Conquest

The Destruction of the American Indios

Translated by Carl Ipsen

polity

This translation copyright © Polity Press 2008. First published in Italian as *Conquista* by Massimo Livi Bacci, Società editrice il Mulino, Bologna, © 2005

Polity Press
65 Bridge Street
Cambridge CB2 1UR, UK

Polity Press
350 Main Street
Malden, MA 02148, USA

ISBN-10: 0-7456-4000-1
ISBN-13: 978-07456-4000-6
ISBN-10: 0-7456-4001-X (pb)
ISBN-13: 978-07456-4001-3 (pb)

A catalogue record for this book is available from the British Library.

Typeset in 11 on 12 pt Simoncini Garamond
by Servis Filmsetting Ltd, Manchester
Printed and bound in India by Replika Press PVT Ltd, Kundli

For further information on Polity, visit our website: *www.polity.co.uk*

The translation of this work has been funded by SEPS
SEGRETARIATO EUROPEO PER LE PUBBLICAZIONI SCIENTIFICHE

Via Val d'Aposa 7 - 40123 Bologna - Italy
seps@alma.unibo.it - www.seps.it

With the support of the Italian Ministry of Foreign Affairs

Contents

CAMINA EL AVTOR

This book derives from an interest dating back to my youth combined with an effort undertaken somewhat later in life. That early interest focused on the extraordinary history of the New World. It was an interest subsequently fueled by frequent travel, trips, and visits, never long enough to be entirely satisfying but which served nonetheless to keep the interest alive. The later effort instead came in 1998, when a sabbatical leave allowed me a year of residence and research in that New World: in North America as a guest of the Chair of Italian Studies at the University of California at Berkeley, in Cuba, and in Brazil at the Universidade Federal de Minas Gerais in Belo Horizonte and at Unicamp in the city of Campinas. I have enjoyed many discussions and exchanges with colleagues at these three generous institutions, discussions which have both confirmed and contradicted my various working hypotheses as well as opening new paths of research.

Traditional quantitative methods are of little help in seeking out the causes and mechanisms of the demographic catastrophe of the Indios (used here to refer generally to the indigenous peoples of what became Latin America). There is little in the way of numeric data and what there is is often unreliable and always incomplete. Those data allow for the construction of hypotheses and interpretations, but not, alas, firm conclusions. The role of the demographer, then, in the analysis of the American catastrophe would seem to be limited by a scarcity of sources. Fortunately, though, the broader surviving documentation is rich and complex. Conquistadors and soldiers, clerics and lawyers, government officials and merchants wrote memoirs and reports, issued verdicts and sentences, and carried out investigations. The religious, juridical, and philosophical debates over the nature of the New World and its inhabitants informed these documents left by Europeans. Meanwhile the native populations themselves have left important testimony and other eloquent traces regarding the tragedy. Centuries of historical research have informed our understanding of the catastrophe, building, modifying, and destroying various theories and paradigms over time. This book, then, represents a sounding in that large sea in search of facts and other evidence useful for the construction of a demographic interpretation of the catastrophe. The *Leyenda Negra* of the Conquest, dating from the first decades of the sixteenth century, was fed by eyewitness testimony of the cruel and merciless subjugation carried out by Europeans; it would later be used to attack both Spain and the Catholic Church. It was an interpretation of the Conquest that contributed to the ethical and political debate, but not one that helps us sort out the relative weight of the various factors that brought about the disastrous decline of the native population over the course of the sixteenth century. On the other hand, recent epidemiological revisionism, which identifies European diseases as the exclusive cause of the demographic decline, minimizes and denies the economic, social, and so demographic disruption inflicted on the American population by the Conquest. It is an interpretation that overlooks the fact that there was no single actor in the American tragedy, but instead a large cast that mediated the encounters between the conquerors and the conquered.

The catastrophe was not inevitable. It was not the necessary consequence of contact between the Europeans and the Indios, but rather the outcome of a series of factors that included the methods of the Conquest and the nature of the subjugated populations. In some areas it led to total extinction, in others to a long and sustained decline, and in still others to an initial shock followed by rapid recovery.

In the world of scholarship, the exchange of ideas and the advice of friends and colleagues are an important asset. I would like in particular to thank Nicolás Sánchez-Albornoz, Carlos Sempat Assadourian, Francesco Barbarani, Carlo A. Corsini, Ernesto J. A. Maeder, Luciano Matrone, Letizia Mencarini, Floriano Papi, Cecilia Rabell Romero, David Reher, and Stefano Turillazzi, who have read parts of the manuscript, offered advice, and helped me obtain needed material. Special thanks go to Maria del Carmen Diez Hoyo, who directs the excellent Biblioteca Hispánica in Madrid, and who with generosity and friendship has helped me to avoid getting lost in the labyrinth of Hispano-American literature.

1 In which are described three voyages that changed the face of a continent, the American population at the time of contact, the demographic catastrophe of the Indios, the sorrowful increase of the Africans, and the expansion of the Europeans

Three voyages lie at the heart of the complex population history of the American continent in the modern era. The first, the oldest one, was undertaken 15,000 or 20,000 years ago by a Siberian hunter who crossed the frozen Bering strait with a few companions and set foot in Alaska, initiating a slow migration that over the next 1,000 or 2,000 years led to the settlement, albeit sparsely, of the entire continent all the way down to Patagonia. That voyage stretched 20,000 kilometers and progressed at the fair pace of 10 or more kilometers per year in unknown and not always welcoming lands.[1] The 30 or 40 million people who we believe inhabited the Americas 500 years ago descended from these first migrants and those who followed them in successive waves. We know very little about this migration beyond what archeologists and paleontologists have been able to reconstruct and hypothesize on the basis of slowly and painstakingly gathered bits of evidence.

The second voyage was that of a certain sea captain from Genoa. Of average height and about forty years old, he was a great sailor, courageous, dogged in the pursuit of his goals, and favored by excellent political and religious connections. About his voyage – it was not the first European voyage to the Americas – we know practically everything. It was a quick crossing. Christopher Columbus with his three ships and crew of ninety set sail with a favorable tide from Palos at the crack of dawn on August 3, 1492.[2] The crossing of the Atlantic began, after a long stop at the Canary Islands, on the morning of September 6 at La Gomera and ended with the sighting of the island of Guanahaní (later renamed San Salvador) at 2 in the morning on October 12, thirty-six days later.[3] It was Columbus's voyage of course that initiated permanent and continual "contact" between the two shores of the Atlantic. It was a dynamic sort of contact, a process insofar as the frontier of European exploration and settlement, while moving rapidly, took decades to reach the majority of the native populations and one or two centuries to reach the most isolated ones.

The third voyage was that of an unknown person, presumably a man. We do not know if he was a sailor or a simple deck hand, a passenger or a royal official. We do know that he disembarked at Santo Domingo in Hispaniola and had one important trait: he was infected with smallpox, and from him that disease spread throughout the island. Two Hieronymite friars, Luis de Figueroa and Alonso de Santo Domingo, who were then administering the island, wrote to King Ferdinand on January 10, 1519, that in December alone smallpox had claimed the lives of "one third of the Indios, and they continue to die."[4] It was the first serious epidemic in the New World, one that would spread throughout the Caribbean, and then to the mainland in Mexico and Guatemala and, according to some, still farther south. That individual symbolized and set the stage for the arrival in the Americas of other infectious diseases brought by other anonymous carriers, diseases that were previously unknown there – measles, scarlet fever, diphtheria – and that were highly destructive because the Indios lacked the relative immunity which the Europeans instead possessed.

The first voyage laid down the demographic basis of the continent's population at the beginning of the modern era; the second initiated permanent contact with Europe and the establishment of long-term domination; the third added new and formerly non-existent weapons to the disease arsenal of the New World. Contemporary accounts of the Conquest and the process of contact describe the rapid decline of the native populations and offer complex interpretations. For the most part, they emphasize political, economic, and social causes (exploitation, violence, uprooting, expropriation) over natural ones (disease and epidemic). Modern scholars instead have dramatically re-evaluated the role of the new diseases and in the most extreme cases have attributed to them sole responsibility for the demographic catastrophe.

This book explores the demography of indigenous America and its catastrophe. The first chapter attempts a synthesis of the numeric data, an evaluation of the human resources which the voyage of

Columbus put at risk. It is a technical argument, though one with many ideological and historic implications. Simplifying, we can say that the estimates of the so-called low counters from the first half of the twentieth century have been replaced by those of "high counters" in the second half.[5] The differences between the two schools are fairly limited for the late sixteenth century, when censuses (generally for the purpose of taxation) and other documentary sources narrow the margins of error and imagination. Neither do the two schools differ over the fact that the population of the continent suffered a precipitous decline, though there are profound disagreements about the causes. The larger differences instead regard the scale of that decline between an unknown initial population size at the time of contact (1492 in the Caribbean and the following decades on the mainland) and a fairly well-known aftermath (from about 1570). The differences exceed an order of magnitude: from less than 10 million to over 100 million.[6] The technical details of the estimates, themselves the object of intense debate, are beyond our scope. A general observation will suffice. The estimates of the high counters suggest a more catastrophic decline: starting from a year B, when the population can be estimated with a degree of certainty, we work backward to a year A, the moment of contact several decades earlier. The more rapid the decline (and so the more disastrous the tragedy) the greater the estimate of the population in year A. In order to explain such a rapid decline, one that can be attributed neither to the swords of a few conquistadors nor to social and economic factors that act more slowly, the high counters favor the epidemiological explanation as the primary one and so tend to discount other potential factors that may have disrupted the indigenous demographic system and so contributed to the population decline. Only disease could adequately explain the decimation of the native population between contact and a century or so later; indeed, the most extreme estimates suggest that the population declined to a mere one-twentieth of its pre-Columbian size by the end of the sixteenth century.

Modern estimates of the size of the American population at the moment of contact (see table 1) vary from a maximum of 112 million to a minimum of 8 million (a ratio of 13 : 1). The last systematic revision was carried out by William Denevan in 1992 and came up with the figure of 54 million, a bit lower than his earlier estimates from 1976 in the heyday of the high counter era.[7] In light of new information and estimates (for the Caribbean and North America), there are good reasons to consider plausible a still smaller population, perhaps around 30 million, and so equal to about one-third of the population of Europe at the time. Only by about 1800, then, did the population of the Americas return to those levels of three centuries before, though by then it was a population augmented by an influx of Africans and Europeans. But we are getting ahead of ourselves. At the moment of contact the human resources of the American continent were considerable. Two-thirds of the population were concentrated in Meso-America and the Andean region; other regions were more sparsely settled, and the most remote ones were inhabited by nomadic groups.

There is certainly an important difference between those who believe that the American population was reduced to a tenth of its original size between 1500 an 1650 and others for whom the final size was closer to one-half or one-third, though in either case the decline was catastrophic. Similarly, the impact of the bubonic plague in Europe was catastrophic even if it killed "only" one-third of the population between 1348 and the first decades of the following century, when the epidemic waves that washed over the continent ebbed and became less frequent. Figure 1 helps us to get an idea of the evolution of population in the Americas over the centuries following contact by comparing the relative weight of native Americans (100 percent at the time of contact), Europeans, Africans, and mixed-race groups between 1500 and 1950. The total population, in rapid decline throughout the sixteenth century, only returns to its original level by around 1800, but by that time native Americans no longer formed the majority. As a result of immigration, white Europeans instead represented about a quarter of the population and black Africans, brought across the Atlantic in chains, about one-fifth. The remainder were racial blends of various sorts. We need to keep in mind, though, that these distinctions were more social than biological or demographic. Those described as "white" in the censuses and other documents included many who counted an Indio or black ancestor. Similarly there were many mixed-race people counted as "Indio" or "black." Law, custom, and census practices, on top of genetics and demography, determined the assignment of individuals to each of these groups.

Just the same, the general trends lead to several conclusions. Alongside the catastrophe of the Indios stands that of the black Africans. Although brought over in their millions from Africa, they constituted a relatively small percentage in 1800. Undeniable instead is the "success" of the Whites who, though deriving from modest immigration flows, numbered about 8 million in 1800.

These general observations are worth pursuing a little further, as differential demographic development is an important indicator of the impact of contact between groups that had different biological characteristics, organizational capacities, technological knowledge, and resources. The American encounter was highly asymmetric for the actors involved, and that asymmetry contributed to the demographic outcome. The famous fourth chapter of Darwin's *The Origin of Species* bears the title "Natural Selection; or The Survival of the Fittest." Given biological variations favorable to humans, "can we doubt (remembering that many more individuals are born than can possibly survive) that individuals having any advantage, however slight, over others, would have the best chance of surviving and procreating their kind?"[8] We will not fall into a crude Social Darwinism if we extend this observation regarding individuals to groups that come into contact for the first time, groups that as a result of that contact find themselves with widely differing outlooks relative to survival and reproduction. The contact first between Europeans and Indios and later between Europeans and Africans strongly influenced the ability of each group to survive and reproduce, and so altered their rates of growth and relative sizes. The Europeans generally found favorable conditions: good climate, especially in the temperate zones, abundant land and food, and low levels of epidemic disease owing in part to low population density. For the Indios instead the conditions for survival and reproduction worsened dramatically, especially in the first two centuries following contact. They encountered new diseases, suffered major economic, social, and territorial dislocation, and were forced to cope with ecological changes that compromised their survivorship. They were also partially absorbed into the European reproductive pool. For Blacks, brought by force from Africa to work as slaves in America, the loss of freedom negatively affected both survival and reproduction. Specifically, lower levels of reproduction followed from an imbalanced ratio between the sexes, restrictions on the formation of couples, and the more or less forced absorption of black women into the European reproductive sphere.

Commentators contemporary to these events described the different conditions of these three major ethnic groups in expressive ways. On the rapid growth of the English colonists in North America, able to double their size every twenty or twenty-five years, Adam Smith wrote:

> Labour is there so well rewarded that a numerous family of children, instead of being a burthen is a source of opulence and prosperity to the parents. The labour of each child, before it can leave their house, is computed to be worth a hundred pounds clear gain to them. A young widow with four or five young children, who, among the middling or inferior ranks of people in Europe, would have so little chance for a second husband, is there frequently courted as a sort of fortune.[9]

The factors of this rapid growth were scarcity of labor, abundance of capital (that is land), and favorable living conditions. Twenty years later Malthus would add to this list of causes the "greater degree of liberty and equality" enjoyed by the North American colonists.[10] Bartolomé de Las Casas, the vigorous Dominican defender of the Indios, described a much different situation for the natives in the thousands of pages he wrote during his long life. At the beginning of his *Brevísima relación de la destruición de las Indias*, for example, one reads:

> There are two main ways in which those who have traveled to this part of the world pretending to be Christians have uprooted these pitiful peoples and wiped them from the face of the earth. First, they have waged war on them: unjust, cruel, bloody and tyrannical war. Second, they have murdered anyone and everyone who has shown the slightest sign of resistance, or even of wishing to escape the torment to which they have subjected him. This latter policy has been instrumental in suppressing the native leaders, and, indeed . . . it has led to the annihilation of all adult males, whom they habitually subject to the harshest and most iniquitous and brutal slavery that man has ever devised for his fellow-men, treating them, in fact, worse than animals. All the many and infinitely varied ways that have been devised for oppressing these peoples can be seen to flow from one or the other of these two diabolical and tyrannical policies.[11]

Nor did Gonzalo Fernández de Oviedo offer a substantially different picture. Oviedo was the other official historian of the Conquest, as well as a fierce rival of Las Casas, and had a highly unfavorable opinion of the Indios. Their disappearance from the island of Hispaniola (and from the other Antilles) was caused, according to Oviedo, by the unbearable conditions they encountered in the gold mines: "Given the wealth of the mines and the insatiable greed of the colonists, some overworked the Indios while others did not give them enough to eat."[12] But the main cause he identified was the *repartimiento-encomienda* system, namely the servitude to which they were subjected and the consequent uprooting they suffered when their communities were destroyed. "The way in which governors and *repartidores* moved the Indios about, transferring them from one master to another, each greedier than the next, all this created the conditions that brought about that people's total destruction."[13] The oppression of the conquerors, then, combined with their cruelty, was the true cause of depopulation, destroying communities and depriving the natives of their land, their freedom, and their traditional ways of life.

The African component – more than 10 million Africans were brought as slaves to the Americas between 1500 and 1870 – arrived already severely reduced by the frightening levels of mortality suffered between the moment of capture and arrival in the New World. Survival and reproductive capacity, moreover, were compromised not only by a regime of backbreaking labor, especially in the sugar plantations of the Caribbean and Brazil, but also by obstacles to marriage. Giovanni Antonio Andreoni, a Jesuit from Lucca known as Antonil, was perhaps the most acute and reliable observer of the situation in Brazil at the beginning of the eighteenth century:

Some masters oppose marriage between slaves, while raising no objections to their illicit unions. In fact, some openly approve of the latter and even arrange them, saying "You, João, will marry Maria at a certain time," and leaving them to converse as if they were husband and wife . . . others, once slaves have married, separate them so that for years they live as if single, a situation that is unconscionable.[14]

The problem then was that the property owners, while permitting illicit or casual unions, did not encourage and even blocked marriage among their slaves and so compromised family stability and reproduction. The outcome negatively influenced the balance between births and deaths.

These observations are supported by the available data, imprecise though they may be. The rapid decline of the indigenous population is indisputable. That decline bottomed out in the course of the seventeenth century, after which there followed a gradual recovery in the course of the following century. It led to extinction in some areas, disastrous declines in others, and more or less serious reductions in still others. The causes and interpretations of those declines are the focus of the chapters that follow. Within the scope of this variety, between 1600 and 1800 the traumatic impact of the Conquest lessened; populations acquired immunities; institutional relations and ruptured social networks were re-established. The decline stopped; the demographic system normalized; and the population curve turned upward.

As to the other two groups, Whites and Blacks, we have quantitative estimates from around 1800, thanks to the US censuses and renewed interest for statistical documentation on the part of Spanish, Portuguese, and British colonial administrations. The population stock at that date was the product of immigration (forced immigration for Africans) from the time of contact and the balance of births and deaths for the two groups since that time. The greater the ratio between the population in 1800 and the immigration flow over the previous three centuries, the greater the reproductive success of the group in question. If the ratio is equal to 1 – current population is equal to total immigration (assuming no return migration, certainly the case for slaves) – then births would have just balanced deaths for the period. If the ratio is greater than 1, then births have exceeded deaths; if it is smaller than 1, then the survival of the group has relied on continued immigration. Obviously these are rough measures, but ones that effectively synthesize the demographic experiences of these groups.

The difficulties encountered by the Europeans in America were many, and the first conquistadors suffered high mortality. When Columbus returned to Hispaniola on his second Atlantic crossing, ten months after leaving the first settlement of thirty-nine Europeans there, all had perished. Of the 1,200 crew members on that second voyage, which left from Cadiz on September 25, 1493, only half were still alive when the admiral returned to Spain two and a half years later. According to Las Casas, 1,000 of the 2,500 men and women who disembarked with Governor Ovando in April 1502 died within a year.[15] Similar experiences were repeated in Mexico, Central America, the estuary of the Río de la Plata, in Brazil, and in Perú.[16] Wars against the native populations and even between the conquistadors themselves, hunger, illness, an often hostile environment, and mishaps of all sorts exacted a high cost in human life. Such was the cost of the initial conquest and exploration. Once they had established themselves in a position of dominance, however, the Europeans generally enjoyed living conditions favorable to demographic growth. In fact, the European migratory contribution to the population in America over the three centuries between first contact and 1800 was relatively modest as compared to the total population at the later date.

The numbers in table 2 describe the situation for French migration to Quebec, British to North America, Spanish to Iberian America, and Portuguese to Brazil. Once again, these are rough figures, especially those for net immigration, which give us at best an idea of the scale of the problem, one from which we can draw a number of conclusions. We need also to keep in mind that the population that remained in Europe doubled over this same period. Under equivalent conditions we would imagine that the immigrant population in the Americas should increase less, given that immigration was spread out over three centuries from 1500 to 1800, and so population on average had less time to increase; we would expect a ratio under 2. Instead we find that the reproductive "success" of Europeans in the Americas was much greater. Over all, an immigration flow of little more than 2 million produced by 1800 a stock of 8 million, an almost fourfold increase. That success was greatest in Quebec, where 25,000 immigrants had by 1800 grown to a population more than seven times larger. It was considerable elsewhere as well, with population to immigration ratios in 1800 of nearly 5 for Whites in the United States, over 3 for Spaniards in Central America, and about 2 for Portuguese in Brazil, though in this last country the mixing of Portuguese with natives and Africans was certainly higher than elsewhere. This is not the place to interpret the reasons behind the apparent north–south gradient in these figures or the apparent greater success of North American Whites compared to those in Iberian America. Climate and disease may have played a role, or perhaps the fact that, while the North American colonies were largely made up of farmers much in need of family labor, those in Latin America instead consisted of urban, merchant, administrative, and property-owning classes, less inclined to have large families. Finally the different levels of ethnic mixing may have played a role.

We can explain the demographic success of the Europeans as compared to the populations from which they derived, and even more compared to the native American populations – who in spite of recovery numbered in 1800 only a fraction of their number in 1500 – with reference to factors already mentioned. Immigration certainly exercised a degree of selection relative to physical hardiness; the material conditions of life in America were generally superior to those in Europe; food was abundant, and scarcity, when it occurred, more often due to human rather than natural causes; the availability of natural resources was considerable; the cost of slave labor and that of the Indios, often organized in work gangs, was low. The much-studied French Canadians enjoyed lower mortality than the populations they left behind in Normandy and Brittany, while violent death at the hands of Indians was a rare event indeed. The women married young and experienced higher fertility. Both family size and survival rates to adulthood were also higher.[17] In a word, those checks on population growth in Europe, well described by Malthus, did not operate in America. Although peripheral to our concerns here, the total European human investment in America is also interesting to note. We can express this investment in terms of the ratio between total migrants and the populations in the countries of origin in 1800 (see table 2). That ratio is a mere 1 per 1,000 for France, the most populous country in Europe at the time (save Russia), but one which for complex historical reasons played a small role in European migration. It reaches a maximum for Portugal (172 per 1,000), a small country that contributed to the population of Brazil, a territory about a hundred times larger. Spain and Great Britain had similar and intermediate ratios (well below 100 per 1,000). By 1800, instead, the various European populations in America by nationality corresponded to 40 percent of the population of Great Britain, one-third that of Portugal, one-quarter of Spain, and a tiny fraction of France (see column 6 in table 2).

The most tragic fate of all was that of the Africans (see table 3). It is estimated that more than 7 million slaves were transported to the Americas from the African coasts aboard slave ships. And to those 7 million we need to add several million more who were seized in their villages, but perished during the trek to the coast, in the coastal depositories, or during the long crossing.[18] As compared to the total of this forced migration, the black (and mulatto) population in 1800 was just 5.6 million, and so smaller than the stock of arrivals. The Caribbean islands received the bulk of this population, about 3.9 million slaves, but counted only 1.7 million African inhabitants in 1800. Brazil received 2.3 million slaves, while the African and mulatto population there in 1800 numbered under 2 million. The remaining million or so went to continental Spanish America and North America, where they experienced better conditions of survival and reproduction. In Brazil and still more in the Caribbean, which together absorbed a large majority of the African population, the demographic system of slavery was maintained only by the continuous importation of still more human supplies to fill the gaps left by high mortality – mortality little compensated by limited reproduction. The stock to immigration ratio is less than 1 – with a minimum of 0.3 in the British Caribbean – except in Spanish America (which accounts for only one-tenth of the total) and, most notably, in the United States. In the US the reproduction rate of the slave population was high (about eight children per woman); the average age at first conception less than twenty; and the length of breastfeeding and birth intervals shorter than in Africa.[19] The system there did not interfere excessively in the formation and stability of couples, though the material and logistical obstacles might have been considerable. Meanwhile mortality there, while higher than that among Whites, was not nearly so unfavorable as in the Caribbean or Brazil.[20] A variety of indicators suggest a demographic system compatible with high natural increase.

The reasons behind the tragedy of the Africans in the Caribbean and Brazil – destination of six out of seven slave ships – can be ascribed to the living conditions that accompanied the loss of freedom, the methods of capture and transportation, the backbreaking labor of the sugar plantations, and the poor dietary and climatic conditions. For several Caribbean islands there is solid evidence of reproductive rates well below those of the US, as unions were less frequent, birth intervals were longer, and the childbearing cycle was shorter.[21] There is also evidence of high mortality, especially during the initial period of adjustment; it is estimated that between one-fifth and one-third of slaves there died within three years of arrival.[22] Nonetheless, the fragmentation of that population, dispersed among a myriad of large and small islands, makes for a complex and not always clear picture.

Consider the Brazilian case. All agree that the slaves there suffered high mortality. It was generally held, for example, that the productive life of a young plantation slave ranged from seven to fifteen years, numbers that find confirmation in their frequent repetition.[23] Nonetheless mortality levels are almost impossible to ascertain given a host of factors that enter into the equation: the age at arrival in Brazil; whether the end of productive life is caused by illness, incapacity, or death; the granting of freedom (not unusual); escape (fairly frequent); and the eventual inability to keep track of individuals (following sale, escape, etc.). How one takes into account these factors affects the results in significant ways. Census data from 1872 – a date that puts us at the end of slavery, but the data are surely indicative of earlier situations as well – allow us to put the life expectancy of male slaves in Brazil at eighteen years, as compared to twenty-seven for the whole of the Brazilian population (or thirty-five for slaves in the United States in the mid-nineteenth century).[24] In the region of Bahia, similar estimates for the end of the eighteenth century yield twenty-three for men and twenty-five for women.[25] Between 1838 and 1872 (during which time the slave trade was formally illegal but widely practiced just the same), the ages of 440 slaves found aboard captured ships were recorded, as well as their ages at death. The males survived on average fifteen years and the females ten, values that correspond to the frequently cited seven to fifteen range. Mortality was especially high in the first years of adjustment.[26]

While there is no question that slave mortality was high (significantly higher than the already considerable mortality of the free population), there is open debate about the causes. The hard work of the sugar plantations – the primary agricultural enterprise through to the end of the eighteenth century – carried out under rigid and often harsh control, is frequently cited: planting, plowing, cutting the cane, transport, crushing, distillation, processing, and the portage of wood over long distances to fuel the cooking vats. It was work that went on year round; during the nine months of production, the mills and vats were in continuous operation, employing men and women from dawn to dusk and in peak periods even at night.[27] And while it is reasonable to believe that slave owners did not want to squander their precious investment, it has nonetheless been suggested that two years of work repaid the initial outlay and that after about five years the return on that initial investment was surely double.[28] Apparently there was, however, an interest in getting the maximum return in the minimum number of years. The slave diet consisted of basic foods and seems to have been adequate and varied: corn (maize), cassava, beans, dried meat, sugar and its derivatives, and fruit. Moreover, the slaves were allowed to cultivate a small personal garden to supplement their food rations. On the other hand, the *senzala* (large rectangular dormitories in which men and women were separated) were undoubtedly filthy and poorly maintained. Accommodation, not to mention adequate care, of the sick was minimal, and the number of slaves unable to work at any given time because of acute or chronic illness, blindness, deformity, or work-related injuries (probably frequent) was high. Certainly the living conditions of the slaves could vary as a function of the attitude of the slave owner – from the benevolent paternalist to the cruel cynic – but it was in any case the production system that made the slaves' lives brutally hard.[29] In a society that did not encourage procreation and family life and that forced women to engage in hard labor, youth and infant mortality were also, it is generally agreed, high – though there are no reliable data or convincing comparisons. Beyond the material factors that constituted the direct causes of the high mortality, there were others that are more difficult to evaluate. The Brazilian slave regime included restrictions that inhibited the development of family and community solidarity and contact between slaves from different plantations. It made it impossible for both the individual and the community to experiment and elaborate efficient mechanisms for survival in the face of external threats, and so increased their vulnerability. It is of course difficult to incorporate this vulnerability factor in a quantitative measure of survivorship, but that does not mean that it should be left out.

Nor were the high mortality losses compensated by slave fertility. To begin with, the male to female ratio for those brought over from Africa was 2 : 1. And all the sources – plantation owners, travelers, members of religious orders – agree in lamenting the rarity of slave births. We have already cited Andreoni on the way in which large property owners created obstacles to family formation and stability among their slaves. The following century, Saint Hilaire would remark:

When the abolition campaign [abolition of the slave trade] began in Brazil, the government ordered the property owners of Campos to cause their slaves to marry; some obeyed, but others replied that it would be pointless for slave women to marry because they would never be able to care for their children. Immediately following birth, these women were obliged to return to work in the sugar-cane fields under a fiercely hot sun, so that when part way through the day they were permitted to return to their children they could not produce adequate milk to nourish them. How could these poor infants survive the cruel misery with which white greed adorned their cribs?[30]

As long as there was an ample supply of slaves on the market and their price was low, it made more economic sense to buy them than to encourage reproduction and the raising of children. Moreover, law and custom forbade breaking up a slave family for the purpose of selling one of its members; reproduction took women temporarily out of the labor force; black *boçales* (new arrivals from Africa) were easier to manage than black *crioulos* (those born in Brazil); and so on. Still other factors further complicate the picture: the intrusion of slave owners into the sexual lives of their female slaves, and so the production of many mulatto children (who remained slaves), and the removal of those women from the slave marriage pool; the restriction on contact between slaves of different owners and so the consequent limitation on choice of partner; and, generally speaking, the organization and rhythm of work. Finally, African customs that did not favor monogamy likely encouraged temporary unions rather than more stable ones.

Our attempt to sketch out the demographic pictures of Indios, Whites and Blacks is necessarily imperfect, not only because of the weakness of the quantitative data available, but also because the divisions between the groups, while legally precise, were crossed over from the start. From the moment of contact, white men coupled with native women and then later with black slave women; there was also of course mixing between natives and Blacks. As is well known, the Spanish and Portuguese migration was largely male and generally accepting of unions with natives and Blacks. As a result, the demographic analysis of the three groups – roughly described here and summarized in figure 1 – is compromised by the mixing between those groups that began as soon as the Europeans set foot in the Americas. The violent death of the thirty-nine crew members Columbus left behind after the first voyage was caused by the rape of indigenous women, as a local informer later described: "As soon as the admiral left, they began to fight and argue, even drawing their knives on one another. They took the women they wanted and whatever gold there was and went off each on his own."[31] "Hernán Cortés, Francisco, Gonzalo and Juan Pizarro, Pedro and Alonso de Alvarado, Diego de Almagro, Sebastián de Benalcázar, and almost all the conquistadors, from captains to soldiers, fathered mixed-race offspring."[32] And so the creation of a mixed-race population found its origin in relationships that ranged from violent rape to occasional sex to concubinage to marriages celebrated in church.

There was, moreover, a specific hierarchy of *mestizos*: those who were fully integrated into Spanish society and succeeded even in joining the military or the clergy, mixing with Whites and so eventually diluting or canceling out the indigenous blood; those who remained *mestizo*, carrying with them the inherent conflict between their two backgrounds, a conflict that often showed itself in social nonconformity and left its mark on both history and art; those who maintained the link to their mothers and so the native community and, while occupying a lower social station, would become reassimilated into Indian culture, with the result that over the generations the white blood would be canceled out.[33]

Mixed marriages were encouraged in order to eliminate or at least reduce concubinage and to strengthen important ties with *caciques* and native leaders. In 1514, the *repartimiento* of Alburquerque in Hispaniola revealed that, among the wives of 186 Spaniards, 121 were born in Castille and 65 were native to the island.[34] In Los Angeles (Bogotá) in 1534, out of 81 heads of family, 20 had married indigenous women; and we can find similar proportions in Jaén (Audiencia of Quito) in 1606 and Panamá in 1607.[35]

In the first phase of the Conquest, the children of a white man and an Indio woman (*mestizos*), whether legitimate or illegitimate, were considered white; subsequently only legitimate offspring were assimilated into white society. "But it is important to keep in mind that the concept of whiteness itself did not imply racial purity at any point in the history of Latin America. *Mestizos* crossed with Spaniards were called *castizos*, while *castizos* crossed with Spaniards were Spaniards. In other words, individuals with one-eighth indigenous blood were considered white."[36] Moreover, individuals with

Map 1   *Political organization of America, 1500–1650*

one-sixteenth black blood were also considered white. Generally speaking there was pressure to enlarge the white category, a process often aided by bureaucrats. In the population registry for the Mexican city of Texcoco we find: "Manuel Hilario Gómez, Spaniard, or so he affirms, though of suspicious coloring," and "Juan Antonio Mendoza, very dark *mestizo*, 60 years old, married to Josefa Flores Miranda, a very dark Spaniard."[37] In another example a bureaucrat, annoyed by the repeated requests of a mixed-race individual with obviously African features, wrote in his register: "Dark skinned; considers himself white." In sum, the population of Whites grew, because of natural increase but also because of the incorporation of natives and to a lesser extent Africans. The Indio category in turn exercised a degree of attraction relative to the African, given that the child of an Indio woman and a black slave acquired the "free" status of the mother and so moved up an important step on the social ladder. The slave and black group instead did not exert this sort of attraction and, after the end of the slave trade, had to rely solely on natural increase to maintain its existence.

At the beginning of the nineteenth century, and so before the great migration of that century, the demographic future of the Americas was laid out. Over the course of three centuries a trickle of conquistador-adventurers, colonists, and immigrants had fed the dominant communities and allowed English, Spaniards, and Portuguese (and to a lesser extent French and Dutch) to control an entire continent politically and economically. Those communities had grown rapidly so that, by 1800, 8 million Europeans constituted about one-third of the entire population of the Americas. Moreover, they would serve as the magnet for another 60 million Europeans who would cross the Atlantic in the century after 1840. The native populations instead survived in the least accessible regions and in those where the pre-Columbian societies had withstood the impact of the Conquest, while the African population survived and grew because of the slave trade rather than natural increase. Contact had profoundly altered the demographic capacities of the three ethnic groups, improving the conditions for European growth, pushing the Indios to the brink of destruction, and paralyzing the growth of the Africans.

The relative demographic success of these three groups – including the creation and growth of the mixed-race populations – can be read in two diametrically opposed ways, though both are correct. The first is the classic interpretation according to which changes in environment and living conditions influenced survivorship and modified demographic behavior. New diseases destroyed the health and increased the mortality of the Indios. Abundant land and the success of plants and animals imported from Europe insured an ample diet to Europeans accustomed to precarious harvests at home. The backbreaking labor of the plantations compromised the survivorship of the Africans. Hence contact generated advantageous conditions for the Europeans and disadvantageous ones for the Indios and Africans.

The other reading of the American story is different. Contact generated profound changes in the individual and collective prerogatives of the several groups, in particular regarding access to power and so the freedom of individuals, clans, and groups. This is most evident in the case of Africans, who were deprived of basic demographic prerogatives: to move about, establish family ties, and reproduce. Yet for the Indios as well the state of servitude to which they were subjected, relaxed somewhat by the *Leyes Nuevas* of 1542, had a profound impact on their ways of life and the choices available to them. Economic dislocation and forced labor seriously limited the ability of communities to access potential resources, especially in subsistence situations with little possibility for accumulation. Social dislocation sundered communities and networks of solidarity and so weakened defenses in the face of calamities, scarcity, and external attacks. Forced confinement in villages altered the natural environment and limited mobility, an essential tool of survival and defense for all societies. In villages deprived of common lands, production and subsistence regimes were altered. These are characteristics well known to historians and anthropologists; their evident links to the demographic situation are explored in the chapters that follow.

2 A humble Franciscan, two combative Dominicans, an Italian humanist at the court of Spain, a remorseful viceroy, a naturalist "alcalde," a Europeanized Inca and an Inca fallen on hard times, a conquistador observer . . . different witnesses and a common analysis of the catastrophe

There is no doubt that the American encounter resulted in a devastating decline of the Indio population; the questions that persist regard the scale of the disaster, its duration, and of course the causes that brought it about. The first of these questions cannot be definitively resolved, as the size of the population at the moment of contact (based on different sorts of data for the different parts of the continent) is at best conjecture – conjecture that may be more or less reasonable and thoroughly researched, but conjecture just the same. The precise scale of the decline, then, eludes us, and we have to make do with those phases for which we have sufficiently solid data. The question of duration presents another problem. Generally speaking the decline began with the establishment of stable contact with Europeans, but it is unclear when the downward curve ended and the recovery began. In Spanish America, which possesses the best quantitative data, there is rich documentation from the period after military operations ceased and during which colonial holdings were consolidated; during the latter half of the sixteenth century and the beginning of the seventeenth, the colonial administration took shape and implemented a rationalized system of tax collection. After that period, however, during the rest of the seventeenth century and for much of the eighteenth, data are scarce, and so determination of the endpoint of the decline is difficult. Finally, there are the causes of the demographic catastrophe, which are in fact the central focus of this book and so will occupy us for much of what follows. But they are also the specific topic of this chapter, where we will review the opinions and theories of a number of contemporary observers – officials, members of religious orders, soldiers, colonists, and travelers – who acted, saw, and listened. These individuals recorded and commented upon what they witnessed for a variety of reasons: as a function of their religious, official, or commercial role in the colonial program, out of simple curiosity or idealism, and for practical considerations. Each had of course his own point of view and his own limitations. They were active in the century following the Conquest and so were able – when not witnesses themselves – to gather information from those who had experienced the events first hand. As we shall see, their accounts reveal that the catastrophe was a complex process, not easily reduced to one or two factors, but instead owing to multiple causes. The historian faces a challenging task in seeking to find some order among these and to determine priority.

That it was a catastrophe is beyond question. In Hispaniola, Cuba, Puerto Rico, and Jamaica, the Taíno population was practically wiped out in the space of two generations. Alonso de Castro wrote in 1542 that, on the island of Hispaniola, "the Indios are extinct." According to Oviedo, in 1548, "there remained a few hundred." For López de Velasco, around 1570, there were still two villages with no more than fifty people in each.[1] In Mexico, passing over for the moment the hazardous estimates regarding the initial period, the population probably declined by about half during the last three decades of the sixteenth century, a drop that followed upon the certain decline of the first fifty years of the Conquest.[2] Between 1570 and 1620, the population of what is today Peru likely halved, but the biggest decline came in the two decades after the arrival of Pizarro.[3] We could go on and on, but the story would be the same: in the Yucatán, along the mainland coasts of the Caribbean, in Guatemala, in Panama, and in Chile. The vast amount of surviving documentation – considered at greater length in the chapters that follow – is unchallenged and unchallengeable.

As already mentioned, the Conquest itself took place rapidly considering the size of the continent and the small number of Europeans. Nonetheless, stable contact between Europeans and Indios was established over the course of a century: in the 1490s for Hispaniola; in the first decade of the sixteenth century for the rest of the Caribbean islands; in the 1510s and 1520s for Mexico and Central America (the fall of Tenochtitlan-México[4] to Cortés and his men took place on August 13, 1521); in the 1530s in Perú (the confrontation at Cajamarca and the capture of Atahuallpa by Pizarro took place on November 15, 1532). It took many more decades to extend control to northern Mexico (beyond the mining centers), to the Yucatán, to other parts of Central America, to Chile, to the lands surrounding the Paraná–Río de la Plata estuary, and to the vast interior of Brazil. The negative demographic effects of contact – there are those who claim that in some cases European diseases actually preceded the conquistadors – began and ended at different times in different places. It is believed, for example, that the native population in Mexico began to recover around the middle of the seventeenth century, while the same would not occur in Perú until the following century. Around 1570, the cosmographer and royal geographer López de Velasco, who on the basis of colonial reports compiled an inventory of Spanish settlements in America, counted 23,000 resident families (*vecinos*) in 225 Spanish cities or villages. The vast majority of these were in the viceroyalties of New Spain (Mexico) and Perú (Peru, Ecuador, Bolivia, and Chile).[5] Limiting our precision to an order of magnitude, we can estimate that there was at the time about one Spanish family for every 100 native families. Half a century later, the traveler-official Vázquez de Espinosa cataloged 77,600 Spanish families in 331 villages and cities; by that time the ratio had about tripled due to the doubling of the Spanish population and the decline of the Indios.[6] These figures should be kept in mind given that the demographic impact of the Conquest surely bore a direct relationship to the size of the European population.

Brother Toribio da Benavente was one of the twelve missionary Franciscans who first came to Mexico following Pope Adrian VI's bull granting a broad mandate to the mendicant orders. The "twelve" arrived in 1524, less than three years after the fall of the capital. Energetic and motivated, they traveled, learned the language and preached in Nahuatl, founded churches and monasteries, and baptized and converted the Indios. Toribio took for himself the name of Motolinia (humble in Nahuatl) as testimony to his evangelical method and program; he died in 1569. His *Historia de los Indios de Nueva España* was probably written in the period 1540–50, while the text that has survived is based on a longer work that was lost.[7] Motolinia is especially interesting for our purposes because his work begins with a description of the "ten plagues" that afflicted the country and its inhabitants, "both native and foreign." They constitute then a catalog of the causes for the destruction of the Indios and synthesize the reasons behind the disaster, defining categories that remain useful. We will return to them more than once in the pages that follow.

1 Smallpox: The disease arrived in Mexico in 1520 with the expedition of Pánfilo de Narváez (coming from Cuba). Its impact was surely devastating. "When the smallpox began to infect the Indians, there was so much sickness and pestilence among them in all the land that in most provinces more than half of the people died, whereas in others the number was somewhat smaller." Many hold that smallpox was an important factor in the defeat of the Aztecs. Given that the next chapter focuses specifically on the role of disease, Motolinia's precise and convincing description will do for now. Following smallpox, it was the turn of measles: "Eleven years later a Spaniard arrived who was stricken with measles. From him it was carried to the Indians."

2 War and "the great number of deaths that occurred during the conquest of New Spain and especially of Mexico."

3 Famine: "Owing to the great war, the fields were not sown, some of the Indians defending the land and assisting the Mexicans, and others siding with the Spaniards. Moreover, what some sowed others uprooted and laid waste. Hence there was nothing to eat."

4 "[T]he *calpixques* or overseers and the Negroes: When the land was apportioned, the conquerors placed in the *repartimientos* and towns that were granted them in *encomienda*, servants or Negroes, who were to collect the tributes and look after the granaries." The *calpixques* were cruel oppressors and the cause of hardship, violence, and escapes.

5 "[T]he heavy tributes and services which the Indians rendered," the measure of which was based upon "a great quantity of the gold which they had collected over a period of many years" in their temples and sepulchers and entrusted to their lords. Initially the demand for gold was so constant that, "in order to be able to meet their obligations, the Indians would sell their children and their lands to the merchants. Failing to meet their obligations, very many died in consequence, some from torture and others from cruel imprisonment, since they were treated inhumanly and regarded as lower than beasts."

6 The gold mines: "The Indian slaves who up to the present have died in these mines cannot be counted. Gold, in this land, was

adored as a god in the form of a calf." The hunger for gold and so for instant wealth was a cause of the catastrophe continually cited by contemporaries.

7 "[T]he building of the great city of Mexico . . . So great was the number of people engaged in the work that a man could hardly pick his way through the streets and over the causeways, though these are very broad. During the work of construction some laborers were killed by rafters, others fell from a height, and others lost their life under the buildings they were dismantling in one place in order to erect them elsewhere." Or again: "It is the custom of this land – not the best in the world – that the Indians do the work and at their expense search for the materials and pay the stonecutters and the carpenters. If they do not bring their own food, they must fast." During the first decades of the Conquest, churches, monasteries, and other grand buildings went up in a fury of construction in the most important cities – Santo Domingo, México, Lima, Cuzco – and employed native labor.

8 The enslavement of the Indios in order to send them into the mines: "So great was the haste with which in some years slaves were made that from all parts there entered Mexico great flocks of them, like sheep, so that they could easily be branded." Nor did these include only those who according to the "barbarous laws" of the Indios were already slaves. "On account of the haste with which the Indians were made to bring such a large number of slaves every eighty days as tribute, many of these slaves died. Accordingly, when the number of available slaves was exhausted they brought their children and the *macehuales*, who were of a lower caste and were similar to vassal laborers; and of these they brought as many more as they could find and assemble; whereupon they intimidated them to such an extent that they would admit they were slaves."

9 "[T]he provisioning of the mines," mines often situated in remote and sparsely populated regions: "To these mines Indian carriers would travel seventy leagues and more in order to bring sustenance. The food which they carried for their own use sometimes gave out, either on the way to the mines or on the return trip before they reached home. Some carriers the miners detained for some days in order that they might help extract the mineral, while others would be employed in building houses or

rendering personal service. During this time the food would
give out and the Indians would either die there in the mines or
on the road."

10   "[T]he dissensions and factions among the Spaniards living in
Mexico": This was the plague that placed "the land in the
greatest danger of being lost," though the civil wars that devastated Perú for twenty years were more serious than the conflicts in Mexico.

Motolinia's list is exhaustive, and we can find in it all the factors
that enter into the current debate over the causes of the disaster of
the Indios in Mexico and elsewhere. Moreover, the ten plagues
follow, at least partially, an order of chronology and importance.
The first three – disease, war, and famine – all made themselves felt
during the first three years of the Mexican conquest and took a devastating toll. More generally we can assign the ten plagues to four
groupings: new diseases; the violence associated with war
and conquest, with the putting down of rebellion, and with civil
wars – violence that brought with it want and famine; forced labor
for public works, mining, transport, and personal services generally;
and the loss of traditional freedoms and so the social dislocation that
caused.

The plagues of Motolinia are more than enough to paint in the
most somber tones the *Leyenda Negra* of the Conquest. That
"Black Legend" was no polemical invention of Las Casas, later ably
exploited by Protestants and other enemies to vilify Spain, as has
been maintained for centuries, but rather the common opinion of
thoughtful Spaniards involved in the early history of the expansion
in America. Motolinia, moreover, was a great rival of Las Casas. In
a passionate and harsh criticism of Las Casas's activities, Motolinia
wrote to Charles V in 1555: "I marvel at the manner in which Your
Majesty and your councilors have put up for so long with a man so
troublesome, disruptive, and inappropriate. Wearing the garb of a
religious man, he is at once tempestuous, argumentative, short-
tempered, offensive, and harmful."[8] And yet Las Casas himself
would surely have endorsed the analysis of the ten plagues.

When Toribio, not yet renamed Motolinia, arrived in Mexico, Las
Casas (the son of one of Columbus's men) had already been in
the New World for over twenty years. He arrived in Santo

Domingo in 1502 with the great expedition of Governor Ovando. Initially under the command of Diego Velázquez and engaged in the repression of the Indios of Xaraguá, he was himself an *encomendero*, but then converted to the cause of the Indios and joined the Dominicans.[9] In 1510, fifteen members of that order arrived on the island, including Antonio de Montesinos and Pedro de Córdoba. It was this group that denounced the inhuman conditions to which the Indios were subjected. That protest made its way to the court and convinced Ferdinand and his councilors to issue the *Leyes de Burgos* in 1512. During his long life, Las Casas wrote incessantly and traveled frequently between Spain and the New World; he exercised great influence over Regent Cardinal Cisneros, Charles V, the court, and the Council of the Indies; and he inspired the passage of the *Leyes Nuevas* in 1542 intended to better protect the Indios. He defended and affirmed the rationality of the natives and their ability to live independently in an ordered society, and to understand and sincerely embrace the true faith. His moment of conversion came on December 21, 1511, the fourth Sunday of Advent, in the Cathedral of Santo Domingo (recently completed with forced Indio labor), and in the presence of "admiral Diego Columbus, and all the jurists and royal officials" of the island. The sermon was delivered by Antonio de Montesinos, according to prior agreement among the friars, on the theme of St. John's preaching "ego vox clamans in deserto":

This voice [of Christ in the desert of this island] . . . says that you are living in deadly sin for the atrocities you tyrannically impose on these innocent people. Tell me, what right have you to enslave them? What authority did you use to make war against them who lived at peace on their territories, killing them cruelly with methods never before heard of? How can you oppress them and not care to feed or cure them, and work them to death to satisfy your greed? And why don't you look after their spiritual health, so that they should come to know God, that they should be baptized, and that they should hear Mass and keep the holy days? Aren't they human beings? Have they no rational soul? Aren't you obliged to love them as you love yourselves?[10]

This medieval invective played an important role in determining the course of the Indios policy of the court and later of the Council of the Indies; but that policy progressively lost its potential impact as it crossed the ocean – in its implementation by offi-

cials in America, in its application over a huge territory, and in the
face of unscrupulous conquistadors and colonists. As a sort of
counterpoint, nearly half a century later (1556) and thousands of
miles away, the troubled Marquis of Cañete, third viceroy of Perú,
wrote to Ferdinand II:

Not all problems can be resolved, especially that regarding the treatment
of the Indios at the hands of the *encomenderos*, which is worse than ever.
Please realize, Your Majesty, that it will take more than a viceroy to assure
that each *vecino* does not rob, mistreat, and work to death these people.
And this behavior is so widespread that, however hard I make my heart,
it breaks in two to see that which takes place . . . and the Indios are being
used up; if God does not intervene, they will suffer the same fate as those
of Santo Domingo, where the same things took place.[11]

Returning to Las Casas, certainly his half century of writing on
the topic was colored by the passion of an activist and apostle. He
was a "partisan" insofar as his mission was the defense of the
Indios, and he succeeded in accruing political dignity to his cause
by engaging royal authority against the feudal power of the
encomenderos. Nonetheless, Las Casas's analysis of the mechanism
of the destruction of the Indios found confirmation in other
accounts, both less partial ones and still others opposed to Las
Casas's mission. Moreover, it is based on his personal experience,
on direct reporting, and on a large quantity of documents to which
he had access thanks to his considerable authority. His *Brevísima
relación de la destruición de las Indias* may have been written in
1542; published in Seville in 1552, it was known to the court and
enjoyed huge success outside of Spain, going through dozens of
translations, into Flemish, English, French, German, Italian.[12] Its
central thesis is laid out at the beginning of the book and has
already been discussed in our previous chapter. There were two
primary causes of the catastrophe: the direct violence of war and
the oppression of servitude. In presenting that thesis he avers: "At
a conservative estimate, the despotic and diabolical behaviour of
the Christians has, over the last forty years, led to the unjust and
totally unwarranted deaths of more than twelve million souls,
women and children among them, and there are grounds for
believing my own estimate of more than fifteen million to be nearer
to the mark."[13] His figures seem incredible, and Las Casas is often
unreliable when it comes to numbers, though it is interesting to

note that they do correspond fairly well to those of the more recent school of high counters. Cook and Borah, for example, estimate the population of New Spain at 25.2 million in 1519 and 6.3 million in 1548. Imagining, had there been no Conquest, a stationary population with equal numbers of births and deaths, then the net population loss resulting from contact with the Europeans for Mexico alone amounted to 19 million in 29 years, considerably more than the 15 million proposed by Las Casas for all of Spanish America over four decades.

What then was the cause of the catastrophe? In the first place, the wars of conquest – in Santo Domingo, Mexico, Guatemala, Perú – and the massacre of Indian warriors protected only by their "flimsy and ineffective" weapons: the brutal raids of Pedrarías Dávila in Darién and Nicaragua, of Pedro de Alvarado in Guatemala, of Nuño de Guzmán in Panuco, and of Juan Ponce de León in Puerto Rico. And everywhere Indios were enlisted to fight other Indios. Beyond the direct impact of the violence, these wars also caused want and famine as fields were destroyed and crops confiscated; and it was impossible for the Indios, often constrained to flee, to plant new ones.

Servitude provoked still greater disasters because of uprooting, oppression, and exploitation, most often in the pursuit of gold:

After the fighting was over and all the men had been killed, the surviving natives . . . were shared out between the victors . . . The pretext under which the victims were parceled out in this way was that their new masters would then be in a position to teach them the truths of the Christian faith; and thus it came about that a host of cruel, grasping and wicked men, almost all of them pig-ignorant, were put in charge of these poor souls. And they discharged this duty by sending the men down the mines, where working conditions were appalling, to dig for gold, and putting the women to labour in the fields and on their master's estates, to till the soil and raise the crops, properly a task only for the toughest and strongest of men. Both women and men were given only wild grasses to eat and other unnutritious foodstuffs. The mothers of young children promptly saw their milk dry up and their babies die; and, with the women and the men separated and never seeing each other, no new children were born. The men died down the mines from overwork and starvation, and the same was true of the women who perished out on the estates.[14]

The exploitation of the Indios took a variety of forms, including the transportation of goods ("they were treated as beasts of burden"), people (on hammocks or litters), wood and tools for ship construction, and artillery. The most extreme form of domination was enslavement – contrary to the *Leyes de Burgos* – accomplished by means of raids or instead by exacting slaves as tribute payments from the *caciques*. Moreover, Las Casas makes an acute demographic observation: the social dislocation caused by a radical change of work regime (men in the mines and women in the fields) and the separation of couples brought about a crisis of reproduction.

In the thousands of pages written by Las Casas – in his accounts, memoirs, pamphlets, letters, and proposed "remedies" (prominent among the last being abolition of the *encomienda*) – we can find no end of descriptions of violence and oppression. Yet Las Casas, one might argue, was a partisan, an apostle, an activist, and a fighter. How can we not suspect that he manipulated the information to strengthen his own case?

And yet we have seen that the account of Motolinia is still more dire than that of Las Casas. And that of Oviedo, nemesis of Las Casas and repeatedly attacked in his writings, is not much different. Oviedo is a significant literary figure who came to the Indies in 1514 after having served in the Italian Wars under *El Gran Capitán*. He saw action in Darién (Panamá) and Nicaragua, and then in 1532 obtained the post of *alcalde*, a plenipotentiary authority, at the fortress of Santo Domingo, where he was also commissioned to write a history of the Indies. We have, thanks to Oviedo – disciplined and a good observer – a thorough, accurate, and systematic description of New World flora and fauna. Like that of many of the early conquistadors, his opinion of the Indios was dismissive, as we can read in the following passage:

When he discovered these islands, the admiral [Columbus] found [a million Indios] here . . . in this year of 1548 there are probably no more than 500, counting large and small, who are natives or descended from the original race and progenitors. Given that the mines were very rich and the greediness of man insatiable, some overworked the Indios, while others did not give them enough to eat. One has to add that the natives are by nature lazy and depraved, little inclined to work, gloomy, cowardly, despicable, evil intentioned, dishonest, and fickle. Many of them . . . took poison to avoid work; others hanged themselves with their own hands, while still others contracted disease, especially a pestilential smallpox which struck the whole island, so that in a short time the Indios were wiped out. At the same time, a great cause of death among these people was the continual traffic in them conducted by governors and landowners; given the passage from one owner to another and from one master to another, from a greedy owner to a still more greedy one, that traffic was a clear cause and evident tool in the total destruction of these people. For all of the reasons I have indicated the Indios died.[15]

Although he never crossed the ocean himself, Pietro Martire d'Anghiera, a learned Italian humanist at the court of Spain, had a broad range of acquaintances and contacts from whom he carefully collected information on the New World over a period of several decades on behalf of his patrons. He offered a balanced reflection of well-informed opinion about the Conquest. In the fourth book of his *De orbe novo* he has this to say about Hispaniola:

Although there is much gold there, the search for it has been nearly abandoned because there are no miners. The natives, whose work is used for extracting the metal, have been reduced to very few. At first, cruel wars killed off a large number. Then famine followed, killing many more, and was especially severe in the year they dug up the roots of the yucca trees, used to make the bread of the *caciques*, and also failed to plant maize, the usual food of the common people. The survivors were instead attacked by previously unknown illnesses that in 1518 like a pestilential wind contaminated them as if they were a flock of scabid sheep. And to tell the truth they were also decimated by our greediness for gold. Typically, after planting their crops they were accustomed to dance, fish, and hunt rabbits, while instead we pitilessly forced them to dig up the earth, pass it through a riddle, and gather up the gold . . . And that should suffice on the deadly hunger for gold.[16]

These dramatic passages bring other elements to light: suicide, cited in numerous other sources (though hard to imagine as truly widespread, it does seem to have been frequent enough and a sign of the disorientation of the conquered), and the inability to adapt to hard labor. A population accustomed to a subsistence agriculture that was not too onerous found itself instead oppressed by a sort of work that, while it might have been usual for a European peasant hardened by the hundreds of generations of heavy field work that had passed since the adoption of agriculture, was unbearable for the Taíno (in the Caribbean case). A despicable and lazy race little inclined to work, concluded the insensitive Oviedo.

In 1571, the Jesuit José de Acosta arrived in Perú; he served as the order's provincial there and traveled the country from end to end. From the writings of this acute observer, we can derive yet another important aspect of the demographic disaster:

The lowlands run along the coast as throughout the Indies; they are normally very humid and hot and so presently the least healthy and most sparsely populated. And yet in the past there were numerous populations of Indios there, as described in the histories of New Spain and Perú; native to those regions, they reproduced well and thrived.[17]

In Perú, the coastal populations lived off fishing and the cultivation of fields that because of the dryness of the soil had to be irrigated by specially dug canals.

Today the population of these coasts and lowlands is so reduced that out of thirty parts at least twenty-nine have been lost, and many believe that the Indios who remain will not survive for long. This fact is ascribed to several causes: by some to excessive work; by others to the different foods and drink they have consumed since adopting Spanish customs; and by still others to excessive drinking and other vices.[18]

The greater decline of the coastal populations still needs to be explained. The impact of the Spanish may have been greater there; it may have been owing to the destruction of a fragile productive system based on irrigation; or it may be that the imported diseases were more virulent there. Certainly the highland populations dreaded going down to the coast because of the negative consequences associated with the different climate and with tropical diseases.

The Inca Garcilaso de la Vega was the son of a noblewoman, who raised him in Cuzco, and one of the first conquistadors. An accomplished man of letters, he traveled to Spain in 1560 at the age of twenty, and provides a detailed description of the Incan canal system:

The channel that passes through the whole region called Cuntisuyu empties into the province called Quechua which is at the limit of that district: it has all the things I have mentioned, and I have inspected it with great care. These works are certainly so great and wonderful that they exceed all the description and praise that one can devote to them. The Spaniards, as foreigners, have taken no notice of these marvels, either in caring for them, or esteeming them, or even referring to them in their histories. On the contrary, they seem to have let them go to wrack and ruin either deliberately, or what is more probable, through complete indifference. The same may be said of the irrigation channels used by the Indians to irrigate their maize fields, two-thirds of which have been ruined. Today – and for many years back – the only channels in use are those which they cannot avoid maintaining because they are essential. There are still traces and relics of the large and small channels that have gone to ruin.[19]

The destruction of delicate irrigation systems, like that of the great network of roads – "Of all this great structure all that remains is what time and war has failed to consume"[20] – was certainly both cause and consequence of the decline of population, especially along the coast.

Another negative impact of the Conquest was the more or less forced displacement of populations from one region to another, with the attendant and traumatic climatic and environmental changes. It is well known that the Incas organized many forced migrations, often to populate their own recent conquests:

As has been said, the Incas ordered that when Indians were moved thus from one province to another, which they called *mítmac*, the regions should also be selected to have the same sort of climate, so that the change should not cause them harm, it being realized that to transfer them from a cold climate to a hot, or vice versa, caused them to die. It was forbidden therefore to move the Indians of the sierra to the llanos, or they would certainly have died in a few days.[21]

The Spaniards lacked this sort of awareness.

In 1535, three years after the murder of Atahuallpa, a fifteen-year-old named Pedro Cieza de León, originally from Estremadura, disembarked at Cartagena in the Indies. For thirteen years Cieza was involved in various military and administrative functions related to the Conquest and the control of vast areas of present-day Colombia and Ecuador; he took part in the founding of cities and in disputes, including military ones, between Spaniards. In 1548 he went to Perú with the powerful forces of Benalcázar to support Viceroy Pedro de La Gasca in combating the insurrection of Gonzalo Pizarro and ending the civil wars. Cieza won the confidence of La Gasca and was named the Official Chronicler of the

Indies. In this role he traveled the length and breadth of Perú, consulting official documents and gathering statements, before returning to Spain in 1550.[22] It is this Cieza, traveler and first-hand witness of the realities of Andean America, who interests us, in particular his observations regarding the populations he encountered there. His reflections on rapid population decline cover a host of localities and a vast territory that stretches from Panamá – "the natives are few because wiped out by the poor treatment they have received from the Spaniards and the diseases they have contracted" – to Lake Titicaca ("it is well known that once upon a time there was a large population of Indios here at Pucara, while today almost none remain").[23] Map 2 shows the sites of depopulation as described by Cieza. In some cases he simply offers testimony to the drastic decline: the Pearl Islands, the Tumbez valley, the valleys around Antioquia, the region between Popayán and Pasto, the Guarco valley, the Jauja valley, Pucara. But in most cases he attributes the decline directly to war (those against the Indios and the civil wars between Spaniards assisted by Indios). So it was in the Rio Magdalena valley, in the valleys between San Miguel (Piura) and Trujillo and between Trujillo and Los Reyes (Lima), in the valley and province of Chincha, between Nazca and Tarapacá, in the province of Arequipa, in the region of Cajamarca, and in that of Andaguaylas. In some cases he refers specifically to the Incan wars, as for the depopulation of the Vilcas valley; in others he refers to both war and pestilence (as in Puerto Viejo, where he explicitly states that the population "diminished more from war than from disease")[24] to war and famine following upon the abandonment of farming (between Cali and Popayán), or to the pestilence which spread throughout Perú in 1546. There are also frequent references to depopulation resulting from the flight of Indios in the face of the Spanish conquistadors: in Culata de Urabá, where the Indios who had fled from Darién replaced the natives who had themselves fled; in the province of Popayán; in the territory around Ancerma; between Antioquia and Arma ("when the Spaniards arrived, the natives retreated into the Cordillera");[25] in the Lima valley, which had been densely populated but where "today there are few native Indios, as their fields and irrigated lands have been occupied and they have emigrated, some to one valley and others to another."[26] Cieza, witness to much of the two tumultuous and bloody decades that followed upon the arrival of

Map 2 *Journey of Cieza de León and cities that he cited as suffering severe demographic decline*

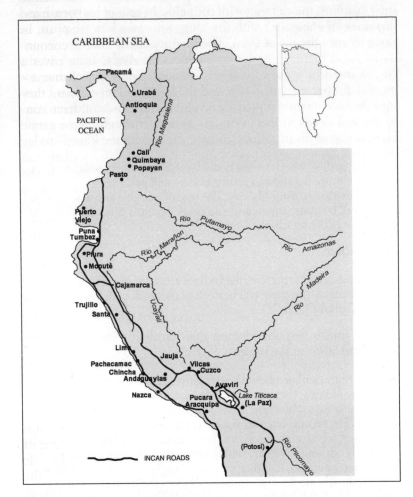

Pizarro, seems to have had little doubt in positing war and its indirect consequences in first place among the causes of the demographic disaster.

At the age of eighty, an Inca gone to wrack and ruin returned home after thirty years' service to the king. A bizarre fellow, he had left wealthy and returned impoverished to his desolate and destroyed homelands: Andamarcas, Soras, Lucanas. In his own peculiar way he describes the events of the Conquest, the history of the Incas, their customs, the cultivation of the fields; he tells of his voyage and imagines an encounter with the king, who asks him what can be done to cure the ills of Perú. The identity of the anarchic, imaginative, and picturesque Guamán Poma de Ayala, author of the *Nueva corónica y buen gobierno*, remains controversial; but the incisive if ungrammatical text and the lively and ingenuous drawings that accompany it provide a vivid picture and condemnation of the evil deeds of the Conquest as seen through native eyes.[27] Here is one of his imaginary conversations with the king:

"Tell me, author, what is wrong nowadays? Why is the population declining and why are the Indians getting poorer and poorer?"

"I'll explain to Your Majesty. The best of our girls and women are all carried off by your priests and the other Spanish officials. Hence the number of half-castes in the country."[28]

And another:

"As matters stand at present, the Indians are in the process of dying out. In twenty years' time there will be none of them left to defend the Crown and the Catholic Faith."[29]

The Indios fled abandoning their lands for fear of the work gangs and labor in the mines.

"Tell me more, author, about these fugitives [from the mines]."

"Your Majesty, they can be divided into three categories. First there are the runaways who leave their villages to become thieves and highwaymen. The second category consists of strangers within any particular community, who feel themselves to be outcasts, abused and ill-treated by everybody, without any living soul to whom they can turn in their trouble. They are so poor, too, that they are unable to pay their taxes. In the third category, finally, are the unfortunates who are employed as servants in the households of the landowners and administrators and who wish to escape. If things continue as they are now, Your Majesty, you are likely to lose all your Indian subjects, indeed to lose everything you possess."[30]

So Guamán focuses on the harm done by the Spanish intrusion into the native communities and insists upon the need for Indios to be governed by Indios, for the Spaniards to remain in their own cities, and for the end of racial mixing and the unfortunate expansion of the *mestizo* population. He forcefully underscores the profoundly disruptive impact of the Conquest on the residential and social aspects of Indio settlement patterns; the drawing of native women into the reproductive and social sphere of the Spaniards; and so the growth of a *mestizo* population and consequently the decline of the native one.

The ten first-hand reports described here are a tiny sample of those that have survived.[31] They do not explain why the demographic disaster took place, which is to say they do not provide a coherent interpretive model of the decimation of the native Americans. They do suggest, however, that the impact of the Conquest was widespread and entailed the various biological and social components that together maintain the demographic equilibrium of a collectivity. They suggest that the loss of that equilibrium and the long and disastrous decline were the result of a variety of causes, several primary ones (including of course the new diseases) and many secondary ones that combined and interacted in different ways depending upon particular local conditions and events. We need then to reverse an approach that has been used in researching these problems. Rather than coming up with a model and trying to apply it to local situations, we need to return to the healthy historical practice of studying local situations in order to construct a model that fits them.

The new diseases imported from Europe had an enormous destructive impact almost everywhere. But that impact must have been felt primarily in the initial phase when the viruses spread among populations lacking immunity and so totally vulnerable. The survivors, having acquired immunity, were not susceptible to subsequent epidemics, and so the destructive force of the diseases should have gradually declined to European levels; it may even be that over the generations selection factors rendered them less virulent and serious. Presumably the new diseases had no significant effect on fertility, so should not have reduced the reproductive capacity of the collectivity.

The impact of the wars of conquest and the civil wars was a function of their duration and extent and the degree to which the natives were drawn into them. Some areas escaped those conflicts altogether; in others they were devastating. Nor was the destruction of war limited to the direct effects of violence; it produced instead indirect effects that were still graver and of longer duration: the collapse of agriculture and famine, the destruction of resources and infrastructure, migration and dislocation. In those cases where the violence affected men and women differently, reproductive capacity was also diminished.

The "deadly hunger for gold" is an overriding theme of the Conquest. Certainly only that hunger can explain its speed. In the first phase, that rapacious greed was the direct cause of deaths, slavery – which brought about the desertion of the Lucayas Islands (Bahamas) – misery, and the breaking up of families; in a word complete destruction. Gold was the true cause of the destruction of the Taíno – "in order that they seek after gold, all [the natives] must die," according to Fray Pedro de Córdoba;[32] it affected all aspects of the demographic system, raising mortality, disrupting unions, lowering fertility, and depopulating large areas. Subsequently, gold, silver, and mercury were at the center of a complex system of labor exploitation with less direct demographic consequences – mining deaths were presumably no more frequent than during the European Industrial Revolution – providing we exclude emigration and/or escape from the zones subject to forced labor.

European domination and the subordination of the Indios had yet another effect of great demographic importance: the more or less forced removal of women from the Indio reproductive pool and creation of *mestizo* populations. In a broad view of American demographic evolution, the *mestizos* compensated for the decline of the Indios. But the disequilibrium that development created in the native communities caused a decline in reproduction and weakened recovery following the demographic crisis.

We can characterize the first phase of the Conquest as a sort of appropriation by the conquistadors of both the means of subsistence and the labor of the Indios, as the natives were obliged to supply, nourish, and serve the new arrivals. In those populations depending on a subsistence economy, the Conquest meant a net loss of resources and a decline in the ability to survive. When the numeric ratio between Europeans and Indios was very small, the negative impact was limited, but it became heavy as the ratio increased. In more structured societies, such as those found in the Andes and in Meso-America, that were able to accumulate resources and where tribute systems (in work or goods) already

TRAVAXA
ZARAPAPAHALLMAIMITA

enero, coprcraymiquilla

labrador
hacauacamayoc

enero - capai raymi   *encro*

TRAVAXO
ZARAPTVTACAVAIMI TAN

febrero pauaruacayquilla

gran tazones de
noche tuta caxa

oxeador de noche
tuta zara uacayouay

febrero - pauparurnay   febrero

TRAVAXOS
ZARAMÃTAORÍTOTACAR
coymitã marzo pacyapocoyquilla

marzo – pachapucuy   marzo

TRAVAXO

ЗARAPVCOI ЗVVAMÃTA

utacayelqaymeta,,abril ynrazaymequeda

fabracos
paryaia
aottua

abril. — ynca caymi   abril

TRAVAXO
ZARACALLCHAIARCVIPA

.cha muyo · aymoray quilla

rigasoriallhac

mayo — hatun cusqui   mayo

TRAVAXOS

PAPAALLAIMITAPA

rpa pinto haucayausqui quilla

labra dor
pachaca

junio — haucayusqui   junio

TRAVAXA
ZARAPAPAAPAICVIAIMO

ray pulio sdocra comachquella

collcacamayoc
sispensiro

pulio — chacraconacuy

TRAVAXA
HAILLICHACRAIAPVIC
VI

pacha agosto yapuyquilla

ayau haylli yau ayau hay llvau
ayau hay lli yau ayau yaylliyau
chaymo ya chay miprala

labrador

ahaylli

ahaylli

agosto — hacra yapuy

agosto

TRAVAXO
ZARATARPVMITAN

setienbre coyaraymiquilla

cienbrador de mays zaratarpoc

setienbre — coyaraymi

setienbre

TRAVAXA
CHACRAMÃTAPISCO

carcoy pacha tienpo deoxean dela sementera enpotereyno
utubre·oma caymi quilla·

pasian·arariuro·pachaca
o jeador

otubre — omocaymi   ctubre

TRAVAXA
ƷARACARPAÍIACOMVC

choy · rupaypacha — nobienbre ayamarca quilla

carpai zipas como nidaltacaquita riega

cocha · yaco
agua delpozo
para regar

nouienbre — ayamarcay   nouienbre

TRAVAXO
PAPAOCA·TARPVIPACHA

dezienbre - capac yntiraymiquilla

labrador depapas

dezienbre - capac yntiraymi   deciembre

existed, the impact could be absorbed to some extent by the ability to increase production. And while the number of the conquistadors and early colonists is fairly well known, the size of the indigenous population at the time of contact is unknown. The larger we imagine it to be, the less we are able to explain the demographic collapse as a function of the undoubted appropriation of indigenous energy and resources by the conquerors.

These considerations can be translated into a simple model which allows us to calculate how much the conquistadors took from the native collectivity.[33] It can be used for the island of Hispaniola in the following manner. In 1502, Governor Ovando arrived in Hispaniola with 2,500 colonists, who joined the few hundred who were already there. Let us estimate, then, that the European population numbered 3,000 and that around the same date the native population had halved relative to the moment of contact and so numbered about 150,000. We can also assume that the purely subsistence economy of the Taíno produced no surpluses; everything that was produced was consumed. Finally, let us assume that every European consumed on average three times that of a Taíno. Recall that Las Casas, undoubtedly inspired as always by his polemical zeal, wrote:

And since the Indios normally did not work; nor did they care to procure more food than they needed for themselves and their families . . . and any Spaniard ate more in a day than an entire native family ate in a month, because not only were they not content with what was necessary but there was much left over and waste without any rhyme or reason.[34]

It seems probable that the conquistadors helped themselves to whatever they liked without worrying much about waste, so that estimating per capita consumption at three times that of the natives is surely conservative. The percentage of production, then, needed to support 3,000 Europeans was equal to 12 percent, calculated as follows. The Europeans needed three units of production per person, or 9,000 in total; but since these units had to be produced by natives (because the conquistadors did not work) who themselves needed to survive, the conquistadors appropriated (for themselves and for those who were working directly for them) 18,000 units of the total product of 150,000: $18,000/150,000 = 12$ percent. In the case of Hispaniola, though, we need to take into account another aggravating factor: one-third of the adult males (about 8 percent of the total population or 12,000 men) were sent to work down in the mines and so had to be supported by the production of another 12,000 farmers. In this case the subtraction of native resources grows to 28 percent. While a 12 percent reduction in per capita consumption was serious, a 28 percent reduction was certainly unsustainable. Again we can understand the degree to which the initial population size influences our interpretation of the catastrophe. In the case of Hispaniola, if the population had been ten times larger – as some maintain – the appropriation impact would be an order of magnitude smaller and so practically nil. In Mexico and Perú around 1570, the weight of the European population must have been about 1 percent; both societies enjoyed developed agriculture and were able to save, accumulate, and invest, so that the direct impact of the appropriation was limited, even though at a local level that impact might be strongly negative.

The model sketched out here is purely abstract and static. It serves primarily as a guide to the interpretation of the consequences of the Conquest. Together with that abstract model, four lines of a poem serve to sum up the sense of this chapter. They are searing lines taken from the *Chilam Balam di Chumayel*, a volume of prophecies written by Mayan priests probably a few decades after the Conquest:

> They [the foreigners] taught us fear;
> they came to deflower the flowers.
> So that their flower could live,
> they ruined and sucked the lymph from our flowers.[35]

3 A tireless traveler disrupts a continent, but a quarter century too late. From the Caribbean to Perú: a brief history of a long voyage and of the suspected assassin of Huayna Capac, father of Atahuallpa. The true and presumed sins of smallpox and other crowd diseases

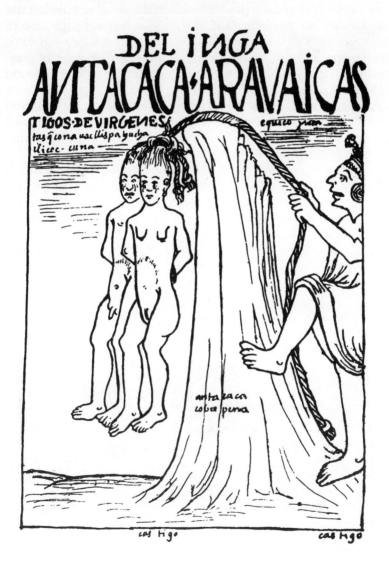

On January 10, 1519, the Hieronymite brothers who had been sent to Hispaniola with a broad mandate to govern the island in crisis wrote an anguished letter to King Charles: "In December of this past year, while [the Indios] were returning to their villages from the mines, it was the will of Our Lord to strike them with a pestilence of smallpox that has still not ceased; it has killed and continues to kill almost one-third of the Indios." After having lamented that, "if this pestilence lasts for another two months or more this year, we will no longer be able to mine any gold on this island of Hispaniola" (a potential wound to the king's finances), they added: "We have been told that a few Indios have begun to die of smallpox also on the island of San Juan [Puerto Rico]." And finally: "A few Spaniards have also fallen ill with smallpox but they have not died."[1] This is the earliest documentation of the arrival in the New World of one of the major protagonists of the catastrophe of the Indios – a protagonist accompanied by a host of other actors, also new to the American population: measles, scarlet fever, diphtheria, mumps, and typhus (of which, however, there was a pre-Columbian variety in the Americas). This chapter, however, will focus primarily on smallpox for two complementary reasons: it was the most violent and deadly of the new diseases, credited with far more disastrous effects than the other Old World maladies; and the discussion of smallpox can by extension be applied to the other diseases with which it shares many characteristics.

These were new pathologies for the American context, and so the native populations were "virgin territory," as they had not acquired any of those defensive immunities that develop over time as humans and the pathogens interact.[2] The Indios were all "susceptible" to contracting the infection and initially suffered from high to very high mortality; with time, by mechanisms we describe below, the effects gradually diminished. To understand the impact of smallpox, we need to carefully explore its epidemiological nature and why it was a new disease. Then we can trace its progress and repeated outbreaks in the New World, though not without first saying a few words about why it might be that the disease arrived only in 1518, twenty-six years after first contact. Except for the last, these are all arguments that have generated great interest, and the available documentation is generally well known and authoritatively discussed in a large body of literature. Our task will be to derive a synthetic narrative out of those sources. Nonetheless, we do have to confront a number of controversial questions: Was smallpox the real cause of the catastrophe? What were the circumstances that aggravated or attenuated (in different cases) the deadly effects of the epidemics? And what were those effects in the short and the long term?

We can turn again to the *Chilam Balam di Chumayel* for a picture of the time before the Conquest:

> There was no sin then,
> there was no sickness,
> there were no aching bones,
> they did not suffer from fever
> there was no smallpox . . .[3]

Could it be that before contact with the Europeans, the New World, free of smallpox and the other pathologies discussed below, did not know infectious disease at all and so that constraint which elsewhere insured high levels of mortality and consituted a check to demographic growth? This is a complex question since, lacking any written or pictorial documentation, we need to rely on paleo-pathology, a highly specialized discipline which has many limitations; primary among these is the inability to detect those diseases that do not leave any traces on bones (of which smallpox, for example, is one). Rather than venture into this difficult territory, we will limit ourselves to the conclusions of several specialist studies. For the southwest of the present-day United States, for example, it has been confirmed that the pre-contact populations were surely prey to a host of bacteria and viruses: staphylococcus, streptococcus, several forms of herpes and hepatitis, polio, whooping cough, and rhinovirus. They probably also suffered from fevers caused by ticks, tularemia, amoebic dysentery, tuberculosis, and treponemal illnesses. Meanwhile, turkeys and domestic animals could transmit parasitic infections such as salmonella and shygella.[4]

In summary, then, the bioanthropologic studies reported here provide unmistakable evidence of a substantial disease burden suffered by Native Americans prior to 1492. Much of this is due to chronic bacterial infections, while the remainder includes the effects of traumatic, degenerative, and congenital conditions. Their prevalence, severity, and chronology fluctuated enormously, were probably static in any one community only transiently, and responded to both biological and environmental conditions.[5]

Table 4 lists pathological infections for the indigenous populations of the Amazon according to whether they were indigenous and endemic to those populations, were developed as a result of contact with animals (zoonotic), or were introduced into the region. In other social and environmental contexts, the picture could be significantly different.

So it appears that pre-Columbian America was not quite the earthly paradise lamented by the Mayan priests – without sickness, aching bones, and high fevers – though it was free of smallpox and measles. It was instead a world characterized by high and fluctuating mortality, not vastly different from that of the Eurasian world with which it came in contact. Moreover, if we consider post-contact indigenous populations for which we have reasonable data, we can see that life expectancy at birth in non-epidemic years was nonetheless very low. Among the Guaraní at the Jesuit missions in Paraguay, of whom we will speak more in chapter 8, life expectancy in "good" years fluctuated around twenty-five, lower than in Europe.[6] Nor were epidemic-style mortality crises unknown in pre-Columbian times. Fray Bernardino de Sahagún transcribed and translated (with some variations) invocations to the gods made by *Huehuehtlahtolli* ("the ancient word") elders and priests; they include the following:

The pestilence brought great destruction and massacre to all the people; and what tears most at the heart is that children, innocent and without blame, who want nothing more than to play with stones and build little mounds of dirt, are now dying one atop the other, collapsing on the ground and against the walls . . . The force of this pestilential fire has now entered into your people like a fire on the prairie, spreading hot flames and smoke.[7]

According to the account of the Yucatán gathered by Diego de Landa, around 1500 "there came an epidemic of pestilential fevers that lasted for twenty-four hours; then on its abating the bodies of those attacked swelled and broke out full of maggoty sores, so that from this pestilence many people died and most of the crops remained ungathered." Similar episodes can be found in the native sources of Meso-America, as for example the great famine and epidemic mortality of 1450–4.[8]

Smallpox, like measles, scarlet fever, and mumps, is defined as a "crowd disease." This prosaic term is used to designate certain pathologies (not only those described here but also others ranging in virulence from plague to influenza) that first developed among animals, and in particular those that live in flocks or herds or in any case in dense groups. The development of agriculture including fixed settlements, and domestication created cohabitation between animals and humans and so a bridge for various viruses and microbes from one species to another. Interaction, evolution, and adaptation were such that, over the millennia, pathogens developed among animals gradually migrated to humans.[9] Molecular biology provides confirmation of this phenomenon, identifying the similarity between the measles and smallpox viruses and, respectively, bovine plague and cowpox. Analogously, influenza seems to derive from similar diseases found in pigs and dogs, malaria from birds and poultry, and tuberculosis again from cows, not to mention HIV/AIDS and its presumed origin in monkeys. The array of crowd diseases was less rich in the Americas than on the Eurasian continent, both because humans had arrived there more recently and were spread more sparsely and because the continent lacked large animals that lived in herds or flocks, apart from turkeys and bison in the north, llamas and alpacas in the south, and dogs throughout. Interaction between humans and animals, then, was limited, and hence the absence in the New World of a number of diseases of animal origin, such as smallpox.[10]

Smallpox is a respiratory virus that is transmitted when a healthy person comes into contact with a sick person and that person's surrounding environment.[11] There follows a latent period of twelve to fourteen days during which the infected person shows no symptoms and is not infectious. At the end of that period a high fever breaks out, accompanied by an increase in the quantity of the virus present in the body, shivering, nausea, vomiting, and strong, at times unbearable, back pain; later on there may follow great difficulty in swallowing and eventually death from septicemia. It is during this second period, lasting at most twelve days, that the sick person is infectious, and most infectious of all in the first few days following the latent period. By about the fourth day, the illness causes eruptions – on the forehead, face, neck, trunk, and extremities – that after a few days turn into groups of pustules (to the point of being confluent) that are typical of the disease and ooze, dry up, and then fall off, leaving deep marks on the skin. The infectiousness of smallpox is very high; it is increased by dense living conditions because transmission of the virus requires nearness to the sick person – who during the infectious period spreads the virus by breathing – or to bedding or clothing that has recently been in contact with him or her. Although theoretically possible, other forms of transmission have not been confirmed and so are highly improbable. Among those who are not immune, mortality from the illness varies with age: high among small children (40 to 60 percent), lower for five- to 25-year-olds (20 to 40 percent), and growing to as high as 50 percent or more for those over fifty. Nonetheless, its deadliness seems also to depend on social factors. Individuals who contract smallpox and recover acquire permanent immunity. For measles, which also claimed many lives, lethality was much less, around 10 percent of those who got sick.

Epidemiologists have constructed sophisticated models to describe the outbreak, spread, and subsiding of epidemics, charting their progress and levels of contagion, mortality and recovery. A few of the basic elements, in a simplified version, will help us to understand the mechanism at work. When smallpox is introduced into a "virgin" population that has never been exposed to the disease before, everyone is susceptible to infection. The percentage that actually contract the disease depends on a host of factors, including population density, lifestyle, the frequency of contact among people, and chance. Those who are infected run a high risk of dying (20 to 50 percent according to age as described above), but those who recover acquire permanent immunity. In small communities, epidemics tend to burn out given a lack of fuel, so to speak, as individuals either die or recover, acquiring immunity. In order to reignite, the infection must be reintroduced from outside, but that can only happen when a sufficiently large group of susceptible individuals has been reconstituted (either new births or non-immune immigrants). Hence the periodicity of epidemics. When, instead, a population group is large enough, the infection can become endemic, remaining active and never burning out, because there is always someone who is sick and so producing the infection; every year smallpox will claim a certain number of lives. Such was the case in the large European cities of the seventeenth and eighteenth centuries. We do not know, however, when smallpox became endemic in the great American population centers such as Mexico City and Lima.[12]

Consider a numeric example employing a hypothetical Indian village of 1,000 non-immune inhabitants and imagine that all the population is infected with smallpox (an extreme case, as someone is always away; some escape infection by chance; and others are "resistant" and do not get sick). If the average mortality among the sick is 40 percent, then we will have 400 deaths and 600 survivors who, having contracted the disease, are now immune. In order for a second epidemic to break out, a certain number of years will have to pass so that new births can create a susceptible population, and the contagion will need once more to be introduced from outside. Alexander von Humboldt repeated the commonly held view that smallpox reappeared in the Americas every fifteen to eighteen years.[13] For our example we will use a fifteen-year interval. If we assume our population is stationary between epidemics and that 40 percent, or 240 individuals, are not immune (because aged under fifteen, and so born after the first epidemic), then we will have another 96 deaths from the second epidemic (0.4×240) and an overall mortality that has dropped from the 40 percent of the first epidemic to 16 percent ($96/600 \times 100$). Using the same parameters for a third epidemic after another fifteen years would give us 81 deaths (overall mortality again of 16 percent) and 423 survivors. Thirty years after the arrival of smallpox, the population would have been reduced to a bit over 40 percent of its original size – a decline that qualifies as truly catastrophic.

Nonetheless, this example is an extreme one for three reasons. First of all, when smallpox arrives, not everyone is infected; chance, nature (there are always individuals whom the contagion fails to infect), or separation and distance from the sources of infection are always such that a significant proportion of the population is not infected. Presumably that proportion increases with time as individuals learn to recognize symptoms and avoid contact. The second reason is that our hypothetical level of mortality among those who are infected is high. We chose the maximum level of 40 percent, while it can be lower and in any case tends to decline after the first epidemic. In this regard, there are two groups of factors, biological and social, that play a role in lowering mortality. First, there is a selection process according to which those who recover are naturally more resistant to the virus and transmit that resistance to their offspring.[14] And there is also social adaptation according to which after the first epidemic the sick are no longer left on their own without food, water, or support, and so the rate of recovery increases. In recounting the epidemic of 1520, Motolinia wrote: "Many succumbed also to hunger because, all taking sick at the same time, they were unable to assist one another. There was no one to give them bread or anything else."[15] The third reason derives from an almost universal law that has been confirmed in numerous historical cases. After an epidemic there is a demographic "rebound," namely a notable excess of births over deaths. Births increase as new unions are formed among survivors who have lost their spouses, while deaths decline because the epidemic has eliminated many of the weaker members of the population – infants, old people – leaving behind those with, on average, a lower risk of dying. So following an epidemic, populations generally do not remain stationary (as in our example).[16]

Now we can modify our model imagining that (a) in each epidemic 70 percent of the non-immune population is infected (rather than 100 percent); (b) the average mortality among those infected declines from 40 percent in the first epidemic to 30 percent in the second and third; and (c) in the interval between epidemics the population grows by 15 percent (less than 1 percent per year). Applying these parameters, after thirty years the population would number 901 rather than 423. The demographic recovery between epidemics would be almost sufficient to balance the destruction wrought by the disease. This model can be made much more sophisticated by changing the intervals between epidemics; introducing age structures, mortality schedules for normal and epidemic phases (including for other crowd diseases), and fertility schedules; and taking into account reciprocal interactions between the various phenomena, but the results while changing numerically would tell a similar story.[17] We can return then to two essential points. Smallpox certainly provoked a disaster on its first appearance, as the entire population was potential fuel for its destructive force. The extent of the damage inflicted by its more or less regular return, instead, depended not only on the number of susceptible individuals but also on the degree of infection, the recovery rate of the sick, and the ability of the demographic system to respond; moreover, selective factors must have lessened the vulnerability of the non-immune population over the course of generations. In sum, the fate of the Indios depended on biological factors, but also on demographic and social factors, and even chance. If in some societies (the Greater Antilles) the Indios disappeared, that was not necessarily the fault of smallpox. If in others there was a more or less rapid recovery, that might come about in spite of smallpox. We shall return to this argument in the course of the chapter.

The descriptions left by contemporary witnesses of the impact of smallpox correspond well with the epidemiological treatises. Here is a version, originally in Nahuatl, repeated by Fray Bernardino de Sahagún:

When the Spaniards left Mexico . . . a great plague spread among us, a general sickness. It began in the month of September [1520]. A great devourer of men spread among us. Some were covered with it and it spread all over the body. On the face, on the head, on the breast. It was a very destructive sickness. Many died. No one could move. They could only lie down, stretched out on their beds; they could not turn their neck or make other movements with their body. They could not eat, either lying down or by turning to one side or the other. And if they moved, they shouted out. For many, that illness of pustules, contagious, hard, compact, meant death. Many died, but many died simply of hunger. They died of hunger; no one took care of anyone else; no one worried about anyone else. On some the pustules were spread apart; these suffered less and not so many died. Though many were left with disfigured faces . . . Others lost their sight and remained blind. It raged for sixty days, sixty deadly days. It began in Cuatlán. By the time it became apparent it was already fully developed. Then the pestilence moved toward Chalco. At that point it weakened but did not stop entirely.[18]

Here then are the symptoms: the body covered with pustules, the inability to move about, different sorts of eruptions and different levels of mortality, the rapid spread and quick termination of the epidemic. According to Bernal Díaz del Castillo and López de Gómara, it was a black man stricken with smallpox who disembarked with the expedition of Narváez – sent to put down the insubordination of Cortés – and started the epidemic:

When Narváez and his men disembarked, there was among them a Negro with smallpox who spread the disease among those in the dwelling that housed him in Cempoala, and so it passed from one Indio to another; and as they were many and slept and ate together, the disease spread quickly throughout the entire region. Most of the cases resulted in death; in many villages claiming half the inhabitants.[19]

We can also follow the trajectory of the disease (see map 3). It broke out first in Santo Domingo in December 1518, spreading almost immediately to Puerto Rico and then Jamaica and Cuba. It arrived in Mexico with Narváez in April–May 1520 and moved gradually inland: Tepeaca, Tlaxcala, and finally Mexico City in September–October. In the valley of México it raged for two months and then moved toward Chalco.[20] In the great capital city, Cuitlahuac, Lord of Ixtapalapa and successor to Montezuma, died of smallpox just eighty days after taking command of the empire. And smallpox is generally credited with an important role in the overthrow of Tenochtitlan-México. In the words of Bernardino Vázquez de Tapia, a companion of Cortés, writing twenty years later:

On that occasion there came a pestilence of measles and smallpox so hard and cruel that I believe it killed one-quarter of the Indios in the whole country. It aided us greatly in the war and was the reason that it ended so quickly, since, as I have said, that pestilence killed many people, including soldiers, lords, captains, and valiant warriors, whom we would have had to oppose as our enemies, but whom Our Lord miraculously killed and so took out of our way.[21]

The subsequent itinerary of the epidemic, or pandemic, of smallpox is uncertain. According to Fray Diego de Landa, the leading authority on the Mayan lands, the Indios had been struck by "a pestilence with great pustules that rotted the body, fetid in odor, and so that the members fell in pieces within four or five days."

Map 3 *Smallpox, 1519–24*

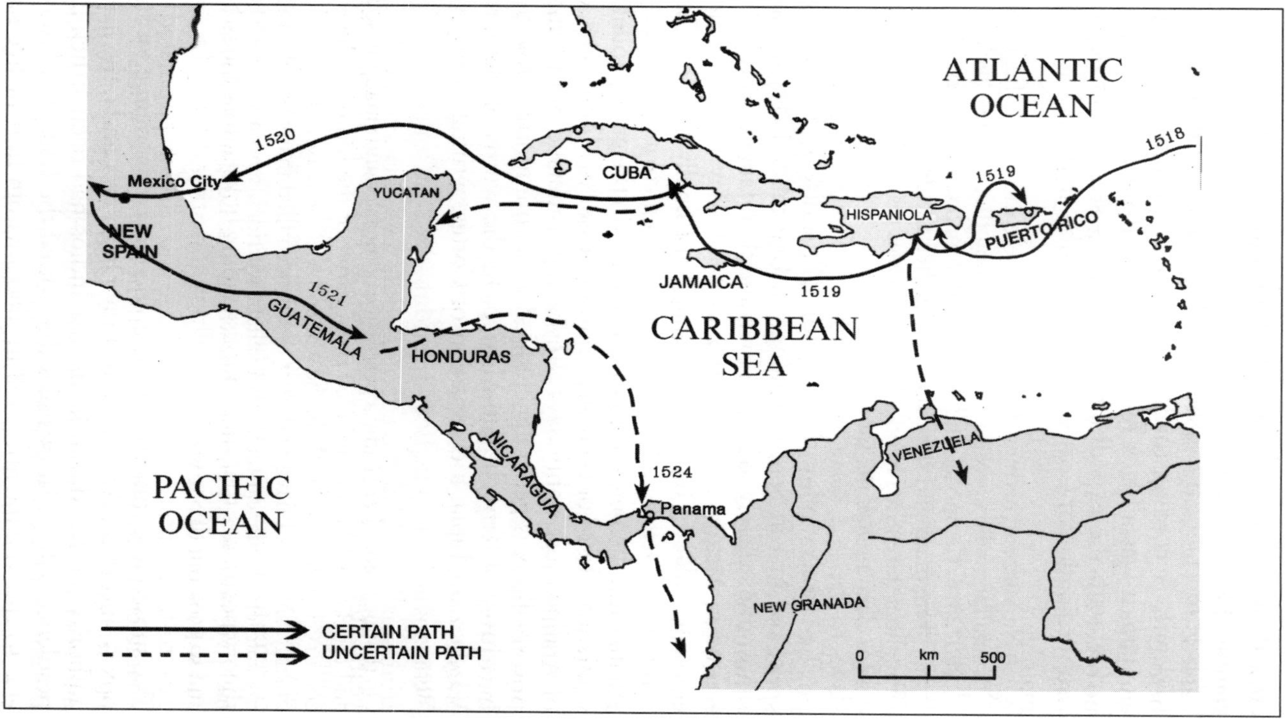

Writing at an uncertain date, sometime in the 1560s, Landa continues: "Since that last pestilence more than fifty years have now passed."[22] The date, then, is unclear; it could have happened before the arrival of Narváez. The pustules sound like smallpox, and likewise the "fetid" odor is typical of the disease; but we have no other confirmations. Assuming that it was smallpox, did it then pass from the Yucatán to Central America and the Caribbean mainland? It is hard to know, for as we get farther from the initial centers of the Conquest, Santo Domingo and Mexico, documentation becomes scarcer and our information less reliable. There are references to high mortality in Guatemala in 1519–21 but the cause is unclear.[23] Further south the only reference comes from a 1527 document, according to which it was necessary to bring slaves to Panamá, Nata, and the port of Honduras because smallpox had killed the Indios.[24] Historical documentation, then, of the spread of the epidemic that began in Santo Domingo ends at the isthmus of Panamá, if not in the Yucatán. The conjecture of some historians, however, does not stop there but instead revives and suggests – some claim it as certain – that the disease continued its southward journey, crossing the isthmus and traveling down the Pacific coast to arrive in Ecuador, and then climbing up to Quito, where it killed Huayna Capac, the last great Incan king and father of Atahuallpa, several years before Atahuallpa himself was taken prisoner by Pizarro (1532).[25] The European epidemics then would have preceded the conquerors. It is a hypothesis based on the most fragile of evidence, in the first place the reports of Juan de Betanzos and Cieza de León regarding the death of Huayna Capac from smallpox. The two conquistadors were writing about twenty years after the arrival of the Spanish and were using questionable sources.[26] It may also be that the term *smallpox*, which Betanzos in any case does not use, could have been employed in a generic sense to refer to an epidemic or mortality crisis. In the second place, the theory postulates that the tenuous trading links across the isthmus made possible the spread of smallpox and other diseases by direct, face-to-face contact.[27] In such a huge and sparsely populated area, characterized by few and intermittent contacts, it would be difficult for smallpox to spread directly. Discontinuities of settlement and contact, and the difficulties of spreading in humid zones or during the rains, would have easily interrupted the propagation of the disease, requiring that it be reintroduced from outside.[28] That smallpox which afflicted ancient Perú in the 1560s and devastated the coasts of Brazil in 1562–5, threatening the survival of the new settlements there, was a new pandemic.[29] It is then highly likely that smallpox really had nothing to do with the undoubted demographic disaster suffered by the Incan Empire.

In central Mexico, a densely populated region with a developed network of communication, smallpox spread quickly, though the first epidemic seems not to have extended beyond the Tarascan Empire. Jesuit witnesses, for example, confirm that it did not arrive in Sinaloa and Sonora till 1593.[30] Further north, in what would become the southwest United States, it arrived still later, perhaps with the completion in 1607 of the *Camino Real* that went from Mexico to Santa Fe. In the Northeast and Canada, instead, smallpox was brought by the Dutch, English, and French; it broke out among the Mohawks in 1633, spreading from there to Quebec and among the Huron people.[31]

In recent decades the supporters of the epidemiological theory have been anxious to prove that the new diseases, especially smallpox, can explain the disappearance of the Taíno from the Greater Antilles. As we have already pointed out, the first certain documentation of smallpox in the New World comes from Hieronymite friars. At that time (1518), the speed with which the natives were becoming extinct was clear to all. Labor had become scarce, and after having brought in thousands of unfortunate slaves from the neighboring islands, who themselves soon disappeared, the Spaniards resorted to others brought from Africa. Gold production was in decline, and the colonists were quick to abandon the islands for the more promising mainland. Many scholars hold, with some justification, that the islands must have already suffered the heavy impact of European diseases. Each incoming ship from southern Spain carried men, animals, plants, seeds and goods. "To argue that no disease transfer took place on these voyages is to assume the highly improbable."[32] And yet this may indeed have been the case, at least for smallpox. Alfred Crosby has argued that smallpox arrived in Hispaniola as late as it did because the full course of the disease, from infection to elimination of the virus, lasts one month or less, while "The voyage was one of several weeks, so that, even if an immigrant or sailor contracted smallpox on the day of embarkation, he would most likely be dead or rid of its virus before he arrived in Santo Domingo."[33] Crosby's observation is of fundamental importance for our discussion and merits further consideration. To accomplish that we need to review some basic aspects of epidemiology and of the history of navigation combined with a few simple mathematical operations.

In the case of smallpox, the latent period – during which the infected individual is not contagious – lasts twelve to fourteen days; after that the infection breaks out, and for a period of ten days the virus can be transmitted to another individual. After those ten days the survivor is immune for life (and no longer contagious). So there are twenty-two to twenty-four days between when the infection enters the body and the acquisition of immunity. For measles – another disease that was deadly for the Indios – the latent period is nine to twelve days and the outbreak of the infection lasts five to six days, so there are fourteen to nineteen days between infection and immunity.[34]

Now we can consider the data gathered by Huguette and Pierre Chaunu at the Archive of the Indies in Seville on the maritime traffic between Spain and Hispaniola. Between 1506 and 1518 the number of ships that weighed anchor in Seville and the nearby ports was 204 (or about sixteen per year), ranging from a minimum of six in 1518 to a maximum of thirty-one in 1508.[35] These were on average ships of about 100 metric tons that could carry fifteen passengers and a crew of thirty, or forty-five people in all.[36] Assuming that they all went ashore, we can estimate that 9,000 people disembarked on the island for longer or shorter stays. Between 1492 and 1505, it may be that a similar number went ashore (1,200 on Columbus's second voyage, 1,000 with Bobadilla in 1500, 2,500 with Ovando in 1502). Given then a round figure of, say, 20,000 Europeans who disembarked on the island between 1492 and 1512, we can imagine that the probability that one of those had smallpox was greater than zero. But how much greater? There lies the problem.

In order for an epidemic of smallpox to break out in the New World, three conditions had to be met. The first is that an infected person had to get on a ship. If that person survived, he would have been able to infect another person on board during the twelve- to fourteen-day period. Considering the upper limit of fourteen days, that infection could take place between the eleventh and twenty-fifth day of the crossing (if embarkation took place on the first day of the latent period) or between the first and the fifteenth day (if it took place on the last). Given that the average duration of the voyage between San Lucar de Barrameda and Santo Domingo was forty-eight days (between a minimum of forty and a maximum of sixty-eight), our hypothetical smallpox patient would either be dead or recovered before he arrived. So, in order for one or more infected persons to disembark at the end of the voyage, the virus would have to pass along to another passenger or sailor, starting a series of infections. Given the tight quarters, contagion on board was likely (though not certain) if there were other non-immune people on the ship. The second condition, then, is that the infected person (or persons) should arrive on the island. And the third is that, once disembarked, that person (or persons) should pass on the contagion to other people and so start the epidemic.

Briefly, then, in order for an epidemic to break out on the island a series of three conditions had to be met: 1) an infected person had to board a ship in Spain; 2) the infection had to spread, and another infected person (or several persons) had to survive and disembark in Hispaniola; 3) the infected person (or several persons) had to start an epidemic on the island. According to the rules of probability, the total probability that an epidemic should break out is the product of the probabilities of each of the three conditions: *P(total) = P(1) × P(2) × P(3)*. What might *P(1)* have been (the probability that an infected individual boarded a ship)? It is of course impossible to say with any precision, but we can estimate an order of magnitude and be satisfied with that for the time being. Smallpox was surely endemic in Seville at the time, and in the network of centers that surrounded that city; and we can estimate that it was responsible for 10 percent of deaths there, as it was in London and other large European urban centers in the seventeenth and eighteenth centuries.[37] According to the census of 1591, there were 18,000 families (*vecinos*) in Seville and another 96,618 in the rest of the province (Cadiz, Puerto Santa Maria, San Lucar de Barrameda, Jeréz de la Frontera, and the adjacent countryside).[38] From that data we can estimate, and an approximation will do, that the population of the area of Seville was about half a million at the beginning of the sixteenth century. If we imagine that the annual death rate was thirty per thousand, then it follows that the number of smallpox deaths per year would be

$$500{,}000 \times 0.03 \times 0.1 = 1{,}500$$

or 125 per month. Using this figure and imagining that the case mortality rate of smallpox in Seville was 25 percent, or one death for every four cases, then we can conclude that there were $125 \times 4 = 500$ persons who came down with smallpox each month. Each sick person could transmit the virus for about ten days if a survivor, but only for three to four days if he died. We can, however, rule out that those who showed symptoms would have been able, or allowed, to board ship, both because of the weakness and prostration brought on by the disease and because of the obvious nature of those symptoms (facial pustules). Continuing our calculation, we can estimate the risk that a person with a latent smallpox infection (and so not yet contagious) boarded ship, and so then suffering the outbreak of the disease and becoming contagious during the voyage. If we assign an average length for the latent period of twelve days, we can calculate that in the region of Seville there were each day $(500 \times 12)/30 = 200$ people with latent infections. It is in this group that we can look for the infected sailor or passenger traveling to the Indies. We need, though, to add another restriction. In those areas where smallpox was endemic, the majority of those stricken with the disease were small children (at most early adolescents) – judging from statistics for the seventeenth and eighteenth centuries, 90 to 95 percent.[39] Passengers and crew instead were drawn from the adult population (at youngest adolescent), so the infected population at risk of embarking (not children) then has to be reduced by an order of magnitude, from 200 to 20. Out of half a million people, then, there were each day twenty adults capable of transmitting the disease once on board, or four per 100,000 ($20/500{,}000 = 0.00004$). Now we can return to the docks of Seville from which departed each year sixteen ships with forty-five people aboard; the risk then that there was an infected person among these is

$$0.00004 \times 16 \times 45 = 0.0288.$$

There are good reasons to suspect that this figure is too high; the number of adults stricken with smallpox was generally less than the 10 percent indicated above, and while the disease may have been endemic in the crowded city, it was not likely to have been so in rural Seville, and this too would lower the overall risk. This probability then refers to the likelihood that an infected individual boarded a ship. The other two events also still had to occur. Namely, our smallpox sufferer had to infect other people on board (though a good number of those would have been immune as they came from a region where the disease was endemic), and, once ashore in the New World, those who caught the disease on board ship had to start an epidemic (a more likely event given that the natives were all susceptible). The probabilities that these last two events should take place, while high, are in any case less than 1, and so we can justifiably suggest that the combined probability of all three events occurring was not more than 0.02 (2 percent). In the simplest model, the average waiting time until an epidemic should break out in Hispaniola is equal to $1/0.02 = 50$, or half a century.

Those who are quantitatively inclined can refine this elementary mathematical exercise, but given that we are working with conjectures and hypotheses it is probably not worth the trouble. We can, instead, draw two useful conclusions. The first is that the "delayed" appearance of smallpox in the Caribbean – the epidemic broke out "only" in 1518 – is what we would expect. The second is that the Taíno were unlucky, since they got smallpox twenty-six years after the arrival of Columbus, rather than fifty. Though if the epidemic had arrived in 1542, it would have found few Taíno left as they were already well on the road to extinction.

The impact of an epidemic disease – such as smallpox, measles, diphtheria, typhus and others – does not depend only on the existence, or absence, in the population of acquired immunity. In addition to biological factors there are social ones that play a role in determining the gravity of the disease, as well as actions and behaviors that speed up or slow down the spread of the infection. We have already referred to these factors but need to say a few words more. They can be grouped into three categories: (a) those factors that affect the introduction or reintroduction of the disease into each community; (b) those that influence its intensity, namely the percentage of the non-immune who contract the disease; and (c) those which influence the rate of recovery.

The introduction of the infection depends upon the frequency of contact with areas where the disease is endemic or where there is an epidemic underway. In the second half of the sixteenth century, the continent was fairly well integrated, though there were areas that remained isolated (some continue to be so to the present day, such as the Amazon basin or the Orinoco). Traffic with Europe was regular and continuous, while that within the continent intensified. At the same time, population density declined severely over the course of the century, and this presumably reduced the frequency of contact. Population distribution probably also played a key role. Daniel Shea has noted the difference between central Mexico and the Andes. Mexico had a dense population settled concentrically around its capital city, and there smallpox spread rapidly through that network thanks to the high levels of communication and contact. In the Andes, settlement followed a "comb"-like pattern, distributed along the ridge of the Andes and down its valleys, which run parallel to one another (and perpendicular to the ocean) like the teeth of a comb. There we would expect disease to spread more slowly, with a good possibility of interruption, for example between one valley and the next.[40]

Still other factors and behaviors influence the spread of a disease once an infection has been introduced into a community. Density of settlement, frequency of face-to-face contact, type of agricultural work, outings for fishing and hunting, and the possibility of getting away from the group are all elements that, case by case, will help to determine the frequency of infection. Certainly one of the factors that increased the risk of infection was the policy of "reductions," namely concentrating the Indios who lived in sparse settlements into planned villages in central locations for the purposes of control, indoctrination, and administration. There were hundreds of reductions, from north to south, carried out by missionary orders, and we shall return to these below. But there were also reductions carried out by the administrative authorities, especially after 1570 in Perú, where the viceroy, Francisco de Toledo, made them a centerpiece of his administration. There is no doubt that the speed and rate of contagion increased significantly as a result. Naturally other actions might counter the effect of the reductions.[41] Padre José Cardiel, a Jesuit at the head of one of the thirty missions in Paraguay (we shall encounter him again below), tried to minimize the rate of contagion during a smallpox epidemic in this way:

[The smallpox] was such that if one person fell ill then he infected everyone else in the house. I arranged, then, for the construction of a good number of huts outside of the village, but nearby, and another group well built and farther away. When anyone fell ill, we moved them to the first set. If the illness was not smallpox, and one can tell after a few days, we sent him back home. But if it was smallpox we sent him to one of the more distant huts, and we burnt the one he had been staying in and built a new one.[42]

This was an intelligent strategy that could well be suggested by a modern epidemiologist.

As to the third factor, certainly patients were not helped by the medications and treatments given to, or inflicted upon, the sick according to the medical beliefs of the day. Nonetheless, the trauma of the initial epidemics was gradually overcome. For almost all cases about which we have documentation, those early scourges provoked flight, the abandonment of the sick, and social breakup. Certainly the practices described with obvious satisfaction by Padre Antonio Sepp, another Jesuit in Paraguay, regarding the care of smallpox sufferers in his mission were probably the exception:

At mid-day all [of the sick] received broth and half a pound of well-cooked meat instead of bread, which had begun to run low . . . At two in the afternoon I had each given some fresh water mixed with lemon juice and sugar in order to revive their livers, which were scorched by the fever . . . I had them fed once again when the sun set, this time some chopped meat and cassava tort. By opposing their innate voracity with this frugal diet, I succeeded in keeping alive many who otherwise would surely have died.[43]

It is doubtful whether this diet really cured anyone, but abandonment and a lack of food and water, not to mention moral comfort, surely killed many whom the virus might otherwise have spared.

As stated at the outset, smallpox was only the most important of the new and frightening diseases that struck the New World. It may be surprising then to learn that in Mexico, which likely suffered more from the new diseases than other parts of the Americas, the smallpox epidemic of 1520–1 was not followed by other widespread smallpox epidemics for the rest of the century. If there were any, they were not of a general sort and did not produce disasters described by contemporary observers.

The other deadly disease was typhus, almost certainly responsible for the other two major Meso-American epidemics of the sixteenth century, that of 1545–6 and the one that began in 1576. Typhus was a "new" and devastating disease also for Europe. According to the leading hypothesis, it was well established in the eastern Mediterranean and found new fuel in the war against the Moors in Grenada in 1489 or 1490, having been brought by soldiers from Cyprus, where it was endemic. From Spain, it seems then to have spread to Italy, France, and Central Europe, speeded along by wars and the movement of troops.[44] So the scourge of typhus in the New World was not much different from that in the Old. In both cases it was a new disease, and probably more virulent than it would become in subsequent centuries when some degree of immunity or adaptation was achieved. Finally, we should note that typhus is a disease strongly exacerbated by fatigue, malnutrition, crowding, and poverty in general.

4 *A golden nose ring and the tragic destiny of the Taíno. An Indio follows a deer and discovers a mountain of silver. A people in constant movement, over 1,000 miles and at an elevation of 4,000 meters, and the wealth of Potosí. Deeds and misdeeds of gold and silver*

Columbus's first encounter with gold came on December 12, 1492, six days after landing on the island of Hispaniola and three days after having named it and taken formal possession. The admiral sent three sailors ashore who came upon a number of naked natives, "who ran away, but nonetheless they managed to capture one woman," coincidentally "very young and beautiful." They brought her back to the *Santa Maria* and so before Columbus himself. "She wore a gold ornament on her nose, which convinced [the admiral] that there was gold on the island, and he was right." So wrote Las Casas in his transcription of Columbus' diary. In the following days, and until January 16, when he sailed back to Spain, Columbus and his men saw many natives wearing adornments of gold and received it as gifts and in exchange – enough to convince him that there was gold and that all one had to do was look for it. And enough to convince the court to outfit a second grand expedition. Three years later Columbus tried (and failed) to carry out a true organized plundering of gold, imposing on each family the consignment every three months of a *cascabel* (a small bell given as a gift to the natives) full of the yellow metal.[1]

We have already spoken of the "deadly hunger for gold," a description offered by Pietro Martire. That hunger was the overriding obsession of the Conquest, one that tormented leaders and followers, the court and the king. Martire was right to characterize it as "deadly," at least in the initial phase of the Conquest. It was deadly because the considerable risks associated with the first expeditions demanded a rapid and high economic return, justifying violence, abuse, and the employment of a large workforce. As Iberian domination in America established itself and the production of gold rapidly declined – around the middle of the sixteenth century – the search for and production of silver took off instead and rapidly came to exceed in value that of the more treasured metal. Silver production was not carried out so rapaciously as was that of gold, insofar as it required heavy investment and solid management. It was not then so destructive as had been the search for gold, though it inherited that same ill fame, as captured in the following phrase: "What is being sent to Spain is not silver, but the blood and sweat of the Indians."[2]

Before going much further, it is worth reviewing generally the production of precious metals in the Americas. The sources of data are essentially three: payment to the Crown of the *quinto* for all the metal extracted and refined; the activity of the mints; and the shipping of precious metal to Spain as registered by the Casa de Contratación in Seville (see figure 2).[3] Regarding the importing of precious metals, from the beginning of registration in 1503 through 1650, 181 metric tons of gold and 16,866 metric tons of silver were shipped to Spain. Given that the relative values of the two metals range from 10:1 to 15:1, we can estimate that the value of the imported silver was about eight times that of the imported gold.[4] Until the middle of the sixteenth century, it was almost exclusively gold that arrived in Spain, as the discovery of the silver mines in Mexico and Perú and the beginning of production there occurred more or less contemporaneously in the period 1545 to 1555. Until about 1525, the gold imports came instead almost exclusively from the greater Antilles: first from Hispaniola starting in 1494; from Puerto Rico beginning in 1505; from Cuba in 1511; and a trickle from Jamaica (already nearly depopulated) in 1518. Export from the three major islands declined rapidly after 1515, given the sacking of the Indio reserves, the using up of the alluvial deposits, and the rapid thinning of the ranks of indigenous labor. Once the islands were used up and depopulated, attention turned to the Caribbean mainland – initially referred to as the Castilla de Oro – including Darién, Veragua, and Panamá; these too were soon depopulated. Subsequently, gold imports came from Perú, thanks especially to the plundering of the stock accumulated over centuries for religious and ceremonial purposes. The infamous ransom of Atahuallpa – a vast enclosure filled up to the height of a man with precious objects – amounted to nearly 10 metric tons of gold.[5] After mid-century, gold mined in Nueva Grenada and Nueva España replaced alluvial gold (taken out of stream beds) and production reached its peak (43 metric tons imported to Spain in 1551–60).[6] By that time, silver production had well surpassed that of gold.

Why was the search for gold so destructive of the Indios? How many Indios were involved? And why did an activity that is not normally particularly dangerous have such negative effects?

In the first half of the sixteenth century, Spain imported on average about 1 metric ton of gold per year. The total amount of gold extracted must have been much more, as all witnesses attest, given that the incentive to avoid paying the *quinto* was great. Imagining, then, that total production was double that reported, we can ask what size of labor force might have been employed in the hunt for gold; and while we cannot offer a precise response, we can come up with an indirect and conjectural one. Given the methods of extraction prevalent at the time, the annual production of a prospector/miner had an upper limit. Only in exceptional cases might that production reach 1,000 grams; in most documented cases it was instead a few hundred, with a minimum of 100.[7] Taking these as maximum and minimum limits, that would mean an annual workforce directly involved in gold extraction of between 2,000 and 20,000 per year, while the total population indirectly involved – families of the workers, Indios employed in supplying food and other goods for the mining areas – must have been larger by a factor of ten (or more). So that the thousands or tens of thousands of workers directly involved in gold extraction would have drawn in a much larger population in those areas rich in deposits, but often sparsely inhabited. Hispaniola, Cuba, Puerto Rico, and Jamaica were islands with limited populations where the royal ordinances allowed that one adult in three be drafted for gold work. On these islands, and perhaps also on the Castilla de Oro, the scale of human mobilization was significant compared to overall population size. In the district of Popayán (Kingdom of Nueva Grenada, today Colombia), official production between 1546 and 1599 was about 400 kilograms of gold per year. It was the major gold-producing region south of Panamá, and it suffered rapid depopulation (71,000 taxpayers in 1559; 33,600 in 1582).[8] It has been estimated that one-third of those taxpayers were involved directly or indirectly in hunting after gold, to the considerable detriment of agricultural production. Hard, forced labor, the abandonment of agriculture, an unhealthy climate, and not enough food help to explain why "the life expectancy of the Indios in the mines was very short; they died in large numbers; and births did not succeed even to balance deaths."[9] Elsewhere the effects were either more localized or non-existent.

The technique of extracting gold from alluvial deposits and from the sand in stream beds is accurately described by Las Casas and Oviedo.[10] First, in what looked like a good spot, a trench was dug out about 8 to 10 feet square and about one or two palms deep. Then the earth was taken to a nearby stream, where it was washed and passed through the *bateas*; these were a sort of large wooden bowl at the bottom of which the gold dust and small nuggets would settle. The jobs of excavation, transport, and washing were carried out by different groups of Indios; for the washing women might be used too. "When you ask a worker how many of the washing *bateas* he is operating and he responds that he has ten, this means that an operation of this scale requires fifty workers since there are five for each *batea*."[11] If the results of the first dig were encouraging, then the trench was deepened and widened; if not, another spot was chosen for a new one. The Indios were sent to do this work in *cuadrillas* (squads), often traveling several dozen miles away from their villages, for *demoras* (periods of work) lasting up to ten months, and under the command of a Spanish overseer. They had to be supplied with food either from their distant villages or from fields nearer to the mining sites, an undertaking that constituted a heavy burden for those who, while not working the mine, were nonetheless involved in the production, preparation, and transportation of food.[12] When the *encomienda* system was generalized in the first decade of the sixteenth century, the Spanish *encomenderos* were encouraged to send one-third of able-bodied men to the mines, as private greed was complemented by the insatiable appetite of the Crown. As described by Oviedo, the work was not particularly hard, though in a careful and less passionate moment, Las Casas, an eyewitness, describes the destructive mechanisms employed in the search for gold during the time of Ovando (1502–9):

In those times there was a feverish hunt for gold . . . and so the decline and death of the Indios was an inevitable consequence, as they were accustomed to light work, given the fertility of the earth that they farmed almost without effort and so obtained and sustained themselves on its abundant fruits . . . Not only were they by nature a delicate

Map 4 *The mines of Meso-America*

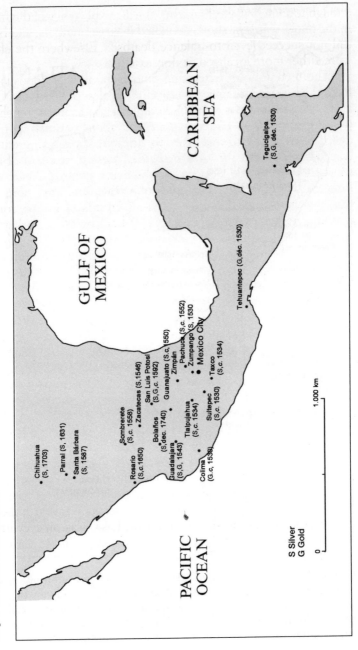

Map 5 *The mines of South America*

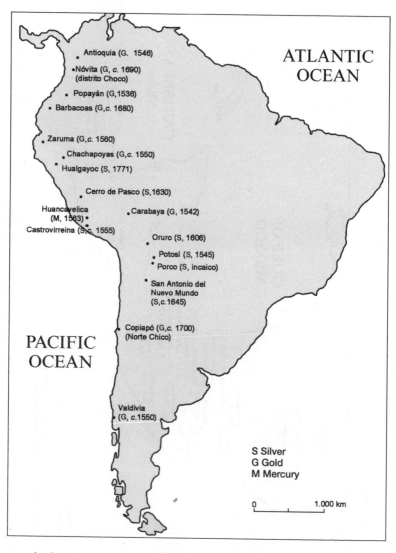

people, but they were immediately put to hard and bitter labor, going directly from one extreme to the other rather than gradually bit by bit, and so it was inevitable that they would not survive for long. And so it was, as during each *demora*, which lasted six or eight months, between one-quarter to one-third of the Indios making up the *cuadrillas* who worked on the whole process, from extraction of the gold from the mines to its melting down, died . . . Those who fell sick . . . were not believed and accused of being shirkers and layabouts trying to get out of work. And when the illness and fever instead became obvious, showing them to be truly sick, they received a little cassava bread and a few *ajes* and were sent back to their homes, which might be 10 or 15 or 20 or 50 leagues distant, but not in the hopes of curing them but rather so that the sick workers would go somewhere else and so not require any care; surely they would not have meted out such a treatment to their own horses had they fallen ill.[13]

Las Casas could be suspected of partisanship, were his claims not corroborated by much other testimony. In the letter to the Monsignor of Xèvres, the Dominicans on the island wrote: "Out of 100 Indios [sent to the mines], no more than sixty returned, and from those mines where the treatment was harshest, out of 300 no more than thirty returned."[14] Nor was it only religious figures who described the disastrous situation of the Indios in the mines and insisted upon the need to reduce and moderate their burden of work; officials such as Gil Gonzales Dávila (the king's treasurer) or the *licenciado* Zuazo on Santo Domingo or the administrators of San Juan (Puerto Rico) also joined in the chorus.[15] The king, the court, and the Casa de Contratación in Seville were also all aware of the situation; on the one hand they admonished the colonists to treat the Indios well, while on the other they encouraged their recruitment for the procurement of gold. It is also worth mentioning that many observers thought that the change of climate and environment was particularly harmful for the Indios. "They sent them where there were thin waters and cold streams and inclement weather, and since they were naked, an infinite number died, leaving aside those who died from the enormous weight of the work and from exhaustion."[16]

In the first decades after contact, the gold economy exacerbated the destructive force of the Conquest and was itself unsustainable in the long run. On the one hand, it was unsustainable because both the gold held in the treasuries of the Indios and that in the alluvial deposits was soon used up; on the other, it was unsustainable because the hunt for gold exercised a traumatic impact on both society and the population, raising mortality and lowering fertility. The mechanism of that destructive force can be outlined according to the following model:

1 The demand for gold led to forced labor involving the largest possible number of indigenous workers.

2 The Indios constituted a fragile labor force. Accustomed to light and intermittent work, they were not steeled to continuous and physically heavy labor of the sort engaged in by any farmer struggling with land reluctant to yield its fruits.

3 The Indios, like other populations accustomed to tropical climates with modest variations of temperature, suffered when these changes became noticeable. The poor working conditions – workers assigned to the *bateas* were constantly standing in the water – increased their vulnerability still more.

4 The distance of the gold deposits from the villages and from the fields made food supply precarious, and the workers suffered from lack of nourishment.

5 Variations in climate, excessive work, and precarious diet increased mortality from endemic diseases – many of them presumably of a respiratory nature. The introduction of new pathogens must of course have worsened the situation, but even without them the picture was strongly negative.

6 Long absences from their villages for most of the year, the greater mortality of men as compared to that of women, and the intensification of female labor in the production and preparation of food were all factors that lowered indigenous fertility.

7 The reduction of the workforce led to the recruitment of still more Indios and so a worsening of the crisis.

8 The avarice of the conquistadors, as described by contemporaries, and the brutality, violence, and cynicism it inspired, also worsened the crisis. That avarice can be explained by the high risks overcome by the first generation of conquistadors and by the perception of future risks, including the possibility that the entitlement of free Indian labor might be taken away from them.

9 The Indian society employed in the search for gold acted like a vortex, swallowing human resources in concentric circles, drawing in population first from the nearby islands and other territories but eventually also from the coasts of Africa.

10 The negative interaction between gold and the Indios played out its destructive effects over a short period of time: at the longest over the course of a single generation; at the shortest over about ten years.

Las Casas describes that, at the end of 1507, Juan Ponce de León crossed the stretch of sea that separates the east coast of Santo Domingo from Puerto Rico, having heard that the Indios had gold. He was well received by the *cacique* Aqueibana, who led him to the stream beds where there was gold, "innocently unaware that he was revealing the knife with which he himself and his kingdom would be killed."[17]

A first aside. In the southern hemisphere, at the center of the Brazilian continent, gold was discovered two centuries later. It was toward the end of the seventeenth century that the *bandeiras* (expeditions) coming from the region of São Paulo discovered gold in the foothills of the Sierra do Espinhaço. A sparsely populated area inhabited by only a few thousand natives, it was named Minas Gerais and attracted thousands of *faisquieros* of every race and combination.[18] According to Giovanni Antonio Andreoni, in 1709 there were 30,000 people in Minas. In 1699, 725 kilos of gold arrived in Lisbon, in 1703 over 4 metric tons, and in 1712 more than 14 (as much in a single year as arrived in Spain in the first two decades of the sixteenth century). Production reached a maximum in the first half of the eighteenth century and then declined slowly. Meanwhile the population had grown to 300,000. Earlier slash and burn agriculture complemented by the raising of some pigs and chickens had given way to more advanced cultivation and animal raising. Gold was not a destructive force, but a magnet that contributed to the long-term development of the region.

An Indio named Gualpa, originally from Cuzco and working for a Spaniard, chased after a herd of deer that:

fled up the side of a mountain that was very steep and covered with a bush called *quiñua* and other dense undergrowth; in order to climb up such a difficult slope, he grabbed hold of a plant growing out of a vein . . . In the hollow of the root he noticed, thanks to his experience in [the mines of] Porco, that the rock was very rich [in silver]; on the ground near to the vein he found several pieces of rock that had broken loose and were not easily recognizable because faded by sun and water. He carried these to Porco to examine them by melting.

This is the description offered by the mining entrepreneur Luis Capoche in his *Relación general de la Villa Imperial de Potosí.*[19] More than half of the silver imported to Spain before 1650 came from the Cerro Rico of Potosí, which rises 600 meters above the surrounding 4000-meter high plateau, and from the city of Potosí situated at its base. At the peak of its expansion Potosí became the most populous city in the Americas and the one in which circulated the greatest riches (in terms of both quantity and flow).

Why are we interested in Potosí? Fray Domingo de Santo Tomás called it the "mouth of hell" that swallowed up every year thousands of innocent Indios.[20] The Augustinian Friar Antonio de la Calancha wrote: "The mills have ground up more Indios than metal as every weight that is coined costs ten dead Indios."[21] In fact, the mines of Potosí garnered ill fame – yet another component of the *Leyenda Negra* – bringing social and demographic disruption to a vast area, more than a thousand kilometers in length and several hundred wide. Again citing Luis Capoche: "The mountain and imperial city of Potosí are situated in a cold region where it snows a great deal; the land is sterile and nearly uninhabitable for its harsh and inclement climate . . . no edible foods grow there except for a type of potato . . . and a grass without grains . . . because it is always cold . . . the terrain is rolling and bare."[22] "For at least 6 leagues surrounding Potosí there is neither fruit nor tree."[23] Dry for nine months of the year, it is inundated with torrential rains for the other three. The survival of the city and of its mining activity depended upon a transportation system for foodstuffs, tools, and other consumer goods coming from afar. A few dozen kilometers from Potosí there were lower valleys that produced meat, wheat, and corn: "Beyond 6 leagues there are valleys with a wonderful climate; there one finds grapes, Spanish and local fruit, sugar cane, melon, cucumbers, and different sorts of vegetables from Spain."[24] Dried fish, sugar, and fruit came from Arica on the Pacific coast, 500 kilometers away. Fresh fish and salt came from Lake Titicaca; lamb and beef from Tucumán, Buenos Aires, and Paraguay.[25] Mining activity consumed huge amounts of fuel, lumber, and other materials, all brought from more or less remote regions. The growth of the city, mining work carried out at a furious pace, and provisioning and transport required a large, available, and cheap labor force.

A brief look at growth in the period that interests us will help us understand better why Potosí and its mines merit a place in the *Leyenda Negra*. The wealth of the Cerro Rico was immediately apparent and, in the twenty years after 1545, thousands of miners arrived, drawn by the hope of gain, and excavated the mountain's four richest veins. In 1546, at the base of the Cerro there were 300 Spaniards and 3,000 Indios. In 1547, the year the city was founded, there were already 14,000 residents.[26] But those veins were quickly exhausted, profits declined, and the Indios returned to their villages. In such an inhospitable region, lacking other sources of wealth and so unsuited for settlement, the workforce had to be brought in from afar. African slaves could not endure the climate and the work. Extraction techniques were primitive; trenches and tunnels followed the veins into the mountain without any sort of order or rule; discarded slag littered the base of the mountain; melting down of the silver (production of which declined rapidly) took place in thousands of small open kilns, fueled by the dry grass of the plateau. The great relaunching of mining activity coincided with the arrival of Viceroy Francisco de Toledo, who came to Perú with a broad mandate to re-establish civil and economic order based on two principles: the improvement of extraction techniques and the supply of labor. The long visit of Toledo in Potosí in 1572–3 concluded with an important accord with the wealthy entrepreneurs of the region. They agreed to invest in expensive equipment to pulverize and wash the ore, making it possible to use an amalgamation process in which the ground ore was mixed with mercury to extract the silver. This technique was considerably more productive than the traditional one and had already been used to good effect in Mexico for more than a decade with mercury imported from Spain. In Perú instead, mercury could be gotten in sufficient quantity from the mines of Huancavelica and so, thanks to a state monopoly, supplied to the entrepreneurs of Potosí at a good price. The amalgamation procedure also allowed extraction of silver from the slag discarded over the previous quarter century. The labor force was to come from the highlands – a strip 1,200 kilometers long and 400 wide stretching from Cuzco in the north to Tarija in the south – according to a system of forced rotation (once every seven years) where the salaries were fixed beforehand. This system took the name of *mita* and the workers were called *mitayos*. The introduction of the mercury amalgamation technique and creation of the *mita* (1573) yielded excellent results: silver production revived and ten years later had grown eightfold.[27] In the last two decades of the century, the largest loads of precious metal ever recorded were shipped into the port of Seville.

The *mita,* then, was the key to Toledo's system, a system that would continue to function for two and a half centuries until definitively abolished by Simón Bolívar in 1825. It found historical precedent in the Incan obligations regarding work for public and religious purposes. The responsibility to provide labor, however, fell not to the individual but to the village or community; ceasing to reside in the village, for example as a result of emigration, also meant the end of the *mita* obligation.[28] Although Indian laws prohibited forced labor, they did make an exception for activities that were publicly useful. Toledo relied on this principle – the production of silver was certainly a priority for the state – and on the opinion of a consultative committee that he convened in Lima; on those bases he issued a detailed ordinance. The king hesitated to give his formal approval, which came only in 1589. The allocation of work obligations for the various highland provinces – the lower elevations were excluded in order to avoid the damaging effects of climate and environment change – were instead first assigned in 1573, revised somewhat in 1575 and 1578, and confirmed by successive viceroys.[29]

In the period that most interests us, until the beginning of the seventeenth century, about 14,000 adult Indios (aged fifteen to fifty) were drafted each year, or 14 percent of the taxpayers in the relevant population; in theory that would amount to an individual *mita* obligation once every seven years. That obligation to work in the mines lasted one year and required one week of labor out of every three, so that the average *mita* labor force was around 4,500. Toledo, who had carried out an accurate census of taxpayers at the beginning of the 1570s, ordered that 17 percent of them come from the district of Charcas (which included Potosí), 16 percent from La Paz, 15 percent from Cuzco, and 13 percent from the provinces of Canchis y Canas (Cuzco) and Condes (Arequipa). In the *Relación* of Capoche (written in 1585), the 13,335 Indian *metayos* came from 125 communities, and each community contingent came accompanied by a captain (usually a *curaca* or local chief).[30] The distances traveled were enormous, from a minimum of a few dozen leagues to a maximum of 180 (almost 1,000 kilometers) for those who came from the district of Cuzco. "The number of people gathered together in this city [Potosí], added to those already resident, was 13,340 Indios; but to reach that number more than 40,000 had to leave the villages, adding wives and children. And the roads were so crowded one imagined the entire kingdom in motion."[31] The Indios traveled with their families and household belongings, accompanied by llamas for transport and eventual sale. Following the instructions of their *curacas*, they gathered in specified meeting places and then proceeded as a group. In 1602, Padre Durán, from the Jesuit mission of Juli, was sent along with another member of the order to witness the departure of the drafted Indios from the province of Chucuito on the southern shore of Lake Titicaca:

This province is required to send 1,900 Indios to the Cerro; the [established] number and proportions leave according to the lists. All are combined into a single list, and they are made to depart in single file across a bridge made of green rushes that spans the outlet of the great laguna of Chucuito [Titicaca], and so there is no way to escape . . . More than 30,000 souls gather at the bridge, the 5,000 bound for Potosí along with others who have accompanied them to this point. And I say 5,000 because, while the workers assigned to the mines number 1,900, they bring along with them their wives and children, their overseers, and their *caciques* and so the total number comes to 5,000. The livestock from that region, used to carry their gear and provisions, amounts to more than 20,000 head.[32]

This crowd of men, women, children, and animals, approaching biblical proportions, undertook a voyage lasting at least a month, proceeding at a pace of 5 or 6 leagues per day (they received a small allowance for each day of travel). The same voyage in reverse took place one year later. In Potosí, Friar Salinas y Córdoba noted that every year 50,000 head of livestock (llamas) arrived, brought by the *mitayos* and loaded down with their provisions. None of them made the return trip, however, "because everything is consumed and eaten in that city."[33] According to Alfonso Messia, the pressed laborers in Chucuito in 1600 numbered 2,200, plus wives and children: "I have twice seen them and can report that there must be 7,000 souls. Each Indian takes at least eight or ten llamas and a few alpacas to eat. On these they transport their food, maize and *chuño*, sleeping rugs and straw pallets to protect them from the cold, which is severe, for they always sleep on the ground. All this cattle normally exceeds 30,000 head."[34]

We have already referred to the 14,000 Indios of the *mita gruesa* (the full annual contingent) who were directly employed in the backbreaking labor of the mines; they worked one week out of three (from Monday to Saturday), and so on any given day 4,500 Indios were doing mine work. Of these, less than a third worked in the tunnels and pits of the mines themselves, while the rest operated the mills that ground the ore, carried out the amalgamation process, and engaged in other activities. According to Capoche the distribution was as follows:

In the mines and tunnels	1,369
In the water-driven mills	2,047
In the horse-driven mills	620
In the amalgamation process	222
In other activities	195
TOTAL	4,453

In theory, the other two-thirds of the *mita gruesa* should have been free to pursue other activities (or to rest). Nonetheless, the authorities drafted a considerable number of *mitayos* for other tasks: the *indios de mese* and *indios de plaza* were used for various services; others transported provisions – for the salt works, for the monasteries, for various officials, for the physician surgeon, to develop new deposits, and so on – amounting to another 1,000 workers. Given then that a large number avoided the *mita* altogether,[35] about half the *mitayos* were directly employed every day, while the other half theoretically enjoyed a period of rest, though that period was generally used by the Indios for salaried work.

The development of mining led to heavy immigration, so that within a century Potosí was the largest city in the Americas, credited with a maximum population of 160,000 inhabitants in 1611, though that is probably an overestimation.[36] It was an immigration fed in part by the many *mitayos* who stayed in Potosí rather than returning to their villages. Cieza de León visited the city in 1549, two years after its official founding, and marveled at the level of commercial activity, and the baskets of goods ranging from coca to textiles from Spain and Flanders. "In the time of the prosperity of the mines, the Indios themselves, and so without the involvement of Christians, engaged in exchanges amounting to 25,000 to 30,000 gold pesos per day, and some days as much as 40,000; an amazing thing as I do not believe there is a market in the world that can match these levels."[37] Less than forty years later, Capoche would write: "the clothing and ornaments of this population are as precious and expensive as one encounters in Madrid . . . the games and lotteries are without number . . . the alms given are so generous that the Jesuit fathers completed building their church and headquarters in just a few years."[38]

An anonymous document from 1602 estimates that there were 46,000 Indios employed in Potosí, of which one-third were in mining and the rest in other activities (see table 5). According to the census of 1611, however, the Indios numbered 76,000.[39] The *mitayos*, then, constituted a minority of the workforce but, insofar as they were directly involved in the highly risky work of metal extraction, they were the irreplaceable economic motor of the *Villa Imperial*.

Did the *Leyenda Negra* of Potosí, described as a "cruel mouth of hell," also signify catastrophe, high mortality, and depopulation? Do we encounter here too a tragic plundering like that of gold in the Antilles? The answer is almost certainly no. The Potosí *mita* – not a unique case in Perú, as we shall see – represented at the same time a centripetal and a centrifugal force that instituted and amplified an annual ebb and flow of 40,000 people. It generated migration but not mortality, geographic dislocation but not catastrophe. David Cook's accurate estimates of population decline for 1570–1620 include a figure of 43 percent for the area he calls "south sierra" – corresponding more or less to that part of present-day Peru included in the Potosí *mita* – considerably less than the 58 percent decline he obtains for the country as a whole.[40] And, as we shall see below, in a number of areas where we can make the comparison, there was in fact demographic expansion between 1570 and the beginning of the seventeenth century. This is not to say that the trials of the voyage and working conditions did not claim a heavy toll in lives, but rather that the overall impact was relative and not devastating.

Working conditions in the depths of the mines were certainly inhuman, as confirmed by the following testimony of Padre José de Acosta. At depths reaching to nearly 250 meters:

they work by candle light, organized in such a way that one group works by day and sleeps by night and the other does the reverse. The rock is hard, and they break it loose with hammer blows, and it is like breaking granite. Then they carry it out on their shoulders up ladders made of three large twisted strands of cow's hide; between the strands are inserted pieces of wood that serve as the rungs so that two people can climb up and down at the same time. These ladders are 10 *estados* in length [about 16 meters] and at the end of one there is another, [and between the two] there are wooden platforms for resting, like landings, because there are many ladders to climb. Each man carries 2 *arroba* [25 kilos] of rock in a sack tied to his back and shoulders, and they ascend in groups of three. The leader carries a candle attached to his thumb to make some light since, as mentioned, it is pitch dark and they have to climb using both hands; and so they proceed for long stretches, as I have already said, that often exceed 150 *estados* [235 meters], which is a terrible thing, the simple thought of which makes one tremble.[41]

The backbreaking nature of the work, large swings in temperature, the inherent danger, cave-ins, and the inhalation and ingestion of mineral dust all combined to cause respiratory illness, silicosis (*choco*), injury, and accidental death. Although there were strict ordinances regarding both the maximum number of trips and load limits for the *apiris* (the porters), those rules were not observed, and daily quotas were often set for the amount of ore transported.[42] The dangers of the mine – cave-ins, landslides, falls – are vividly described in Capoche's *Relación*: "Some leave [the mines] dead and others with broken arms or skulls. In the mills there are injuries every day. And great harm is inflicted by the simple fact of working at night in this freezing land and by the millwork, which is all the more exhausting for the dust which fills one's eyes and mouth. And so the hospital is full of injured Indios, and more than fifty die each year, swallowed alive by this ferocious beast."[43] Tragic as the situation was, a mortality on the order of three or four per thousand per year (there were 15,000 mine workers in 1602) was not that different from that among European miners during the Industrial Revolution: high enough to discourage the Indios from working in the mines, but not high enough to decimate the population.

Certainly the long voyage undertaken by tens of thousands of people across inclement highlands brought with it suffering, exhaustion, and accidents. To the viceroy, marqués de Montesclaros, the Jesuits warned "that because of this constant migration the Indios do not grow and the babies die on the *puna* (steppes) and in desolate regions that are very cold; women do not conceive, and all are stricken with illnesses from which they die, and so their villages are depopulated."[44] Nonetheless, the Indios did know how to protect themselves against the harsh climate. Their means were meager, but they generally traveled with adequate provisions, and there was an element of continuity with the centuries-old practice of moving in work gangs with entire families in tow.[45] Juan de Matienzo, well acquainted with the ways of the Indios, wrote: "It is easy for them to leave their land and homes and go elsewhere because they can carry everything they posses along with them, like snails."[46]

Figure 3 offers surprising evidence for the limited influence of the *mita* on the relevant populations. The data used come from twenty-one communities for which we know the number of tax-payers counted by Toledo in 1572–3 and again from subsequent censuses taken at different dates between 1591 and 1610 (though for the most part in the period 1599–1604), and so on average thirty years later. For these communities we can also calculate the percentage of Indios serving as *mitayos*. A first glance reveals that the number of communities that experienced decline (eleven) is just about equal to those that grew (seven), though the overall population decline was significant (18.8 percent). The surprising result instead is that there is a positive relationship between the level of the *mita* and population change. Namely population grew (or declined the least) for those communities that contributed most heavily to the *mita* and vice versa – the opposite, then, of what one would expect. It could be that the small number of cases (eighteen) and limited size of the population in question (a little more than 31,000 in 1571–3) render the results of little significance, but it may also be that they represent more than a simple coincidence.

As suggested above, the *mita* in Potosí acted as both a centripetal and a centrifugal force, generating a broad migratory movement. We have already spoken about the centripetal force, though it should be added that other mining centers exerted similar attraction – in particular Huancavelica, where 3,000 drafted laborers worked at mercury extraction. In 1623 the ordinary *mita* – the total number of pressed workers was a multiple of this number, three times as we saw in the case of Potosí – numbered 4,304 in Potosí, 1,293 in Castrovirreina, and 667 in Porco, to which we can add another half dozen mining sites employing 100 to 300 Indios each.[47] The centrifugal force, however, requires better explanation. As time passed, and especially toward the middle of the seventeenth century, it became progressively more difficult for the communities and their leaders to mobilize the Indios in sufficient numbers to satisfy their quotas. A first obstacle lay in the lower wages of the *mitayos* as compared to those of the *indios mingados*, or those contracted so to speak on the free market, who enjoyed significantly higher salaries. This discrepancy grew ever larger as a result of the constant pressure of the mine owners to eke out the maximum possible work from the *mitayos* or to withhold their compensation by the evasion and manipulation of the strict rules laid down in the ordinances. Generally speaking, the Indios did not run away from the mines; there were instead many who, rather/than returning to their home villages, as they were required to do, evaded their chiefs and stayed in Potosí or nearby – Indios who lived in the region were exempt from the *mita* – in order to work at a salaried job. It was therefore the *mita* from which the Indios tried to escape, and so the fate of working at a job not compensated by an adequate level of pay. A second reason for the growing inability to meet the *mita* quota was the demographic decline of the contributing communities, the shrinking of the human resources from which to draw the drafted labor. This decline came about for natural reasons – there were serious epidemics in the 1580s and 1590s – but also because of steady emigration caused by the first reason listed above. An Indio who left his village for another, even if otherwise obliged to serve as a *mitayo* – found himself exempt because he was now a *forastero* (someone from outside the community). These mechanisms have been well studied and are based on documentary evidence that is difficult to challenge.[48]

The Indios tried everything to avoid the *mita*. They pretended to be *yanacona* (that is, servants to the Spaniards, and so exempt); they baptized their sons as daughters; they refused to return to their villages after finishing their work in Potosí; they ran away from their villages just before the departure. At the time of Toledo's census, the category of *forastero* did not exist, as every Indio was assigned to a village and the *yanacona* were few. But by the mid-seventeenth century, a partial count of the area subject to the *mita* yielded 64 percent *naturales* (residents), while 14.2 percent were *yanacona* and

21.8 percent *forasteros*.[49] In this way, more than a third of the population escaped the *mita*. Looking again to contemporary observers, here is the opinion offered by the Jesuits in 1610 and already cited above:

When they leave the mines to return to their villages, they escape instead to the nearby valleys where there are farms that will lodge them providing they agree to work for a period of time, or they will go to some other unknown place where they can raise some crops. Because when they return home, rather than being able to rest, they must work at the *tambo*, do drayage for the *corregidor*, or join work crews for the *cacique* or the priest; and their homes, which they left in good condition, they will find instead missing a roof or ruined.[50]

Or from another source:

Barely one-tenth return to the distant villages . . . though they make a show of leaving once the *mita* is finished; when the drum is beaten in the public square, they leave in groups with their wives and provisions and children hanging from their necks; then having walked barely a league they wait for night and return, dividing up so that some stop in the fields, some in the mining settlements, and some in other nearby places.[51]

The communities themselves constantly complained that they were unable to fulfill the *mita* because of population decline and evasion. The province of Chucuito, for example, had a quota of 2,200 Indios but could send only 600.[52] Jeffrey Cole has shown that during the first half of the seventeenth century the *curaca* gradually became unable to fulfill their *mita* obligations, and they were fined a sum equivalent to the salary of an Indio *mingado* hired on the open market for each *mitayo* they failed to send to Potosí. Toward the middle of the century, the weekly number of *mitayos* actually at work was half the official quota established by Toledo (and subsequently reconfirmed).[53]

On a mountain 4,400 meters high overlooking the city of Huancavelica, midway between Lima and Cuzco, lay the mine of Santa Barbara, an important source of mercury. The site was already known to the Incas, who got cinnabar there, used for ceremonial and religious purposes. The exploitation of mercury took off because of its use in the amalgamation process for silver: the mined and cleaned ore was shipped overland to the port of Chincha, then by sea to Arica, and again overland up the 4,000 meters to Potosí. Mercury was essential to the relaunching of silver production. The mining of it was also accomplished by means of the *mita*, using Indios drawn from a range out beyond 100 kilometers. The quota for the last decades of the sixteenth century was 3,000 Indios, subsequently reduced by half.[54] An added risk made the mines of Huancavelica even more frightening than those of Potosí: mercury poisoning. Both the dust inhaled in the mines and the vapors coming from the treatment of the ore could be fatal. Ramirez de Arella, physician at the San Bartolomé Hospital, had this to say on April 3, 1649, before an investigating committee sent to Huancavelica: "The illness derives from inhalation of the dust created by blows of the pick axe and other tools . . . it is pungent and penetrating and invades the respiratory organs . . . above all it attacks the large artery of the lung, causing corrosive wounds which evolve into tuberculosis." Or again, transporting heavy loads for as far as 400 *estados*, "scrambling up and passing from excessive heat to equally excessive cold . . . their lungs compress (as Galen writes) and produce emissions of blood."[55] In 1649, the viceroy, marqués de Mancera, came to an agreement with the mining interests. Point 33 of the agreement created the position of "protector of the Indios" intended to guarantee decent treatment. They acknowledged that violation of the ordinances and high mortality among the Indios worked against the interests of the owners:

The Indios take flight and do not return to their villages, which as a result become depopulated. The *mita* obligation then of those who run away falls on the few who remain. They go to places where they are unknown to parish [authorities], *corregidores*, and *encomenderos*, and the *caciques* have the presumption to declare they are dead and so ask that both taxes and *mita* be reduced. The Indios who stay in the village see that the burdens and obligations will all fall to them, and so they too want to leave, and do leave to free themselves of these requirements. All of this weakens the *mita* and so production in the mines, in the fields, in the raising of livestock, and other services necessary to the survival of the republic.[56]

Here then, in an official document, we see clearly described the centrifugal–centripetal migration mechanism, with its perverse implications for industry and the state, not to mention the Indios.

A second aside. The expansion of mining activity in Mexico, as already mentioned, began between 1545 and 1555 with the opening of mines in Zacatecas, Pachuca, Guanajuato, and, eventually, also further to the north, in Sombererete, Parral, and other locations. Mexican silver production was considerable but through to the end of the seventeenth century remained well below that of Perú.[57] The difficulties and dangers associated with the work were the same as those faced by the *mitayos* in Perú, and, as in Perú, the work was initially carried out by Indios drafted as forced labor (*cuatequil*). The pit of the "la Valenciana" mine in Guanajuato reached a depth of 513 meters according to Humboldt's measurements, and the temperature at the bottom was 34 degrees Celsius. "It is curious to observe how the *mestizos* and Indians employed in carrying minerals on their backs remain continually loaded for six hours with a weight of from 225 to 350 pounds . . . ascending eight or ten times without intermission stairs of 1,800 steps."[58] Yet Humboldt also found that, as in the Peruvian highlands, mining work had not caused depopulation, and that in the mining cities of Zacatecas and Guanajuato mortality was no different than elsewhere. "The physicians who practice in places where there are mines unanimously assert that the nervous affections which might be attributed to the effect of an absorption of oxide of mercury very rarely occur."[59] The major difference compared to the situation in Perú was that the workers were free (forced labor quickly fell into disuse); miners who were unhappy with their employer or working conditions could move on to another post without any complications. This earlier analysis has not been substantially changed by more recent studies. The Mexican mining centers were not located, as they were in Perú, in the midst of an uninhabitable desert. Labor demand probably did not exceed 15,000 (equaled by Potosí alone). Nor was there any labor shortage.[60] In Mexico, then, the mining industry fitted into the larger social and economic system without causing major demographic disruption.

It is no surprise that news of gold created the legend of Eldorado and led to the organization of costly expeditions in search of mythical sources of wealth in unknown and hostile lands. In practice, though, the first round of gold seeking was not particularly romantic. It was instead a plundering of the native stock accumulated over centuries followed by a furious search for surface deposits in the alluvial zones. Both of these sources – that held by the natives and that left by the streams – were used up within a few decades. Inexperience, haste, competition, and weakly organized authority – or what we might more correctly call greed, a lack of scruples, and the absence of rules – made those fatal decades for the Taíno and other peoples of the mainland. Another hidden source of wealth, pearls from the Paria Islands off the coast of Venezuela, was equally ill-fated for the local population, subjected as it was to inhuman conditions for oyster fishing. Until the mid-sixteenth century, the search for gold was a destructive vortex and potent force for depopulation among the small and fragile groups of natives unfortunate enough to be drawn into it.

The demographic impact of silver was substantially different. The native stock was insignificant and silver could only be obtained by means of solid finance and management. Although the work was hard and carried with it serious risks, it did not significantly impact mortality, which was high in any case. One can even go so far as to speculate that, in those regions where mining generated income for natives and their families – as it did in Mexico – it may even have had a positive demographic impact. In those regions such as Perú, characterized by forced labor, the impact was both centripetal and centrifugal, given both the attraction exercised by a center like Potosí and the emigration provoked by the *mita*.

5 Hispaniola, the terrestrial paradise of Columbus and the imagination of modern scholars. One hundred thousand or ten million Taíno? The catastrophe of the Antilles as seen from close up and a credible Leyenda Negra. *People die while animals flourish.*

SETIMO CALLE
TOCLLACOCVAMRA

In the previous chapters we have referred more than once to the sad fate of the Taíno in the Greater Antilles, but it will be useful now to explore more fully that unhappy example. Theirs was a dramatic story, vividly told in the surviving accounts. They were described by Columbus as mild, pleasant, and handsome inhabitants of a terrestrial paradise, a pearl to add to the dominions of their most serene majesties Ferdinand and Isabella. On December 9, 1492, at the inlet named Concepción, Columbus named the island Española, Latinized as Hispaniola (present-day Dominican Republic and Haiti). The sailors who went ashore returned with enthusiastic stories: men and women of a lighter complexion than those previously encountered; a valley more inviting than "the countryside around Córdoba, in equal measure as the day outshines the night."[1] "All the trees are green and heavy with fruit; the fields in flower with high grass; the trails are broad and gentle; the air is like Castile in April; and just like April in Spain the birds and the nightingales are singing; at night other birds warble in the sweetest fashion, which is the most pleasant thing one can imagine, and one hears also the verses of the crickets and the frogs."[2] There was also the promise of gold. The happy inhabitants of this invaded paradise, however, would soon be extinct.

The case of Hispaniola and the Greater Antilles is of primary importance because it was there, during the two or three decades following contact, that a system of domination was implemented that would characterize the entire Conquest. Hispaniola saw the introduction of the *encomienda* and *repartimiento* system, and so the forced labor of the Indios. The expeditions to explore and settle the mainland left from there. The missionary activity of the religious orders also got its start there. And the *Leyes de Burgos* were issued with the Antilles natives in mind, the first contribution to a voluminous legislation aimed at achieving the impossible: reconciling the rights of the natives and the interests of the colonists.

Regarding the topics explored in this book, Hispaniola is also the scientific and ideological battlefield between the "low counters" and the "high counters," relative to the estimated size of population at the moment of contact. Nor are those estimates neutral relative to the interpretation of the subsequent catastrophe. The two schools agree that the population was practically extinct by the middle of the sixteenth century, but the higher the initial estimate, and so the more rapid the subsequent decline, the more inviting become monocausal explanations like the epidemiological one. In a similar way, it is tempting to ascribe the extinction of the dinosaurs to a single cause such as the falling of a great meteorite to earth. For our purposes, it has been argued that such a drastic decline could not be explained by those non-epidemiological factors that Ángel Rosenblat (a notorious opponent of the *Leyenda Negra*) summed up as war, abuse, violence, migration, and changes in styles of life and work.[3] It is reasonably argued that the millions or tens of millions of victims who died following contact could not have been killed by the swords of the conquistadors, the violence of the *encomenderos*, or the hardships associated with new ways of life and labor. There were simply too few conquistadors to commit so many crimes; the conflicts were too limited in number; and the impact of social and economic changes would act more slowly. An epidemic in virgin territory solves everything: smallpox in one blow can eliminate half the population, measles as much as a fifth, and so on. Finally, the estimates of population size at contact are not neutral for another more complex reason already explored in chapter 2. The Conquest laid claim to the natives' resources in terms of both sustenance and labor. The Indios were forced to feed, supply, and serve the new arrivals. As discussed above, in less structured societies not accustomed to accumulating resources and so based on a subsistence economy, the Conquest effected a net subtraction of those resources and so impaired the ability of the population to survive. If the conquistadors were many relative to the native population, then their negative impact would be great. And while the number of the first colonists is fairly well known – and so is a given – the size of the indigenous population at contact is unknown. The larger the size we assign to that population, the smaller the role of the new arrivals, and their unquestioned confiscation of resources, in the demographic collapse. It makes, then, a big difference whether we claim 10 million inhabitants for the island at the moment Columbus landed or instead just 60,000, those being, as we shall see, below the maximum and minimum values assigned by modern scholars.

Columbus's idyll with the natives, if it took place at all, lasted at most a few days and culminated in the friendly embassy sent by the *cacique* Guacanagarí, "one of the five great kings of the island,"[4] on December 22 and the meeting on December 26 with the king himself, who came to offer his condolences on the loss of the *Santa Maria* (shipwrecked on Christmas night).[5] The idyll was certainly over less than one year later when Columbus, after his triumphant return to Spain, dropped anchor once again in Hispaniola with a second expedition of seventeen ships and 1,200 men on November 27, 1493. In the locality of Navidad, where eleven months before Columbus had left a vanguard of thirty-nine men, the admiral learned that they were all dead, presumably killed by the natives from whom they had been stealing gold and women.[6] The new settlement of Isabella was founded on the north coast of the island, and from there several expeditions set out toward the southwest to explore the fertile valley of Vega Real and the mountainous region of Cibao, where gold was discovered. The years 1494–6 saw attempts to subdue the rebellious Taíno, who fled instead into the forest, abandoning their fields while suffering famine and high mortality.[7] The Spaniards sought to impose a tribute in labor and gold, which failed completely, but did manage easily to crush the insurrection. Columbus departed in 1496, leaving his brother Bartolomé in charge of several hundred colonists; Bartolomé in turn founded the new capital, Santo Domingo, on the southern coast. The furious search for gold led to the '*repartimiento*' of native labor among the colonists. Discontent simmered among the Spaniards, however, as many chafed under the rule of the Columbus family, and that discontent quickly turned to open rebellion. At the same time, the Crown wanted to squeeze the maximum profit out of the island (and subsequent discoveries), and the prerogatives assigned to Columbus and his clan became a serious obstacle in that regard. In 1500, Columbus was relieved of his command by a royal official sent to the island explicitly for that purpose; the admiral returned to Spain in chains. He was subsequently rehabilitated by the monarchs, but never returned in his lifetime to Hispaniola; his remains instead were later sent there. In 1502, Nicolás de Ovando went to the island as a fully empowered governor, arriving with a fleet of thirty ships and 2,500 men – the first modern transoceanic migration. He governed until 1508 and in that time subdued the Indios in the peripheral parts of the island, "pacified" (bloodily) any revolts, founded new strategic settlements, imposed tributes, organized the administrative and judicial system, and carried out the first *repartimiento*, distributing native labor among the colonists. Gold production peaked in this period but the native population was visibly in decline. The Spaniards had grown in number from a few hundred before the arrival of Ovando to several thousand when he left in 1508. From a land of plunder it had become a colony. In 1509, Diego Columbus, son of Christopher and married to Maria de Toledo, niece of the king, arrived in Hispaniola with the title of viceroy. In fact, much of the power was held by royal officials loyal to the king and directly responsible to him. Diego ordered a second *repartimiento* in 1510, but it was practically ignored, and a third organized by royal officials was carried out in 1514 and counted barely 26,000 natives. Rapid population decline created serious economic problems: labor was in short supply; gold production as a result dropped rapidly while the alluvial deposits were also depleted; and colonists left for Cuba or other more promising spots on the mainland. Thousands of Indios were seized on the Lucayas Islands (the Bahamas) and quickly swallowed up by the destructive vortex of gold. Denunciations made by Las Casas and by the Dominicans, cited above, persuaded Cardinal Cisneros, the powerful regent following the death of Ferdinand in 1516. Was the *repartimiento* a just way to organize native labor? What was the best form of government for the Indios? How could they be saved without overly compromising the interests of the colonists? Three Hieronymite brothers were sent to Hispaniola in 1516 with the power to govern. Among the measures they took was an ordinance to regroup the surviving Indios in thirty villages. Their plans, however, were overturned by the arrival of smallpox; by that time in any case the surviving Indios numbered only a few thousand. Beginning in the 1520s, the island's economy changed with the arrival of sugar cane and the importation of slaves from Africa. Hispaniola remained

important as a link in the transatlantic trade and for its administrative functions. Two important officials, Zuazo and Espinosa,
described the sorry state of affairs in a letter to the king: except for
Santo Domingo, the Spanish settlements were reduced to ghost
towns by the emigration to other islands in the Antilles, Mexico,
Honduras, and the Castilla de Oro; the Indios, "who were once so
numerous, became extinct in so short a time"; the only hope was
the arrival of African slaves, both for gold extraction and, above
all, to sustain the growing sugar industry. Written on March 30,
1528, that letter serves as a requiem for the Taíno society just
thirty-five years after the first landing of Columbus.[8]

This digression on the history of the island, well known and many
times told, allows us to understand better the demographic drama
that played out beginning at the moment of contact. Estimates
made by modern authors since about 1950 – anthropologists, geo-
graphers, archeologists, historians – range from a minimum of
60,000 to a maximum of 8 million, though this latter is an average
chosen from a wider range (see table 6). The ratio between
maximum and minimum is an incredible 133:1. It is all the more
incredible as all these authors accept as valid the figure of 60,000
for 1508 or that of 26,000 from the *repartimiento* of 1514, so the
discrepancy derives entirely from the first two decades after
contact. For some they were decades of gradual decline, for others
of disastrous collapse. The likelihood of a large population at the
time of contact – 1 or 2 million – finds support in the fact that
numerous contemporary observers of the Conquest offered such a
figure in their histories and chronicles; it carries the authority of
repetition.[9] Many find little credence in these figures, as the authors
were writing twenty or more years after contact and on the basis of
hearsay – in particular a presumed count made by Bartolomé
Columbus in 1495 or 1496, a tumultuous time during which only a
part of the island was under the control of a small number of
Spaniards, who were surely little concerned with administrative
issues.[10] No trace remains of that presumed count. The figure of a
million was first cited by the Dominicans, who arrived on the island
in 1510; it was repeated subsequently by a slew of authors and then
given widespread currency by Las Casas. The debate, above all
philological, requires specialized knowledge; suffice it to say that
the doubts of modern authors appear to be well founded.[11]

As already discussed above, the size of the population at the moment of contact is of great importance to the interpretation of subsequent events. On the one hand, we can claim that to estimate that size is an impossible task; even modern censuses manage to measure the growth of populations in only an approximate way. Just the same, the combination of several elements allows us notably to limit the exaggerated range described above. The first step is to estimate the possible population capacity of the island given its environmental conditions and native production techniques; that way we can determine a demographic ceiling at the time of contact. A second approach will be to estimate gold production and productivity, and from those figures estimate the workforce employed and so the total population. A third will be to look at the organization of Taíno society and at the number of clans, for which we have partial information, and again to infer a total population. Finally, a fourth approach will be to reconstruct the organization of Taíno villages and their presumed dimensions. Information obtained in this way, combined with a number of more technical considerations of demographic analysis based on the first census of 1514, will notably improve our understanding of the contact population.

The authors who visited Hispaniola in the first decades following contact, such as Las Casas and Oviedo, have left interesting descriptions of the principal products of the island, of the farming techniques, and of food preparation.[12] Moreover, those practices had not changed for centuries, so even observations made subsequently can be useful. Naturally, many important details relative to the population capacity of the island remain unknown. What was the productivity of a single harvest, for example? Or how much of the island was farmed? How large a role did fishing and hunting play in the Taíno diet?

Judging from the primitive tools (the *coa*, a pointed stick used for digging and planting), the lack of irrigation (with some exceptions in the drier southwest), and the absence of fertilizer, Taíno agriculture was only moderately developed. The diet of the Taínos relied heavily on the cassava (both the bitter and the sweet varieties) and on sweet potatoes. They also consumed other edible roots, maize, squash, beans, pineapple, and other fruit. They practiced both fishing and hunting, but there were only small mammals on the island. In the western part, the inhabitants survived on hunting, fishing, and gathering; there was no agriculture. The growing of cassava (or yucca or manioc) and sweet potatoes took place in fields called *conuco*, consisting of regular rows of small mounds (*montón*) 2 to 3 feet high with a circumference of 9 to 12 feet and spaced 2 to 3 feet apart.[13] The purpose of the mounds is not entirely clear, but they probably provided humus where it was scarce, improved drainage during heavy rains, and made harvesting easier. On the flat top of the mounds, cuttings of cassava and sweet potato were planted; six months later they could be harvested. The tubers (roots) of the cassava were grated to make a paste from which in turn one could make a nutritious and longlasting bread.

What was the productivity of the mounds? It is again Las Casas who tells us that each native needed 2 *arroba* (about 25 kilograms) of cassava per month and that 1,000 mounds produced 200 *arroba* (2,500 kilograms, or 2.5 kilograms per mound) of cassava bread per year. It follows then that 1,000 mounds would be sufficient to feed 8.33 people for a year (2,500 kilograms total and calculating a per capita consumption of 300 kilograms per year) or that 120 mounds were needed to feed one person. Las Casas's estimates find confirmation elsewhere. The *Leyes de Burgos* of 1512, for example, stipulated that there be 5,000 mounds of cassava and sweet potato (supplemented with maize, other vegetables, and chicken, which the Spaniards had introduced) for every fifty natives, or 100 mounds per person.[14] The Hieronymite fathers instead wrote to the king that, in order to carry out their instructions (to gather the surviving Indios together in new villages), they would need to prepare 800,000 mounds to feed 7,000 natives for a year (114 mounds per person).[15]

In order to get an estimate of population capacity, we have to go through a few more steps. First of all, we have to determine how much of the island (76,500 square kilometers in all, about one-fifth the size of California) was suitable for agriculture. A number of factors suggest that it is impossible that more than half of the island was farmable, and probably more like one-third. To begin with, it is a mountainous island with peaks as high as 3,000 meters, and the regions of savannah and prairie did not conform to an agriculture based on the slashing and burning of forest.[16] We can also eliminate other arid regions and the areas taken up by lakes and streams, as well as that covered by a forest so thick "one could not even see the light of the sun."[17] Moreover, even that third or half was only cultivated on a rotating basis. With the slash and burn technique, the fields are abandoned after a productive period of probably five years as the fertility of the soil is used up. After that, they are left for a long period (twenty to thirty years), during which the forest re-establishes itself and the productive cycle can begin again. If we assume that the period (I) between two slash and burns was twenty-five years, of which five were productive (Y) and twenty fallow (F), and that the farmed area (T) amounted to between 25,000 and 37,500 square kilometers (one-third and one-half of the total), then we can calculate that, in each year, between 5,000 and 7,500 square kilometers were under cultivation (P). We have now almost all of the elements we need for this calculation, though we still need to determine how much productive land was needed per person. We have already observed that, according to several different sources, between 100 and 120 mounds planted with cassava and sweet potato were needed to feed one person. Using the measurements offered by Las Casas, that would correspond to about one-twentieth of a hectare (or 0.0005 square kilometers).

According, then, to Las Casas, and assuming that one-third of the island could be farmed, we can derive the following:

(T) Total area suitable for cultivation (1/3)	25,000 sq. km.
(P) Area annually in production (1/5 of S)	5,000 sq. km.
(I) Interval between slash and burns	25 years
– of which (Y) productive period	5 years
– of which (F) fallow	20 years
(A) Productive area needed per person for survival	0.0005 sq. km.
(Pc) Population capacity (T/A = 5,000/0.0005)	10 million

If one-half of the island were cultivated, the population capacity would increase instead to 15 million. This castle of hypotheses relies on the measures offered by Las Casas for the size of the mounds and other conjectures. Changing the hypotheses – as one can easily do – changes the results. Two modern historians of the agriculture and geography of the Caribbean basin, for example, have come up with estimates very different from A; they find that the average area planted with traditional crops necessary for the survival of one person is between 0.2 and 0.5 hectares (0.002–0.005 sq. km.).[18] Using these figures, the maximum population, assuming cultivation of one-third of the island, declines to between 2.5 and 1 million, or 3.75 and 1.5 million assuming half the island. Even if we were to assume that the entire surface of the island were farmed, the population capacity would still remain well below the highest estimate proposed by two well-known scholars thirty years ago (and included in table 6).

This exercise, falling somewhere between pedantry and conjecture, leads in any case to the conclusion that the population capacity of the island lay well below those of the highest counters, and so those estimates of many millions need to be discarded. The upper limit of our estimates has to be considerably reduced. Having lowered that population ceiling, however, we still need to explore plausible estimates.

We have already recalled Columbus's first encounter with gold, just after the second voyage at the beginning of 1494. Hojeda and later Columbus himself led expeditions from the north coast toward the southwest into the fertile valley of Vega Real and as far as the Cibao mountain chain. It was there they discovered the source of the natives' gold: the alluvial deposits in the foothills and the beds of streams and rivers. The next year they found the rich deposits of Río Hayna. By 1496, when Columbus left, the major gold-producing region of the island had been explored and exploited. On the basis of Columbus's attempt to impose tribute on the "pacified" Taíno at the end of 1495, Luis Arranz Márquez has made an estimate of the population of the Vega Real and Cibao, certainly the most densely populated part of the island and representing about one-quarter of the surface area. Every three months each native adult male was required to pay as much gold as could be held in a Flanders bell (these were intended for falconry, but used by the colonists as merchandise to exchange with the natives). One bell held 3 to 4 pesos of gold (12.5–16.7 grams).[19] An anonymous source, having returned to Spain from Hispaniola, wrote that the tribute had yielded barely 200 pesos (836 grams) of the expected 60,000 pesos (252 kilograms) after three payments, a complete failure. If each payment, then, should have amounted to 20,000 pesos (83.7 kilograms) and each bell contained 3 to 4 pesos, then those paying the tribute should have numbered about 6,000. Arranz Márquez maintains that the tax referred not simply to adult males but rather to the *bohío*, a multi-family hut, and that the expected yield was based on a rough count made by Columbus and his followers during the campaign of exploration and subjugation in 1494–5. In those years, the population was terrorized; many fled into the forest, while others (natives and Spaniards alike) died of starvation and disease. On the basis of these considerations, Arranz Márquez estimates that the population of the region in 1494 was about 90,000 (fifteen people per *bohío*) and perhaps 60,000 in 1496, which corresponds to a total population of the island about triple those figures.[20]

Another way to estimate the population of the island, at the beginning of the following decade, is to follow the method used in chapter 4. If we know the level of gold production and the average productivity of the gold workers, then we can calculate the number of Indios engaged in that work. Imagining that one-third of adult males were so employed – as stipulated in the royal decrees – we can derive the total adult male population, and as that population represents a percentage of the total population that varies within a fairly small range, we can estimate the total population. The gold that officially arrived in Seville in the first decade of the century (1503–10) averaged 621 kilograms per year,[21] though actual production was certainly much higher. The metal that arrived in Spain had paid the *quinto* to the Crown and came from the two foundries in Concepción and Buenaventura, where it was stipulated all the gold collected should be brought. In spite of the regulation that ships transport only gold that had paid the *quinto*, there was surely a great deal of evasion. Putting together other available data, we can estimate that gold production was about 1,000 kilograms per year at the beginning of the sixteenth century, when there were still few Spaniards on the island and before the "normalizing" impact of Ovando's policies exerted their negative influence on the native population.[22] If we assign a minimum level of productivity to native labor of 100 grams per year per person – derived from a variety of sources, including estimates for gold regions in Colombia, Ecuador, and Brazil, where techniques were similar to those of Hispaniola – then a metric ton of gold requires the labor of 10,000 Indios. Since the adult male population must be about one-quarter of the total, and one-third of that population

(8.3 percent) was engaged in mining, we get a total population of 120,000. Naturally, if productivity is higher (in Minas Gerais, at the height of the eighteenth-century gold rush, 46,000 slaves produced 7,500 kilograms of gold, or 160 grams per person),[23] population is proportionately lower. It suffices for now to observe that a population of 120,000 at the beginning of the sixteenth century is compatible with that of about double estimated by Arranz Márquez for 1494–6 and with the conditions of demographic implosion experienced on the island.

On Monday, December 17, 1492, near the estuary of Trois Rivières on the north coast of what is today Haiti, the sailors sent ashore by Columbus "encountered a cacique . . . whom they took to be a 'governor of a province,' and who showed a remarkably acute trading sense with a piece of gold leaf that he owned, as big as a man's hand."[24] The next day "a squire brought a belt which is like those of Castile in shape but of different workmanship, which he took and gave me, and two pieces of worked gold which were very thin."[25] It was at this point that Columbus "learned or understood that in the language of the island *cacique* meant king."[26] And Las Casas, transcribing Columbus's diary, noted: "Until today (23 December), the admiral had not understood whether *cacique* meant king or governor, and if another word, *nitayno*, meant grandee or *hidalgo* or governor; the truth is that *cacique* means king and *nitayno* means squire or *señor principal*, as we shall see below."[27] The Castilian categories of rank, however, could not easily describe the political organization of the island. The *cacique* was normally the head of a village, but there were different levels within that category. Las Casas referred to five principal *caciques* (*reyes*) on the island, as well as a further subdivision into thirty districts.[28] Hernán Colón, the son of Christopher Columbus, lowered the number of principal *caciques* to four, but added that each of them had seventy or eighty other *caciques* under him.[29] Columbus reported that the *cacique* Guacaganarí ruled over five other *caciques*, and that Guarionex – who was the main authority in the Vega Real and who organized the rebellion against the Spaniards in 1496 – was defeated and fourteen *caciques* associated with him were taken prisoner.[30]

The *caciques* ruled over daily life, religious ceremonies, and relations with other villages. They organized communal labor, meted out justice, and were responsible for the distribution of the harvest and storing excess production. The *cacique* lived in the largest dwelling of the village; that structure also served as a meeting place and ceremonial site and housed the *zemis* (Taíno divinities). It faced out onto the principal open space of the village, where games, feasts, and religious ceremonies were held. The *caciques* had multiple wives and wore symbols of their authority. The office of *cacique* was hereditary following the male line. If there were no male offspring, it passed to the son of the *cacique*'s sister; and if she did not have a son to the sister herself.[31] About 10 percent of the *caciques* counted in the Alburquerque *repartimiento* were women. The *cacique*, then, was recognized as the head of a village community that enjoyed a certain amount of social, economic, and perhaps also demographic autonomy.[32]

The size of the groups associated with the *caciques* are conjectural at best, though there are references to several thousand people in the largest villages. Nonetheless, given the usually asymmetric distribution of human groups, the largest of those groups tends to exceed the average by an order of magnitude, more or less. An average size of a few hundred, moreover, is credible on several counts. It is compatible with the social and productive organization characteristic of the Caribbean populations: subsistence agriculture depending on fields near to the villages with little in the way of accumulation and a rudimentary division of labor lacking a caste of warriors or priests.[33] We shall have more to say about this below.

Given that the office of *cacique* was hereditary, we can imagine that even during a demographic crisis that office survived, providing that the whole community was not wiped out, a possible but surely exceptional event. According to the *repartimiento* of 1514 the majority of the *caciques* had only a few dozen surviving subjects. Although their communities had shrunk, they nonetheless kept their titles. So we can presume that the 362 *caciques* identified by name in the Alburquerque *repartimiento* were the same that had existed twenty years before, or else their heirs, and so represented the same number of communities. To that 362 we have to add an unknown, but certainly not large, number of communities that vanished entirely. It is not unreasonable, then, to imagine that at the time of contact the island was organized into 400 or 500 *cacicazgos* averaging several hundred subjects each. Following this line of reasoning to its conclusion, the total population at the time of contact would have been a few hundred thousand (200,000 to 250,000) if the size of each community averaged 500 people.

The few surviving archeological vestiges, contemporary witnesses, and the chroniclers of the era agree in describing the Taíno village as a group of dwellings (*bohíos*) irregularly arranged around a central open space dominated in turn by the house of the *cacique*. In that space the Indios played a ball game (*batey*) and held their other community events. The *bohío* was a hut, usually circular, that could house ten to fifteen people. The *conuco*, planted with cassava and sweet potato, together with fields of maize or other crops, were arranged around the village and provided the staples for survival, supplemented by fruit gathering, fishing in sea or stream, and occasionally hunting.[34]

But how many villages were there and how large were they? According to Las Casas, "on the island of Hispaniola and the islands of Cuba, San Juan [Puerto Rico], Jamaica, and the Lucayas [Bahamas], there were an infinite number of villages, with houses grouped together and many families of different tribes."[35] During the first voyage, the explorers sent ashore discovered toward the "southwest after four and a half leagues a village with one thousand houses and more than three thousand men"; later six men came upon a "fairly large village," 3 leagues from the anchorage.[36] On December 23, the explorers returned from the village of Guacanagarí, which they found "the best and most organized, regarding streets and houses, of those yet seen," with a large population of 2,000 men and "an infinite number of women and children."[37] Yet a careful observer such as Doctor Chanca from Seville, who accompanied Columbus on his second voyage, described Guacanagarí's village as a modest agglomeration of fifty houses.[38] In Cuba, during the first voyage, the expedition sent in search of Cipango found only a modest village (near present-day Holguín) of about fifty houses, 12 leagues inland.[39] On the way there they came across a number of villages "of not more than four houses." And it was again Doctor Chanca who, after the discovery of the deaths at Navidad, went instead to a nearby village of seven or eight houses.[40]

If we leave aside the obvious exaggerations of Columbus (as reported by Las Casas), the villages must have ranged from a few houses to fifty or 100 in the largest ones, with populations between a few dozen and several hundred, and perhaps in a few exceptional cases, in particularly favorable surroundings, as many as 1,000 or more. And yet there is one more bit of useful information taken from a later document, penned when the population of Hispaniola was declining rapidly and the authorities sought to reorganize the survivors in more viable communities. Las Casas suggested to the Royal Council in 1517 that villages of 200 families should be built, and on another occasion he proposed concentrating the natives in villages of 1,000 people, bringing together four, five, or six *caciques* and stipulating that the villages be 5 to 7 leagues apart.[41] The king instructed in 1516 that the Hieronymite fathers build villages of 300 *vecinos*, to which the latter replied: "We have built on Hispaniola thirty villages where we have concentrated the few Indios that survive." And in that same letter, they affirm that they have organized the preparation of mounds to feed 7,000 Indios, implying that the villages numbered 200 to 300 inhabitants each (or 400, if we go by the reference that only seventeen villages were built).[42]

And so, how many were the "infinite villages" mentioned by Las Casas? If every *cacique* headed a village/community, then there must have been 400 or 500 at the moment of contact. Archeological estimates are consistent with this finding, as about 500 pre-Columbian sites have been identified on the island. Those sites include of course some that were abandoned prior to contact, and that number balances out to some unknown degree the sites not discovered.[43] The fertile Vega Real in the center of the island was densely populated relative to the rest of the territory. Hojeda's expedition in March 1494, after having marched for two days through uninhabited lands (from Isabela to Puerto de los Hidalgos, about 12 miles), crossed the Vega Real, dotted with villages "at every league."[44] In other regions – in the savannah and prairie poorly suited for agriculture, in the mountainous regions, in the sterile southwest, and in the impenetrable forests – settlements must have been small as well as few and far between. If we accept the high-counter estimate of 8 million inhabitants, then we need also to imagine 20,000 to 30,000 villages, a figure that well corresponds with Las Casas's "infinite" number. For if these settlements were evenly distributed over the territory, then a traveler would encounter one village for every mile he covered, including in the areas of forest and mountain. Our estimate instead of 400 to

500 villages would imply that our random traveler encounter one village every 7 or 8 miles, and every two to three in the Vega Real. Might that not also qualify as "infinite"?

Have we resolved the mystery of the contact population? Certainly not. But the preceding considerations regarding the population capacity of the island – estimates based on various elements and intersecting, partially independent sources regarding gold production, the number of the *caciques*, the number and size of the villages – do tell us that the contact population numbered in the hundreds of thousands and certainly not in the millions. Going a bit further out on this limb, we can say that the "true" population of the island has the greatest probability of falling between 200,000 and 300,000, and very small probabilities, rapidly approaching zero, of being either above 400,000 or below 100,000.

In the first decade of the sixteenth century, with the extension of the *repartimiento* system to the entire island, administrators and contemporary chroniclers began to offer estimates of the population based on actual counts, however rudimentary and approximate. Las Casas suggested a figure of 60,000 for the year in which the royal treasurer Pasamonte arrived (1508) and 40,000 for the year following the arrival of Diego Columbus (1510). Documentation of the *repartiminento* ordered by Diego in May 1510 has been lost, but the figure of 33,528 Indios is mentioned by Muñoz, who probably had access to the original sources.[45] The so-called Alburquerque *repartimiento*, to which we return below, offers a more secure figure, though 26,188 Indios was certainly an underestimation given that many fled into the forest or spread throughout the island (see map 6). The population in any case was visibly in decline by that point. In 1518, the Hieronymites were preparing villages for 7,000 surviving Indios, who were then struck by smallpox at the end of the year. According to Zuazo and Espinosa, writing in 1528, the only remaining Indios were *naborías*, servants in the homes of the Spaniards, and there were no more *indios de servicio* to work in the fields, produce sugar, and dig in the mines. According to Alonso de Castro in 1542, the island's economy depended upon 25,000 to 30,000 African slaves and the 1,200 resident Spaniards, because "the *indios de repartimento* were extinct." Oviedo estimated 500 in 1548, and according to López de

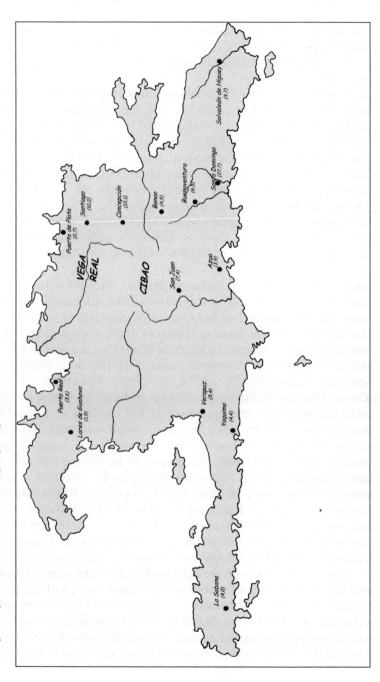

Map 6 *Hispaniola at the time of the Alburquerque repartimiento, 1514.*

Velasco, writing at the beginning of the 1570s, two villages of about fifty Indios each had survived.[46]

We can divide the post-contact history of the Hispaniola Indios into four periods. The first goes from 1492 to the complete subjugation of the island and the first *repartimiento* of 1505. The population suffered a severe shock, but did not lose its original characteristics regarding distribution and organization into communities. At least until 1502 there were few Spaniards, and vast tracts of the island continued to escape their control. If the Spaniards had left at that point, the native population would have been able to recover in spite of the rapid decline it had undergone. The interesting opinion of Las Casas (who nonetheless maintained that the population numbered in the millions at the time of contact) is relevant here: "It is of note that all these island territories began to go to the dogs once news arrived of the death of our most gracious Queen Isabela, who departed this life in 1504. Up to then, only a small number of provinces had been destroyed through unjust military action, not the whole area."[47] In the second period, from the *repartimiento* of Ovando to the departure of the Hieronymite friars and the smallpox of 1518–19, the population was completely enslaved, in practice if not by law, and suffered radical dislocation; the original communities and settlement patterns were entirely disrupted. In the third period, from 1520 to about 1550, the surviving population gradually disappeared: the Indian communities dwindled and the natives became integrated into the families of the colonists and mixed in large measure with the Spaniards, with the Africans brought as slaves, and with Indios brought from other islands, also as slaves.[48] The fourth period is in fact post-demographic. The Taíno population as such became extinct, though Taíno genes continued to be transmitted from generation to generation in the mixed-race population. Such was the fate also of the Taíno language. It too was lost except for the transmission via Castilian and other languages of a few words: hammock, barbecue, cannibal, *cacique*, potato, tobacco, hurricane.[49]

The story of Hispaniola was repeated in Cuba, Puerto Rico, and Jamaica. Although Columbus sailed along the coast of Cuba on his first voyage, that island was only colonized by Diego Velázquez in 1511. It was less densely populated than Hispaniola, with fewer and fewer settlements as one traveled from east to west. Already in 1522, after the smallpox epidemic, the *repartimiento* counted only a few thousand Indios; in 1526 employment of Indios in the gold mines was banned; in 1531 there were reportedly 4,000 survivors, and in 1542 maybe 2,000.[50] In Puerto Rico, the Spaniards arrived in 1508 with Ponce de León. The Taíno there were not so easily subdued, accustomed as they were to doing battle with the agressive Caribs, and many took refuge in the interior. In 1515 the *repartimiento* counted only 6,000 natives and in 1530 little more than 2,000. The limited documentation available confirms their subsequent extinction: in 1540, according to the *cabildo* of Puerto Rico, there were fifty left. Jamaica, which had a small population and almost no gold, and where smallpox did not arrive, the natives were practically extinct by 1540.[51]

The *licenciados* Alburquerque and Ibarra arrived on the island in 1514 – Ibarra died shortly afterward – with the task of carrying out a third *repartimiento* of the Indios. They were strongly influenced by the royal treasurer Pasamonte and the faction hostile to Diego, who had authored the *repartimiento* of 1510. That document has survived and, until we can decipher the mystery of the Incan *quipu*, constitutes our earliest source of census data for the Americas, based not on estimates but on actual counts.[52] A look at it allows us to make a series of observations about Taíno society, regarding among other things the causes and nature of its decline, at a little more than twenty years after initial contact with Europeans. The method employed in carrying out the *repartimiento* itself bears a moment's consideration. It was carried out after the Indios returned to their villages from the mines at the end of 1514. It was preceded by two separate counts: two officials in each district carried out the first by calling together resident colonists, who declared under oath the number of Indios entrusted to them; the second was carried out by two investigators, nominated by Alburquerque, who gathered the declarations of the residents in the farms and mines and then verified those declarations directly with the *caciques* in the villages of each district. The second count gave higher figures than the first and was the basis for the *repartimiento*. It was executed by a group of administrators, including scribes and notaries, led by Alburquerque and carried out successively in each district, starting with Concepción on November 23, 1514, and finishing the following January 9 with Yaquimo. The formula used was of the following sort:

To Juan Fernández de Guadalupe, resident and regent of this city [Concepción], is assigned [*encomendado*] the *cacique* Manicaotex, previously servant to His Majesty the King, together with sixty-five persons in service, thirty-three men and thirty-two women. Also assigned together with the named *cacique* are five elders who are not in service . . . five children who are not in service . . . nine domestic servants [*naborías*].[53]

The *cacique* is always named (Spanish names are more frequent than native ones), while the assigned Indios are divided into those "in service" (adult Indios, divided into males and females in Concepción and Puerto Plata), children (under fourteen years), and the old and infirm (of indeterminate age); servants (*naborías*) are a separate category.[54] In a number of cases, children, the old, or both categories are not mentioned; the question remains whether in those cases they were omitted – they had no evident economic value – or instead simply did not exist.

Table 7 lists the distribution of the 26,188 Indios by status and category and for two distinct groupings: mining districts (Santo Domingo, Santiago, San Juan, Concepción, Bonao, and Buenaventura) and non-mining districts and, alternatively, east and west. That table, and several other tables and figures, is based (with some marginal changes) on the fundamental work of Luis Arranz Márquez.[55] Looking at the table, the small percentage of children jumps out at once, to which we shall return, as does the high percentage of domestic servants (*naborías*). The latter, as far as we can tell from other sources, were primarily women; they were not attached to a *cacique* and so were removed from their original communities. Together with the *allegados* they constituted about 30 percent of the total. Many of them had spent long periods with their masters and so had undergone a certain degree of acculturation. The remaining 70 percent were attached instead to a *cacique*. Figure 4 displays the distribution of the 362 *caciques*, according to the number of Indios they controlled. The average number of Indios per *cacique* was fifty-one, the median value thirty-five, and the modal one twenty-one. Almost one-fifth of the *caciques* had no more than fifteen Indios. For many of these little remained beyond the formal function of command. Figure 4 may in fact be a picture of the distribution that was "lost" at the moment of contact, one that had the same shape but was larger by an order of magnitude. Other elements from the *repartimiento* are also of great interest and help us to explain certain aspects of the demographic catastrophe, as we shall see below: the notable prevalence of men relative to women (among *indios de servicio* in Concepción and Puerto Plata); the low ratio of children to adults; the frequent assignment of Indios attached to one *cacique*, and so one community, to different *encomenderos*; and dislocation, often over long distances.

Thirty years after contact, the Indios of Hispaniola were reduced to a few thousand and were no longer able to sustain themselves demographically. Even if we were to hypothesize a very young age structure at the beginning of the period, low life expectancy, and no births at all during those thirty years, one-third of the initial population would still have been alive rather than this much smaller percentage. To claim then that mortality was the primary cause of the disaster is to state the obvious. Much less obvious rather were the causes of that mortality, and there lies the heart of the debate. To simplify, the tremendous post-contact mortality can be attributed to three categories of cause: (a) direct violence on the part of the Spaniards: indiscriminate killings, wars of pacification, gratuitous cruelty and consequent deaths; (b) direct consequences of the disorder and dislocation caused by the Conquest: abandonment of farming and famine enter into this category; (c) the effect of new diseases in virgin terrain. The essence of the *Leyenda Negra* is summed up in (a) and (b); the revisionists and the high counters instead give absolute priority to (c).

Direct violence was certainly responsible for many deaths, from the so-called battle of Vega Real in 1494 to the violent pacification of Higuey (7,000 to 8,000 dead, according to Zuazo) and Xaraguá in 1502–4.[56] Nonetheless, the conquistadors, for all their cynical disregard for human life, did not plan a genocide. They profited from the work of the natives, and their violence was a function of the imposition of their command and the exploitation of that native labor force. However, gratuitous cruelty was surely inflicted on the Taíno by many early adventurers and was frequent enough to earn the moral reprimand of contemporary observers; but it was not on such a scale as to qualify as a major cause of death.

The second group of causal factors for Taíno mortality (and also low reproductivity, as we discuss below) was surely linked to the disruption of the social system and settlement pattern of the island; the forced relocation of natives from one place to another and from one master to another; the changes in food production and supply for the natives who were forced to support the invaders with their labor; the heavy work in the mines for a population accustomed to light and occasional physical effort; and frequent suicide, mentioned by too many independent sources to be an invention of the chroniclers. Contemporaries saw forced migrations as the cause of famine, disease, and death: "The death of this people was also caused in large measure by the continual moving about of the Indios by governors and officials, their passing from one master to another, each one greedier than the next."[57] The institutional lever of that disruption was the *repartimiento* started by Columbus and institutionalized by Ovando and Diego Columbus. According to Zuazo, because of the *repartimiento*, "Indios from the province of Higuey were forced to go to Xaraguá or La Cabana, places that were hundreds of leagues away from Higuey."[58] The fortress at Santo Domingo was built by workers brought from Higuey after that area was pacified. The king, who was constantly demanding more income, urged officials to build villages near the mines and to put one-third of the Indios to work in the search for gold, at least 1,000 in the king's own mines.[59]

The 1514 *repartimiento* provides data on the scale of the population redistribution. For example, thirty *caciques* and their dependents came from districts different than those of the *encomenderos* to whom they were assigned.[60] The total number of *caciques* was 362, but their people were divided among 498 *encomenderos*, a sign that in a large number of cases groups were divided among two or more masters. The two largest groups were headed by female *cacicas*: Maria de Higuey, who had 443 Indios, and Isabel de Iguanama, who had 341. Their subjects were divided, respectively, between sixteen and eleven different *encomenderos*. In thirty-seven cases the distribution crossed district lines, in that Indios attached to one *cacique* were assigned to two or more *encomenderos* resident in different districts. The community disruption caused by the 1514 *repartimiento* only further exacerbated that owing to the *repartimientos* of Diego and Ovando carried out just four and nine years earlier – not to mention the non-institutionalized ones of still earlier dates. Family and clan networks were sundered or weakened; the material conditions of life changed, as did work regimes; and at the same time new adaptation strategies had to be found relative to new masters. There is no doubt that the effects on survival were strongly negative.

Flight into the bush, or at least into the wilderness, was frequent as natives sought to escape the violence and oppression of the Spaniards. They learned quickly. According to Michele da Cuneo, 1,600 Indios were taken prisoner in 1494 and concentrated in the "city" of Isabela. Of these, 550 were sent to Spain as slaves; others were distributed around the island, also as slaves; and the rest, about 400, mostly women and children and unsuitable for work, were freed. These latter immediately "fled into the woods, seven or eight days march away."[61] In 1494–5, Guarionex and his people from the Vega Real fled from the violence of the conquistadors into the wilderness, abandoning their farms. Gil Gonzales Dávila deemed the dispersion of the Indios and consequent mortality to be among the causes of depopulation, because they sought refuge in the forest "for the smallest reasons."[62] When the Hieronymites took the extreme decision in 1518 to reunite the survivors – not yet struck by smallpox – in thirty new villages, they were seeking desperately to revive the communal life of a society that had been uprooted and dispersed. Paradoxically, that extreme measure was at the same time destructive of what remained of the pre-contact society and the only hope of reuniting the surviving fragments of that society. But it came too late.

Regarding the third group of factors invoked to explain the high mortality – new diseases and virgin populations – we have already offered support for the hypothesis that the smallpox epidemic of 1518–19 was the first. And we have examined how it was entirely plausible that the virus did not arrive before that time in spite of the intense traffic between Hispaniola and Spain. Other unknown viruses might of course have arrived on the island, but none of these would have had the destructive potential of smallpox. In any case, the small amount of material on illness and mortality during the first decades of Spanish domination has been carefully analyzed by David Cook and Francisco Guerra.[63] Unfortunately that material tells us more about the Spaniards than about the natives; it can be synthesized as follows:

1 The 1,200 or so men who arrived with Columbus's second voyage in November 1493 immediately fell ill, and that illness stayed with them for a number of months. Guerra has hypothesized that they suffered from swine flu, owing to the presence of eight

pigs picked up at La Gomera, together with horses, plants, and provisions, and that it constituted the first European illness in the New World.[64] Yet Guerra's hypothesis is pure conjecture, if not fantasy. The only certain point is that the Spaniards were not well when they arrived. In a more recent work, Cook has suggested that the disease was smallpox, brought to the island by one of the four Taíno from the Samaná peninsula whom Columbus had taken with him to Spain at the beginning of the year. According to Columbus, he sent a caravel ashore "to land one of the four Indios whom we had taken from there the year before and who had not died from smallpox, like the others, when we left from Cadiz."[65] So three of the four had died of smallpox, but when? During the crossing, during the preparations for departure, at Cadiz? Or did the expression simply signify that the Indio in question was not dead at the time of departure, as the others were? In any case, the surviving Indio made land in excellent health ("*muy alegre*"), having avoided smallpox or recovered from it. There is a remote chance that he contracted the disease on board and so it was in its latent phase, but the chain of probabilities makes that truly unlikely; that chain would have included the spread of infection on the Samaná peninsula, a distant and sparsely inhabited place, and its transmission to the Cibao region over 100 miles away, in order for it to become the principal cause of death for that year and the succeeding one. Moreover, no surviving document makes reference to smallpox. Doctor Chanca, who sailed with Columbus, does not mention it as a cause of the 1494 disaster; and no one afterward ever mentioned smallpox scarring on the surviving Indios.

Returning to the Spaniards, surviving documents describe that they suffered from a scarcity of food, poor hygiene, and syphilis (the *mal de bubas* was endemic among the Taíno, but lethal to the Spaniards as a result of their promiscuity with native women), and that they were sick for much of the time during the months following landfall. Indeed their state of health would continue to be precarious for many years. As to the natives in those first months, we know next to nothing, except that, of the 550 Indios sent to Spain with Antonio de Torres in January 1494, 200 died during the voyage and others disembarked in terrible condition[66] – owing to the difficulty of the voyage, illness, the effect of climate change?

2 According to Las Casas, the fury of war, famine, and illness killed two-thirds of the natives between 1494 and 1496. Pietro

Martire writes of 50,000 dead from starvation ("and more and more with every day that passes").[67] High mortality at the time was the consequence of active Indian resistance to the Spanish intrusion, from the north coast (Isabela) to the Vega Real, to the mountains of Cibao. Abandonment of the *conucos* and a flight toward the interior spread famine among Indios and Spaniards alike.

3 With the arrival of Governor Ovando and 2,500 Spaniards in 1502 and the intensification of traffic between Hispaniola and Spain, the probability of European diseases arriving and spreading through the island increased considerably. Explicit information on illness and death, however, exists only for the Spaniards. Many of the new arrivals dispersed upon arrival in a mad dash after gold; it was not long before their provisions ran out and, unaccustomed to the climate, they fell ill. In a short time 1,000 died while 500 recovered, though we do not know if they suffered from any specific disease.[68] About the Indios, we know only that their numbers declined precipitously.

4 Except for the smallpox of 1518, we have no specific information on new diseases. The one exception is a statement made by a resident of the island, Hernando Gorjón, in a document dated March 1520; he attributes the depopulation of the island to (among other things) "a pestilence of smallpox, measles [*sarampión*], *romadizo* [a respiratory infection], and other illnesses."[69] Measles is named by another witness in that same document. It may be, then, that measles struck the island before smallpox, though it is also possible that disease arrived after the smallpox epidemic ended, at the beginning of 1519. It may also be that, in addition to measles, the natives suffered from influenza, diphtheria, scarlet fever, typhus, and other illnesses before the fatal smallpox; and yet there is no trace of that in any of the copious documentation left by the Spaniards, who were in any case familiar with those diseases and their symptoms. Is it plausible that an epidemic – with its sudden outbreak, rapid and devastating course, and gradual disappearance – went unobserved? Finally, it would certainly be remarkable if Oviedo and Las Casas, who describe at length the natural conditions of the island and make specific reference to syphilis (Oviedo also refers to the *mal de niguas*, a sort of scabies), should say nothing about diseases pertaining to the Indios.[70]

To conclude, before 1518 European diseases were probably added to those endemic to the island, complicating native pathology and raising mortality, mortality already aggravated by the disruption of Taíno society. That situation is adequate to explain the extinction of the Taíno, even without the onslaught of epidemics that, before 1518, may well not have occurred.

Would that extinction have taken place, had the reproductive mechanisms of the Taíno not been compromised by the Conquest? This is another question without a definitive answer, but it is worth considering as demographic history teaches that the most destructive epidemics are typically followed by a recovery in which increased reproductivity plays a major role. We have already cited the example of the plague in Europe, the most traumatic of diseases. Each epidemic wave was followed by recovery generated by increased fertility. When the epidemic waves became less frequent, less regular, and less synchronous, the population began a sustained recovery. But when the reproductive mechanism is paralyzed or compromised, as in the Antilles, that recovery is impossible.

The *repartimiento* of 1514 throws some light on this question. In two out of fourteen districts (Concepción and Puerto Plata) the *indios de servicio* are divided into men and women. Table 8 gives the numbers of men, women, and children and the ratios of men to women and children to women. Children were theoretically fourteen and younger; the women (and the men) were fifteen and older, but did not include the old, so the vast majority must have been under fifty. Two points catch the eye: there are fewer women than men and the children to women ratio is very low. In explaining the small number of women, one cannot exclude counting errors or mortality differentials or greater success among women than men in avoiding the *repartimiento*. But the more natural hypothesis is that more women than men were employed as servants (*naborías*) in the homes of the Spaniards; many of the youngest girls were of course notoriously the concubines of the Spaniards, and many *cacicas* and daughters of *caciques* were married to *encomenderos*. In other words, the conquistadors claimed for themselves young and healthy women who were as a result withdrawn from the Taíno reproductive pool. In the *repartimiento*, 186 Spaniards identified their wives' origins: 131 were from Castille and 65 were natives.[71]

The problem of unions between Spaniards and natives was a much-debated issue both on the island and in Spain. In 1503 the Crown requested of Ovando that native women taken by Spaniards against their will be returned to their communities of origin. Instructions given to Diego Columbus in 1514 and to the Hieronymite fathers in 1516 permitted and even encouraged marriages between Spaniards and *cacicas* or daughters of *caciques*. In 1518 Fray Bernardino de Manzanedo advised the king that the children of mixed unions be forbidden from leaving the island.[72] In any case, the withdrawal of women (15 to 20 percent, according to the data from the *repartimiento*) from the Taíno reproductive pool significantly reduced the reproductive potential of the natives.

None of this, however, explains the very low ratio of children to women (0.281). In a stable population, that ratio would correspond to a population declining at a rate of 3.5 percent per year. Analogously, the very low proportion of children among the entire population of the island (see table 7), at less than 10 percent, corresponds to a stable population declining at 4.5 percent per year.[73] The small number of children and the low ratio of children to women could in theory be due to under-counting, high infant mortality, or very low fertility; it is impossible to know. Nonetheless, many contemporary commentators referred to the scarcity of children, the frequency of barren marriages, and the negative consequences deriving from the separation of men and women (as during the eight-month stays in the mines). Legislators made timid attempts to protect women and children, forbidding field labor for pregnant women and those with children under three, or banning female labor in gold mining.[74] But these laws were written thousands of miles away in Spain and had to be obeyed by greedy *encomenderos* under the weak surveillance of island officials. Finally, the more general phenomenon of dislocation that we have explored created a situation that was fundamentally hostile to the normal reproduction of the population.

The royal cosmographer López de Velasco confirmed the extinction of the Indios (except for two villages, each with fewer than fifty inhabitants) in the 1570s; he added that there was not even one *encomendero* left because there were no more *indios de servicio*, that the Spaniards numbered only about a thousand, and that the island was predominantly populated by 12,000 to 13,000 African slaves.[75] The demographic future of the island, like that of the Antilles generally, depended then on European migration and the slave trade, a trade that depended in turn on the success of the sugar-cane plantations and the factories for sugar production. Around 1800, in the larger area of the West Indies, the population numbered 1.8 million, of which 1.5 million were black, for the most part slaves, and the rest of European origin.[76]

The natural environment was also much changed half a century after Columbus's landing. The small mammals had disappeared, likely more because of repeated bouts of famine than on account of the Spanish love of the hunt. The *hutía*, a sort of small rabbit, and a mute species of dog domesticated by the natives were both nearly gone by the time of Oviedo. "The Spaniards who came with the first admiral on his second voyage to the island ate all of these dogs because they were dying of hunger and had nothing to eat."[77] By contrast, the animals brought from Spain beginning with that second voyage of Columbus flourished: the eight pigs picked up in the Canary Islands were probably not the source of any epidemic but rather the progenitors of a numerous and wild offspring that multiplied and spread throughout the island. There were many cows who multiplied freely, thanks in part to the open spaces left by the abandonment of the fields. Many were killed, not for their meat but in order to send their hides back to Spain.[78] The *licenciado* Echagoian, judge for the Audiencia of Santo Domingo, wrote in a letter to Philip II (1561) that a few years before there had been 400,000 head of cattle, but that number had declined due to the supplying of ships stopping at the island. Our inquisitive judge also informed His Majesty of an interesting ecological phenomenon. The cows were gluttons for the *guayabo* fruit, which had many seeds that they spread while grazing by means of their excrement. Those plants then multiplied, reducing the pastures, and turning much of the field land back into forest, in turn a refuge for wild animals.[79] Horses, donkeys, sheep, and goats all flourished and multiplied. According to Echagoian, the wild horses were "innumerable." They could be caught with a snare, and the only cost was that of taming them. With the decline of the colonist-conquistador population after 1510, domestic cats and dogs became wild too, and the dogs "are worse than wolves and cause more damage."[80] The packing down of the soil as a result of cattle, horse, and sheep traffic cut down on water infiltration and caused erosion.[81] *Conuco* agriculture was reduced to a minimum as the cultivation of sugar cane expanded.

Humans, plants, and animals: a profound revolution had taken place over the span of two generations.

6 A great and rich city, dreamed of by Columbus and destroyed by Cortés. The modern dispute over the population of Meso-America. Tributaries, tributes, and population. Thirteen brigantines hauled overland and a tunnel in the rock. Men and beasts

On Tuesday, November 8, 1519, six months and sixteen days after having landed near present-day Veracruz, Cortés and his men entered Tenochtitlan for the first time, accompanied by an endless escort of dignitaries. After having met the "Great Montezuma" and his opulent following, Cortés's band passed four days housed in the large building assigned to them, carefully studying the extraordinary situation in which they found themselves. Three hundred men in a huge city that was surrounded by a vast lagoon and connected to the mainland by three roads built over landfill, roads that could be easily cut off. But how big was that city? And how large was the population of the empire over which it ruled? Very large: the Spaniards already knew that. From the coast of the Gulf of Mexico, where there were relatively few settlements, they had climbed up to the highlands, encountering a large number of villages and cities. They had then marched for days in deserted and inhospitable lands till they approached the high mountains that defined the eastern limit of the valley of Tenochtitlan. There they came upon densely inhabited and intensively farmed regions and stopped in two great cities, Tlaxcala and Cholula. After four or five days in Tenochtitlan, Cortés and a few of his men – including Bernal Díaz del Castillo – ventured into the city. In his second *Carta de relación* to Emperor Charles V, he wrote: "The city itself is as big as Seville or Córdoba," and then added, "There is also one square twice as big as that of Salamanca, with arcades all around, where more than sixty thousand people come each day to buy and sell, and where every kind of merchandise produced in these lands is found."[1] The figures offered by Columbus, Cortés, and other conquistadors, intent on impressing their patrons with the importance of their discoveries, have little documentary value. Cortés's account becomes instead much more revealing when he describes in great detail the nature of the goods exchanged, which include not only every type of food – maize, beans, herbs, vegetables, fruit, honey, birds live and dead, rabbits, and fish – but also minerals, adornments and jewelry, wood and coal, building materials, vases of different sorts and sizes, leather and hides with and without fur, cotton thread and textiles of different sorts and design, and paints. Moreover, the sale of certain goods was organized in specific neighborhoods and streets, and the work of artisans was carried out in workshops "like apothecaries', where they sell ready-made medicines as well as liquid ointments and plasters. There are shops like barbers' where they have their hair washed and shaved, and shops where they sell food and drink."[2] Or again, "Everything is sold by number and size, and until now I have seen nothing sold by weight."[3] Bernal Díaz del Castillo offered similar testimony regarding this unforgettable visit forty years later; he begins a detailed description of the market as follows: "I would have liked to describe all the things that were sold there, though two days would not have been enough to see everything and make sense of it all, so full of people was the great plaza surrounded by porticoes."[4]

Tenochtitlan, or Mexico City as the Spaniards would later call it, was then a great city with, according to modern scholars, a population between 100,000 and 200,000. It was characterized by a clear division of labor and a specialized merchant class, earmarks of a large and advanced society. Cities, towns, and villages, densely packed and supported by intensive agriculture, dotted the area around Tenochtitlan, along the shores of the lagoons traversed by numberless canoes, on the plain, and on the slopes of the mountains and volcanoes that defined the valley. A modern scholar, not swayed by a need to exalt the Mexican civilization by exaggerating the number of its inhabitants, has estimated a population of 1.1 to 1.2 million for the central valley (7,300 square kilometers, about half the size of the state of Connecticut); today that region holds more than one-quarter of Mexico's total population of over 100 million.[5]

Estimates for the population of Mexico at the time of the Spaniards' arrival, like those for other parts of the continent, cover a wide range. There is, however, substantial agreement that by the end of the century it lay between 1 and 2 million. Spain was in desperate need of income and spared no effort in evaluating the number of potential taxpayers, so the sources are ample and fairly reliable. Nor is there any doubt that during the sixteenth century population decline was very rapid. As a starting point, we can compare the various estimates made by modern scholars for the population at the time of contact, though the extent of the territory in question is not always the same. We find then the following figures (in millions):[6]

Sapper	1936	12.0–15.5
Kroeber	1939	3.2
Cook and Simpson	1948	11.0
Steward	1949	4.5
Rosenblat	1954	4.5
Cook and Borah	1960	25.2
Dobyns	1966	30.0–37.5
Sanders	1976	11.2
Denevan	1976	18.3
Slicher van Bath	1978	21.4
Zambardino	1981	8.0–10.0
Withmore	1991	13.5
Denevan	1992	13.8

From these estimates we get a median value of about 13 million. The degree of uncertainty for Meso-America is about the same as that for the Andean region, as we shall see in the next chapter. It is a function both of the methodological criteria employed by each author, but also of a number of preconceived convictions.

Our knowledge about the population of New Spain, of its distribution and composition, depends upon the testimony of contemporaries but also and above all on surviving tax and tribute records. Those records, however, do not speak to us in a straightforward way and require a full understanding regarding the criteria of tribute and exemption, the nature and amount of the tribute, the frequency of evasion, the identity of the tributary, and the presumed number of his family members, servants, and slaves. It is an immensely complicated business, in part because of the many changes that were made over the course of the century – given that the Spaniards initially inherited the Aztec tributary system, first modifying it, and then transforming it according to entirely new criteria.

Under the Aztecs (or, more correctly, under the triple alliance of Tenochtitlan, Texcoco, and Tacuba), peasants, artisans, and merchants who had access to common lands (*calpulli*) were liable for tribute; but there were many exemptions: for local lords, officials, military leaders, those who carried out community services (for example in the temples), the *mayeques* (a category analogous to serfs that worked the land of the lord, or served him but did not have access to common lands), slaves, and the old and infirm. Tribute was made in kind and in services, including work in the fields and drayage over land or water.[7]

In the first phase, the Spaniards adopted the Aztec system with a few variations responding to the needs of the new masters (fewer ornaments and feathers, more gold). Tribute was due either to the *encomendero* – Cortés had distributed the territory and the Indios to his faithful comrades in arms – or to the Crown. The greed of the *encomenderos*, men who had risked their lives and felt few restraints, translated into tremendous abuse; they demanded heavy tributes of the *caciques* – quantities of gold or, lacking that, slaves who were branded, chained, and sent to the mines.[8] The corrupt administration of the Prima Audiencia (1528–30) – the government organ that replaced Cortés – made the situation still worse by increasing the tribute in kind and services owed by the communities. The Segunda Audiencia (1531–4) sought to impose order and eliminate abuses, but the tribute continued to weigh heavily on the single communities; in theory it took into account what had been paid under the Aztecs, the characteristics of the community and their land, and the number of inhabitants. Tributes were recorded in the *Matricula de Tributos*, a document that has survived but one that includes only a tenth of the localities in central Mexico.

This system lasted about a quarter of a century, during which time the indigenous population declined, including a rapid drop because of the epidemic of 1545–7. As the tribute remained fixed while the population declined, its weight increased, and so did both protest and evasion. With the *Leyes Nuevas* of 1542, defense of the Indios increased and the power of the *encomenderos* was reduced. Those laws were first partially rescinded, but then re-affirmed in 1549 regarding the ban preventing *encomenderos* from transforming the required tribute into personal service. In an attempt to correct the obvious cases of excess and injustice, the Crown ordered a general inspection (*visita*) that was carried out between 1547 and 1550. A count was made for each community, but they were of varying sorts, relative to dwellings or tributaries, families or adult males, sometimes with a few added details. Those exempt from tribute were not counted, though they represented a significant, and variable, segment of the population. The results of the inspections were gathered in a general volume, the *Suma de Visitas*, that includes half of the almost 2,000 localities in central Mexico. The tributes, however, applied to single communities with large territorial inequalities.[9]

The system we have described, based on that of the Aztecs and gradually revised by the Spaniards, was radically changed starting in 1557. At that point it became essentially a uniform poll tax; each taxpayer paid a fixed quota corresponding to 1 *peso* and half a *fánega* (about 23 kilograms) of corn per year, plus 1.5 to 2 *reales* of silver per community. The tax was paid to the *encomendero* or to the Crown. Married men and their family nucleus paid the full tax; widows and widowers possessing land paid half tax, as did the unmarried of both sexes who lived alone. Essentially excluded were *niños* and *muchachos* (under fifteen years of age) and the old (over fifty).[10] By this system exemptions were drastically reduced; only *caciques* and other high local authorities escaped the tax. As we shall see, the taxation system in Perú was similar. For the period from the late 1550s to 1570, during which the new system was implemented, the documentary sources (*Relaciones de Tributos, Relaciones de las Tasaciones*) cover about 90 percent of the localities in central Mexico, though for different years within that period. On the one hand, this new uniform system of taxation simplified implementation and management and eliminated a number of abuses. On the other, it was also the source of new inequalities insofar as it did not take into account variations in the ability of individuals to pay. Nonetheless, it remained basically unchanged for the remaining history of the colony. For the last third of the century, other documents offer additional information on taxpayers: the *Relaciones Geográficas* (1579–84), which we discuss below, gave information on 10 percent of localities. Other documentation on taxpayers to the Crown (1593) and the *encomenderos* (1597) offer data on half the localities. Finally, there are some documents on the process of concentrating sparse populations (*congregaciónes, reduciónes*) that cover 4 percent of the communities for a period at the turn of the century.[11]

In 1574, López de Velasco, the king's cosmographer, gathered together the available information on the human geography of Hispanic America in his *Geografía y descripción universal de las Indias*.[12] The data were offered for 1570, though much must have referred to earlier years. The summary for New Spain (see table 9) reveals that, according to Velasco, there were about 1,400 villages (*pueblos de Indios*) with 770,000 taxpayers divided into 850 *repartimientos* (543 assigned to *encomenderos* and 307 to the Crown). The total population implied by these figures must have been around 3 million, two-thirds of which would have been concentrated in the large central dioceses of México and Tlaxcala-Puebla. The villages (*cabeceras*) with relatively sparse population numbered on average 500 or 600 taxpayers, while those in the dioceses of México, more urbanized than the rest of the country, were about twice that size. Another 6,414 Spanish families, totaling 30,000 to 35,000 people, "oversaw" this still numerous population.

Starting in the late 1940s, a group of scholars from the University of California carefully evaluated the documentation available in Spanish and Mexican archives in order better to understand the demographic significance of the available material. The results of three decades of work – regarding the population of central Mexico between the "Chichimeca frontier" (see note 6) and the Tehuantepec isthmus – are summarized in table 10 relative to the entire period from 1510 to 1605. The authors, Sherburne Cook and Woodrow Borah, have produced an impressive series of monographs characterized by an innovative use of the documentary material.[13] On the surface homogeneous, the series in fact betrays two separate spirits: one firmly based on the available data for the period 1585–1605 and corresponding for the original date to a figure somewhat below the estimate of Velasco; the other entirely conjectural and characterized by bold, if not rash, estimates for the earlier period. Given the authority of these scholars and their unquestioned scientific merits, their figures have taken on an almost official character and are continually repeated as if by a sort of inertia (not uncommon among historians). For that reason it is important to spend a few pages examining the nature of those estimates; readers allergic to figures and calculations may want to skip ahead to the final conclusions.

We should start with the 1560s, after the tax reform had been implemented: the tax applied to individuals, exemptions had been drastically reduced, and the administrative system was strongly reinforced. As we have already observed above, in the period 1565–70 almost all the localities were inspected, with counts of either taxpayers or the number of *casados* or the number of persons; the latter normally referred to the total population less children under three years of age. In order to determine the total population, Cook and Borah used coefficients derived from an analysis of those cases which offered greater detail. For example, married men – *casados* – were multiplied by 3.3 to get the entire population; taxpayers – including also widows and widowers – were divided by 1.17 to obtain the total number of married persons; total persons were multiplied by 1.11 in order take into account children under three. For about 10 percent of the localities, data are lacking, and so data from earlier or later periods were adjusted appropriately to estimate a population for the period in question. This operation was carried out for eleven regions and then consolidated to get a total population for 1568 (the central year of the inspections) of 2.65 million (a figure compatible with that of Velasco). This then is the architecture of Cook and Borah's estimates and the only really secure evaluation of the population of Mexico in the century following the Conquest. Subsequently, the two authors made estimates for 1580, 1595, and 1605, using population data for each of these years from a limited number of localities (141 cases in 1580, 294 in 1595, and just 40 in 1605 out of a total of nearly 2,000) about which they also knew the demographic situation in 1568. They then applied the resultant depopulation rates for the regions in question (between 1568 and 1580, 1568 and 1595, and 1568 and 1605) to the country as a whole and obtained total population figures equal to 1.891 million (1580), 1.372 million (1595), and 1.069 million (1605). This is a reasonable approach for 1580 and 1595, insofar as it is based on a fair-sized sample, but much less so for 1605 (based on just forty cases, or 2.5 percent of the total). Moreover, the method used, beyond the problem of how representative were the communities used in 1580, 1595, and 1605, assumes that the coefficients employed to get, for example, from taxpayers or married men to the total population did not change over time.[14] Experience suggests that these sorts of hypotheses considerably simplify reality; the ratio between population and families, for example, can change significantly in response to demographic factors such as high epidemic mortality, a changing age at marriage, internal migration, and so on.

In less than thirty years – between 1568 and 1595 – the population of central Mexico declined by nearly half, at an annual rate of –2.35 percent. Presumably the serious epidemic that broke out in 1576 bore the brunt of responsibility for this drop. Even leaving aside the estimate for 1605 (in which we have little confidence), the decline continued for several more decades. We get similar results using original and comparable data for *encomienda* taxpayers in 121 localities in 1569–71 and 1595–9 (see table 11). For these, the speed of the decline was –2.25 percent; in sixty-seven of the 121 localities the total reduction was greater than 40 percent. For seventeen localities assigned to both *encomenderos* and the Crown, Lesley Simpson found that for approximately the same period the relative taxpayers declined by barely 8 percent, possibly because of less exploitation of the Indios in this juridical regime or perhaps because of compensatory immigration. Still unexplored, there remain the questions of the nature and quality of the various enumerations, the degree of evasion, and the issue of geographic coverage. The interests at play, of Indios, *encomenderos*, and officials, were each different and often opposed; and there is reason to believe that the exactitude of the enumerations varied over time. All of which invites us to use a good dose of caution when employing these figures, even for the latter part of the century.

For the period before 1568, table 10 suggests a disastrous, though hardly credible, decline. In 1548 the population would have been one-quarter of what it was in 1519, and in 1568 less than half that of 1548 – in all, a drop in half a century to a little more than one-tenth of its original size. We will come back to the factors that contributed to the decline of the Mexican population. The criteria used to calculate the population in 1519 (before the Conquest) and 1532 (midway through the administration of the Segunda Audiencia, which carried out recalculation of the tributes owed by the various communities) are interesting and helpful for establishing orders of magnitude for a situation of great uncertainty, but not adequate to establish a temporal series. They allow us to assign maximum and minimum limits for that population but not to determine the initial value for a historical reconstruction. The method used by Cook and Borah is essentially to convert the various tributes paid in kind by each province (which ranged from gold to feathers, from cloaks to maize, from beans to cacao) into a standard measure; to determine an average tribute; to divide the standard measures obtained by that average tribute to obtain the number of tribute payers; to estimate the number of people dependent on each tribute payer; to add those who were exempt; and to make estimates for the areas not covered by the tribute.[15] Each of these steps is based on conjecture, intelligent conjecture but nonetheless depending on thin evidence or none at all. The estimate for 1519 is based on lists of tributes for the provinces ruled by the triple alliance. These are taken from a codex (*Matrícula de Tributos*) consisting of sixteen sheets of native paper covered with pictograms to indicate the name of the province and the type and quantity of the required tribute.[16] For example, the twelve villages in Toluca province were required to supply, every eighty days, 400 white cloaks bordered in black and red, 400 cloaks made of *maguey* fabric with red stripes, and 1,200 white cloaks of *maguey* fabric. Once a year, alternatively, they had to pay in tribute twenty-two warrior's outfits, twenty-two feathered shields, the equivalent of three silos (about 200 metric tons) of maize, three silos of beans, three silos of *chía* (a plant with oil-producing seeds), and three silos of *huautli* (a type of beet).[17] Other sorts of goods were also included in the tributes, presumably reflecting the characteristics of various provinces: Oaxtepec had to supply paper, Axacopan *maguey* honey, Jilotepec live eagles, Cahuacán lumber, Ocuilan salt, Taxco copal, Tepecacuilco hatchets, Tlapa gold . . .

The conversion of this variety of goods into a standard measure (without knowledge of the price system), and then to proceed from that measure to an average tribute, to the total number of tribute payers, and so to a total population, requires a series of acrobatic leaps that arrive finally at a population figure of over 25 million for central Mexico in 1519.

For 1532, the estimates are based on similar criteria: for a certain number of localities, the tribute (in kind and consisting of a variety of goods) imposed by the Audiencia is translated into a value (this time a monetary one, in *reales*). A reasonable average tribute is then estimated on the basis of a series of complex conjectures (the tribute applied to the community and not to the physical person of the tribute payer, so there was no individual tax of the sort introduced after 1577). Finally, dividing the value of the tribute by the estimated average tribute, one estimates the number of tributaries.[18] The limitations of this calculation are evident – similar to those that apply to the 1519 estimate – and have been pointed out by William Sanders.[19] Moreover, given that tributes for the period in question (centered on 1532) are known for only a small number of localities (219, or 13 percent of the total), the total population estimate is based on proportions derived from later and more complete counts.[20] The final estimate – 16.9 million, or one-third less than 1519 – is probably too high (for reasons we explore below). It minimizes, then, the decline relative to 1519 (in spite of a cruel war and the first devastating smallpox epidemic) and exaggerates that for the following period (a decline to one-third between 1532 and 1548).

We have already mentioned that, in 1546, the future Philip II, while regent, ordered a general revision of the tributes to which the communities had been subject since the time of the Audiencia. That revision was meant to correct disparities that had only been made worse by the population decline resulting from the serious epidemic beginning in 1545. The results of the inspections (eighty-nine in all, and covering 900 localities) were consolidated in the *Suma de Visitas*.[21] The *visita* enumerated (or in any case repeated the numbers supplied by the local authorities, which is not the same thing) houses, tribute payers, *casados*, persons (not including children under three or four), and widows and widowers. Often only one or two of these categories is included for a locality, from which figure, by analyzing the ratios between categories where that is possible, we can estimate the total number of tribute payers. Even this initial estimate, though, faces intrinsic difficulties given the different criteria employed by the inspectors. For example, the number of *casados* refers sometimes to married "couples" and at other times to "spouses," without further specifics. But the major problem is that individuals counted include only the tribute-paying *calpulli*, namely the non-exempt nuclei, while no mention is made of those who were exempt: *caciques* and other important persons, members of *calpulli* with administrative or religious functions (service in the convents for example), *mayeques*, and slaves (in any case abolished by the *Leyes Nuevas*). We simply do not know how many people were exempt. There is some scanty documentation for a few localities (and for different dates) that does offer quantitative indications, and we know that the *mayeques* were common in the highlands but absent from the coastal areas. On the basis of these few bits of evidence, Borah and Cook assume that tributary *calpulli* constituted 40 percent of the total (the 60 percent of exemptions being divided into 10 percent nobles, 20 percent non-tribute paying *calpulli*, and 30 percent *mayeques*), except in the coastal areas (about one-quarter of the total population), where they would have accounted for 60 percent of the total (10 percent nobles and 30 percent non-tribute paying *calpulli*). Since the *Suma de Visitas* covered only half the localities, estimates for the missing ones have then to be added in.[22] In practice, if we accept as correct Borah and Cook's reconstruction of the tribute-paying population (tributaries and their families), then this figure has to be multiplied by five (based in part on conjecture) to get the total population. If instead the exempt were one-third less than hypothesized by the two authors (entirely possible), then the estimate for 1548 would also have to be smaller by a third, or 4.2 million instead of 6.3 million. For this reason (and others as well), the criticisms raised regarding the ingenious and composite estimates of Borah and Cook are well founded.[23] Comparing their assigned value of 6.3 million for central Mexico in 1548 to that of 2.65 million for 1568 (based on considerably more complete documentation), we are hard pressed to explain so dramatic a decline, 58 percent, or 4.3 percent per year, in a twenty-year period that was epidemiologically uneventful and fell between the great and generalized epidemics of 1545–7 and 1575–7.

Beyond the simple observation that it suffered rapid decline, then, we still know little about the Mexican population between contact and 1568. And can we even say what is meant by "rapid"? Several documents from the early 1560s, the final years of viceroy Luis de Velasco's administration, offer a clue. At that time there was a heated debate over taxation of the Indios, still based on the scheme introduced by the Segunda Audiencia regarding single communities. Indian population decline made revision of that scheme urgent. Some officials and other notables felt it was necessary to tighten up the liberal exemptions granted to various groups. The populous province of Tlaxcala, for example, enjoyed numerous exemptions because its inhabitants had been the principal allies of Cortés in the battle against Tenochtitlan, supplying men, food, material, and protection. Similarly the Indios of Mexico City were exempt from taxation by tradition and because they were engaged in other public services.[24] Viceroy Velasco thought differently; if the Indios of the capital were required to pay tribute, he believed, "they will no longer devote their labor to the city's public works, or to maintaining the bridges, fountains, roads and landfills, which are numerous and require repair almost every year – repairs that would cost a great deal of money that the city does not have."[25] Another document, however, surely written by a high functionary, made the rounds in Spain and described the great benefits that the Crown could derive from the Indios of the valley of México and the adjoining province of Tlaxcala. This document included, among other things, the amount of the tribute due from the various communities and the number of tribute payers, both probably taken from the evaluation made by the Segunda Audiencia thirty years before. It came into the hands of the viceroy himself, and Velasco noted in the margins his own comments, including the current number of tribute payers, which were then copied into a report sent to the king. Here are the two series regarding the number of tributaries:[26]

District	1531–35	1558	Var. %
Chalco	45,000	22,500	−50
Cholula	25,000	13,000	−48
Texcoco	25,000	12,500	−50
Xochimilco	20,000	12,500	−37.5
Huejotzingo	25,000	11,325	−54.7
Tlaxcala	50,000	50,000	0
México	20,000	20,000	0
TOTAL	210,000	141,825	−32.5

Keeping in mind that the round and repeated figures are highly suspicious, the decline would have been about one-third (–1.5 percent per year); eliminating Mexico City and Tlaxcala – the first because, as the capital, it must have received a steady stream of immigration and the second because of its privileged status – for which the estimates are identical, the tribute payers in the other five *cabaceras* would have declined by close to half (–2.7 percent per year), about the same rate that we encounter for the last three

Map 7 *The valley of México*

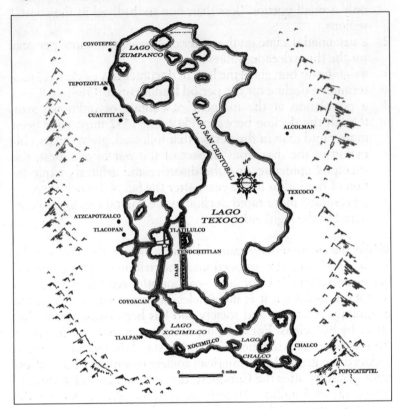

decades of the century. Sanders uses this same document, and incorporates a number of ecological considerations (differential depopulation according to altitude) as well as a few other bits of available information, in order to study the area he refers to as the "central Mexican symbiotic region," namely the valley of México, the populous bordering highland areas of Puebla and Cholula to the southwest and a few sectors of the current states of Hidalgo and Morelos to the northwest.[27] In 1568, this region included almost 1 million inhabitants, as compared to the 2 to 2.5 million estimated for 1530–5, corresponding to an annual demographic decline between 2 and 2.7 percent.

In sum, the reliable information on Mexican demography is limited and consists of the following:

1   a total population around 1568 not far from 3 million, of which only a small portion (less than one-sixth) lived in the coastal regions;
2   a sustained decline on the order of 2 percent or more per year for the three decades following;
3   a significant but, given the lack of documentary evidence, indeterminate decline for the period leading up to 1568;
4   a population at the moment of contact of unknown size, though the decline between 1519 and 1532 must have been more rapid than in the period that followed, given the combination of the disastrous impact of the war of conquest, the smallpox epidemic, and the disorder and arbitrary exploitation of the Indios in the years after the fall of Tenochtitlan;
5   a presumed more rapid decline in the coastal regions as compared to the highlands.

While the documentary material dating before the 1560s – the *Suma de Visitas*, the inspections, and tributary lists compiled before and after the Conquest – cannot offer reliable information on total population, it is nonetheless a rich source for Mexican geography, economy, and society and has been employed to that effect by historians. For our purposes, we can derive a few hints from those sources that help us to understand the mechanisms that reduced the great Meso-American society to a mere 1 million less than a century after the Conquest, down from that indeterminate initial size of 5 million, 10 million, or more. As we saw, for the Caribbean the model is complex, as all the demographic components – survival and reproduction, unions and ethnic migration into the Hispanic population – were traumatized by the ferocious disruption they underwent. The Mexican case, however, was different. The population declined but did not vanish. The economy was transformed but not fully disrupted. Native institutions remained strong, and the Spaniards imposed their reforms within that existing context. The traditional social stratification long remained intact. The Conquest subdued a structured and complex society, but it did not destroy or substantially overturn it. These in any case are some general observations. A more precise understanding of the demographic mechanisms at work may help us to understand better that society's robust resistance in spite of dramatic quantitative decline.

A few useful points can be derived from the *Suma de Visitas* of 1548, even given the inevitable doubts we may have regarding the significance of the various categories employed (houses, *casados, vecinos, mozos, muchachos*, etc.). In spite of the rough nature of the data, the relationship reported between children or young people and the *casados* is an interesting index. In this regard we can rely again on the work of Cook and Borah, who calculated the ratio of children to married couples for 252 districts (of the slightly more than 900 contained in the *Suma de Visitas*). Specifically, they grouped the districts into three different categories according to the definition given of young people. Category A contains the districts that specified who the enumerated "young" were (for example, *niños, muchachos*); category B groups the districts that separately numbered the "ninos" and the "muchachos"; and category C consists of the districts that generically enumerated the "young" with no further detail. The resultant ratios are as follows:

Category A (103 districts): 1.26
Category B (83 districts): 0.96
Category C (66 districts): 1.00

Cook and Borah also noted that the category of the young (or *niños*) generally did not include the *niños de teta* (nursing infants) or children under the age of three. Correcting for that omission, we get the following figures: 1.60, 1.29, 1.33. So, at the time of the *Suma de Vistias*, there were about 1.3 to 1.6 "young people" for every married couple.[28] A ratio of this sort, if maintained over a long period of time, is characteristic of a population in decline. Toward the end of the eighteenth century, that same ratio was about 2.[29] The approximate nature of these figures – the *casados* included old people; it is not clear exactly what age constituted "children" – do not permit us to push these conclusions much further, except to note that, toward mid-century, mechanisms for the renewal of the population appear to have been under considerable stress. But it is impossible to say, for example, whether or not this was a consequence of the epidemic crisis that began in the mid-1540s.

Fifteen years later, in 1562, and so in the midst of a period of epidemiological calm, we encounter a document of great interest that sums up the results of a census of the Indios of Mexico City (the "area of San Juan") and the adjacent quarter of Santiago Tlatelolco.[30] The population at that time was a little less than 70,000, to which must be added 2,000 to 3,000 Spanish families – smaller than the Aztec capital but undeniably the center and motive force of New Spain. The Indian families averaged 4.7 members; the average number of children per married couple was 2.2; and young people constituted 47 percent of the total (see table 12). These parameters are characteristic of a population that has its reproductive capacities intact and has the ability to maintain itself, if not to grow.[31]

Ever since its creation, the Council of the Indies, the most important organ of the Spanish Crown in the Americas, had sought to know the dimensions of the native society by means of reports and inspections. Juan de Ovando was named *visitador* by the council in 1569; together with his secretary (and later the royal cosmographer) López de Velasco, he instituted modern investigative techniques. These resulted in the so-called *Relaciones Geográficas*, multi-faceted reports on the various administrative regions of the American empire. The *Relaciones* consisted of replies to a series of standard questions on a wide variety of topics relating to geography, society, economy, natural resources, religion, culture, and customs. Following several preliminary attempts – the first questionnaire consisted of thirty-seven questions, the second of 200, the third of 135 – a final version with fifty questions was printed and arrived in the Americas in 1577. The replies or *Relaciones* that have survived carry dates ranging from 1579 to 1582.[32] Question 5 is particularly interesting; it asks whether the province had "few or many Indios, and if it had more or less in other times and if the causes are known; and whether they do or do not live in permanently formed villages; and the level and characteristics of their abilities, preferences and ways of living; if there are different languages in the province or one general language that everyone speaks." Question 17 asks "if it is a healthy or unhealthy land or locality and, if unhealthy, what is the cause (if known) and what are the common illnesses and what remedies are taken to combat them."[33]

A systematic analysis of the *Relaciones*, even if solely for demographic ends, would constitute a considerable undertaking. Moreover, from a quantitative point of view they offer at best vague indications regarding population in previous times. The authors included officials, administrators, and other notables familiar with the local situation who employed varying degrees of acumen and diligence in composing their replies. Sixty years after the Conquest, almost no one survived who had first-hand recollections of that earlier period; in many places one has the impression of reading commonplace statements of the sort that might be used for any occasion. For the fifty-nine provinces in the dioceses of Antequera (Oaxaca), Tlaxcala, México, and Michoacán, almost all had experienced, in the opinion of the reporter, strong or very strong declines in population. For almost all the cause was "infirmity" or "epidemics" with a wide variety of indications, both specific – smallpox and measles – and generic, such as pestilence or *cocolitzle* (a generic Nahuatl term) or other terms referring mostly to respiratory and exanthematic illnesses. Also mentioned, however, among the causes are work in the mines and forced labor, insalubrious environments, migration from temperate to hot climates, the concentration of dispersed Indios, and famine. With regard to epidemics, it is interesting to note that a plurality of independent observers identified those of 1520–1, 1545–7, and 1576–80 as the most serious, for both level of mortality and area affected, while other episodes were considered minor and local. Juan Bautista de Pomar (in 1582), for example, attributed the depopulation of Texcoco to "three general pestilences":

It is well known that the general pestilence that took place during the years 1576 to 1580 carried away two persons out of three ... and that another that took place almost forty years ago inflicted a similar massacre, not to mention the first smallpox epidemic that took place while the Spaniards were conquering Mexico City, and that all agree caused more damage than those which came later, leaving aside many other less grave pestilences.[34]

Francisco de Molina and Jorge Ceron Carvajal reported similar details for Tepeaca: "The first [epidemic] was smallpox, about sixty years ago, when the Spaniards first arrived in these lands, and the next would have been thirty-eight years ago and the last three years ago . . . so that of the people that were here when the Spaniards arrived nine are missing out of ten."[35] And, for Tlaxcala, Diego Muñoz Camargo spoke of three epidemics "that I would not know which of the three to say was the greatest."[36]

In other cases, such as that of Veracruz, the discussion is not so much of epidemics as of a general depopulation, as for much of the coastal region. In that regard we should look at the following excerpt in its entirety:

According to what is told by the tradition of the ancient residents of this land, when the Spaniards arrived there were many populous Indian towns and villages within 6 leagues of this city that have declined so much that many are almost completely depopulated, and there remains neither trace nor memory except for the names, while others have so few residents and population today that, compared to what they were before, it is painful to see to what small dimensions they are reduced. So Cempoala, a famous place . . . 2 leagues north of Veracruz, was reportedly once a city of 20,000 families and now has barely thirty houses; and the village that today we call Rinconada and the Indios called Itzacalpan, 5 leagues to the west of this city, was the principal village of more than 10,000 Indios and today has only fifty houses . . . There has then been a very noticeable decline and even disappearance of Indios in this *comarca* since the Spaniards took over, and every day the villages continue to undergo depopulation and the Indios from two or three communities join together to form one in order to protect themselves better, so that one is forced to imagine the total destruction of those who remain. And the Indios have been declining in the way that I describe not because of any specific cause other than the insalubrity of the land and the miserable pestilence of the mosquitoes that afflicts it.

A cycle then was taking place of the sort prophesied half a century before by Alonso de Zuazo, a high official with broad experience, in his letter to the king on the depopulation of Santo Domingo and the coast of Honduras:

Regarding New Spain, I, *licenciado* Zuazo, can offer direct testimony that a great part of the land around the sea ports [of the Gulf of Mexico] is practically depopulated of Indios, who are dead or it is believed will die out in that land just as they have in this [Santo Domingo] in a very short time.[37]

It is possible that the disease load of the hot, humid, and low areas increased significantly with the arrival, presumably from Africa, of the malaria plasmodium, transmitted then by local mosquitoes. That would explain the rapid population decline on account of mortality, low reproductivity, and emigration out of the infested areas. The presumed non-American origins of the plasmodium are supported by a number of considerations, including the fact that in the Americas it is found only in humans and several species of monkey, while in Africa and Asia it is widely spread among primates and mammals generally, suggesting its relatively recent arrival in the New World. Moreover, chronicles and reports from the early explorations of the Gulf of Mexico lowlands and of Darién make no reference to consistent losses though illness and fever. And it has been suggested that if the lands crossed by Cortés and his expedition in 1524–5 had been infested with malaria, as they were a few decades later, they might never have arrived in Honduras. Veracruz itself became unhealthy and dangerous for both Europeans and Indios within a few decades of the first European settlements.[38]

The disastrous effects of the epidemics in Mexico have already been touched upon several times above. Nonetheless, we need to devote a bit more attention to the major actor in the depopulation of Meso-America, a relatively easy task given the quantity of work that has been done on the topic.[39] Our job then will be to offer a balanced summary, keeping in mind that the sources available are to be treated with caution, both because of the state of medical knowledge at the time and because of the often vague descriptions of symptoms left to us (when they are left at all). Moreover, chroniclers and other witnesses rarely gave reliable reports on the effects of the epidemics, offering instead impressionistic descriptions or evaluations of the sort "two out of three died," or round and almost always exaggerated figures. Members of religious orders, the most careful and informed observers, did not keep burial registers and so were no better able than others to offer convincing evaluations. So while there is general agreement about the dates of the epidemics and their extent, there is often uncertainty about their nature and little understanding of their impact.

The author of an excellent synthesis on Mexican epidemiology, Hanns Prem, has categorized the symptoms of the various epidemic outbreaks as described by the chroniclers of the era in the following manner:[40]

- fevers: *calenturas, calenturas tercianas, calenturas cuartanas*;
- fevers with rashes: *viruela* (smallpox), *tabardillo* (typhus), *sarampión* (measles), *sarna* (leprosy);
- respiratory illnesses: *romadizo, tos, dolor de costado* (pains in the chest);

- swollen glands: *hinchanzón de la garganta* (swelling of the throat), *paperas* (mumps), *landres* (swelling of the lymph glands);
- bleeding: *flujo de sangre, cámaras de sangre* (diarrhea), *pujamento de sangre*.

In the case of exanthematic fevers, for example, chroniclers might use more than one term indiscriminately, or else different observers might use different terms, and so they pass on to us the same difficulties of interpretation with which they were coping themselves. In addition, different sets of symptoms might coincide, posing still greater problems of interpretation.

Curiously, it is the smallpox epidemic of 1520–1 about which there are the fewest doubts.[41] As described in chapter 3, this was the continuation of the epidemic that broke out in December 1518 in Hispaniola; from there it spread to Cuba and then, with the expedition of Pánfilo de Narváez in May 1520, to the coast of Veracruz. It then spread inland and in September–October reached the valley of México, where it raged for two months. We know little, though, of its progress after that; according to the Indio tracts consulted by Sahagún: "The plague moved toward Chalco. And then it died down considerably but did not go away completely."[42] Given the centrality of Mexico City and the rapidity of the Conquest, it is reasonable to suppose the epidemic did not encounter obstacles in spreading throughout central Mexico. A singular and concise testimony comes from the first chronicler and direct witness, and also the first beneficiary, Hernán Cortés. Referring to his visit to Cholula in autumn 1520, about a year after the massacre that he himself had perpetrated there, he wrote: "I, with twenty horsemen, went that day to spend the night in the city of Cholula, for the inhabitants desired my presence, as many of their lords had died of the smallpox, which also affects those of the mainland as it does the islanders; and they wished me to appoint new ones on their advice."[43] Certainly a passage with more than a touch of irony if smallpox was, as many maintain, the primary ally of the Spaniards in their conquest of Tenochtitlan.

When it first appeared in the New World, smallpox surely had a devastating impact. While the Hieronymite brothers stated that one-third of the Taíno fell victim to the disease, Motolinia claimed half; but these sorts of conjecture do not get us very far. It is certain in any case that, in addition to the many victims of the war and the very many victims of smallpox, there were those who succumbed subsequently to famine and want; and Motolinia himself referred explicitly to the latter as a "third plague," already mentioned in chapter 2. In preparation for the siege of Tenochtitlan, Cortés concentrated on the systematic destruction and depredation of the coastal areas, whence reinforcements and supplies for the Aztec enemy might have come.[44] The destruction of the city, following upon its defeat, forced the evacuation of survivors at the limit of their endurance, while in the other parts of the valley and surrounding areas hit by smallpox, we can presume that normal planting and cultivation was neglected. The not always compassionate Bernal Díaz del Castillo noted that:

Cortés sent us to visit the city and we saw the houses full of corpses and a few poor Mexicans who could not move . . . and the whole city was as if plowed, the roots of any edible plant having been dug up; they had cooked these together with the bark of some trees and eaten them, and there was no fresh water, only salty.[45]

According to Motolinia, by then resident in the Indies for a number of years, an epidemic of measles broke out in 1531: "a Spaniard arrived who was stricken with measles. From him it was carried to the Indians. Had it not been for the great care that was taken to prevent the Indians from bathing and from using other remedies, there would have been another serious plague and pestilence, similar to the previous one. In spite of all this, however, many died. They called this the year of the small leprosy."[46] This was surely a minor episode, and doubts remain about its cause as there is no description of symptoms.

The second major and widespread epidemic was that of 1545, which dragged on for two or three years. It was largely because of this epidemic that a series of inspections were carried out to recalibrate the tribute obligation, which had surely become excessive as a result. The epidemic was characterized by excessive bleeding, and many present-day interpreters, starting with Zinsser, have suggested that it was typhus. The impact was disastrous. Motolinia speaks of losses between 60 and 90 percent, though surely this was an exaggeration. One also reads of 150,000 deaths in the province of Tlaxcala and 100,000 in Cholula, which, while populous provinces, had total populations of about that size, if not a bit smaller. Sahagún wrote: "In 1545 there was a great and universal pestilence because of which, in all of New Spain, the greater part of the population perished. I was in Mexico City at the time of this pestilence and buried more than 10,000 corpses, and at the end of the epidemic I fell ill myself and was near death."[47] In the *Relaciones Geográficas*, written thirty-five years later, when the memory had not yet been erased by the passage of time, the imprint of the disaster remained profound.

There are also records of other minor episodes: an epidemic of *paperas* (mumps) in 1550 that was apparently not devastating; and indigenous sources refer to a famine in 1559–60 and another crisis in 1563–4 that according to the authoritative royal inspector Valderrama was due to measles. The third disastrous epidemic was the one that began in August 1576 and stretched out, following a remission in 1578, till 1580 and reportedly spread to the whole country. We have reports on this epidemic from a variety of sources, both indigenous and Spanish, though the information on symptoms is fairly confused: fevers, nosebleeds, dysentery. Fray Jerónimo de Mendieta, an eyewitness, claimed that the disease was *tabardillo*, or typhus.[48] But that identification remains questionable and, given the different sorts of symptoms reported, it may have been something else.[49] On November 30, 1576, a Spaniard wrote to his protectress in Spain, the countess di Ribadavia, that the epidemic in Tlaxcala had been raging for six months and reportedly had killed 80,000 Indios; he had lost more than 200 of his own dependents, including several Blacks.[50]

In three letters to the king, Pedro Moya de Cintreras, archbishop of Mexico, allows us to reconstruct the chronicle of the disaster: on November 6, 1576, he describes that the epidemic is winding its way through the dioceses of México and Tlaxcala and after two months has killed 100,000 Indios; on December 10 he notes that it is continuing to spread and has now also stricken *mestizos* and Blacks as well as a few Spaniards; on March 15, 1577, he writes that finally, toward the end of December, mortality among the Indios of the city has begun to decline, but the epidemic continues in other villages of the region and has spread to the remote areas of Michoacán and Nueva Galicia, and to the mines of Zacatecas and Guanajuato, as had already occurred in Pachuca, hitting the silver production there particularly hard.[51] This last bit of news surely saddened the king more than the previous ones.

A little before that, on February 27, the Jesuits of Mexico City had written to the king that, in the preceding eight to nine months, the epidemic had killed 600,000 Indios.[52] Six years later, in a summing up, the archbishop would claim that half the population had died.[53] The *Relaciones Geográficas*, written just after the epidemic had run its course, give an overall impression of devastation, depopulation, and crisis.

The last two decades of the century seem to have been less traumatic, though in 1588 there was high mortality because of a maize shortage; famine was widespread, especially in the regions of Tlaxcala and Tepeaca and in the valley of Toluca. Finally, in 1595–6, there was another general epidemic of measles and other exanthematic diseases and of mumps, "because of which hardly a man was left standing, though thanks to the clemency and compassion of our most benign Lord, not so many died as is usual with other diseases."[54] According to Viceroy Montesclaros, measles in 1595 spread through all the provinces as far as Guatemala and, worse still, had exercised a negative effect on the personal service provided by the Indios.[55]

There are yet other factors that should be included in an ideal explanatory model of the incidence of epidemic pathologies in the Americas, both those that were new and those that were revived by the grafting on of European biology. Given the limits of the available documentation, we cannot achieve that ideal, but there are nonetheless a few more useful factors to consider. A number of important variables surely played a role in determining the severity and the spread of the epidemics: the geographical lay of the country, the communication network, population density, and the types of settlement.

For example, dense demographic concentration in the valley of México and surrounding areas, at the center of the country, surely was a factor in speeding up the spread and rate of contagion for the simple closeness of individuals, families and settlements; and the system of roads that radiated out from the capital must have facilitated the spread of diseases out to the periphery. For diseases imported from Europe and arriving at Veracruz or other ports on the east coast, progress toward the interior was guaranteed by the intense traffic between the capital and those ports; and from the capital they could spread to other parts of the country.

We have already explored the contrasting case of Perú in chapter 3 (and will return to it in chapter 7). Yet it is impossible to flesh out these hypotheses without a detailed epidemiological geography, and that, for the colonial period, is lacking.

From the beginning of the Conquest, both the Spanish colonists and the Crown (and also the Church) shared an aversion for dispersed settlements spread throughout the territory. And yet that sort of settlement was typical not only in areas characterized by primitive agriculture supplemented by hunting and fishing, but also in areas with more developed agriculture but where the nature of the territory was not conducive to denser settlement. From the moment of his arrival in Hispaniola, Governor Ovando worked to construct an "urban" structure as far as possible throughout the territory of the island, which might consist of settlements of a few Spanish families around which the Indios could be concentrated. In an extreme attempt to unite the few surviving Indios into significant groups, the Hieronymite fathers in 1518 sought to bring them together into thirty villages; construction was only partially completed when smallpox struck. The motivations for concentration of the Indios were at once mundane and religious: mundane because their organization into stable villages with a minimum degree of dispersion allowed for more efficient control, easier collection of tribute, and a simpler identification and management of the Indios for activities relating to transport, production and service; religious because the task of evangelizing – the responsibility not only of the religious orders but also of the *encomenderos* or the Crown to whom the Indios were assigned – was more easily accomplished when the natives were concentrated in villages as opposed to spread out over the countryside in farms and isolated settlements. Undergirding the process was the idea, formally expressed in the *Leyes Nuevas*, that the natives were naturally capable of "political" behavior, including living in large, organized, and hierarchical collectivities.

The greatest success of the policy of concentration was achieved with the Guaraní in the valleys of the Paraná and Uruguay rivers in the seventeenth century (chapter 8). In New Spain, at the time of the arrival of the Spaniards, there was already a fairly widespread urban organization in place. It consisted of small independent or semi-independent states, each organized around a principal settlement (*cabecera*) with a market, ceremonial center, the leader's house, the nobility and priests, all surrounded by the common people. The rest of the population lived in small groups close by the fields.[56] In addition to Tenochtitlan, the Spaniards came across other cities of a certain importance, such as Cholula, Tlaxcala, or Chalco. Nonetheless, in spite of a developed urban structure, the push to reorganize settlements – which was strong and revolutionary in Perú – affected Mexico too. Royal ordinances of 1551 and 1558 repeated the invitation to proceed with the concentration of dispersed population. The *cabaceras* were frequently relocated to more convenient and easily reached locations; but "at the same time, in the 1550s and 1560s many Indians in outlying estancias were convinced by persuasion or force to abandon their ancestral homesites and move either to a *cabecera* or to a relocated *pueblo sujeto*."[57] The importance of this first redistribution of population is not clear; according to some its impact was modest, limited to groups transferred for reasons of defense from inaccessible areas to the plains, or else limited to an urban restructuring of disorganized settlements.[58] A second and more extensive program was carried out over the period 1593–1605. In part it was motivated by the population decline caused by the crisis of 1576–80, and so the need to reorganize the dispersed survivors into larger and socially more stable units. The reductions or congregations were carried out after inspectors had evaluated their advisability and chosen suitable sites, and following approval by the authorities.[59] The Indios themselves rebuilt the village in the chosen spot, with the usual gridwork pattern and central plaza surrounded by public and religious buildings. In many cases the spot chosen for the concentration of the Indios might be the *cabecera* village itself. The abandoned homes were then burnt down, though there were instances of protest and attempts to return to the areas left behind, movements that had to be approved by a succeeding ordinance. In any case, these ordinances surely increased the country's level of urbanization, cut down on the dispersion of settlements, and opened up large tracts for the establishment of extensive *estancias* by the Spaniards.

The religious orders raised loud protests against this process – pursued with enthusiasm by the viceroy Conde de Monterrey – which they held responsible for great suffering and a source of abuse on the part of the appointed administrators. The echo of this protest made its way to the king, who issued an ordinance (dated December 3, 1604) specifying the criteria and limits of the new congregations, which were not to be formed if the Indios already lived in communities, but should be restricted to Indios living in isolated and inaccessible places. Monterrey's successor, the marques de Montesclaros, however, sought in any way possible to halt this change of course, which he feared would increase disorder; and so he made public only that part of the ordinance referring to the ownership of abandoned land. He also tried without success to blunt the opposition of the religious orders, and in a letter to the king accused them of deliberately falsifying the number of the Indios; that falsification, Montesclaros claimed, was the true explanation for the apparent population decline and so of the reduction in tribute paid.[60]

Regardless of the importance of the congregations, high population density in central Mexico and the valley of México, the large metropolitan capital, a developed network of cities, the natural attraction of urban centers for dispersed populations, and a good transportation system that radiated out from the capital all contributed to the spread of the new diseases. The degree to which each of these factors had an impact on the demographic balance, though, is impossible to say.

The earliest phases of the Conquest reveal the colossal amount of work the Indios were forced to do for their new masters. In 1520, Cortés, having barely escaped violence at the hands of the people of Tenochtitlan, reorganized his forces and planned a precise siege and attack of the city. In order to conquer the defenses of the city, situated as it was in the midst of a lagoon, it was necessary to be able to navigate that lagoon and support the land forces. However, putting together a "fleet" over 300 kilometers from the coast was no simple undertaking. The Spaniards were able to take advantage of the abundant labor provided by their Tlaxcaltec allies to support the military operations. Under the guidance of the master sawyer Martin López, lumber for the construction of thirteen brigantines was prepared in Tlaxcala and then transported over 70 kilometers by thousands of Indios, with a secure escort, to the vicinity of the lagoon.[61] There the ships were mounted, armed (with hardware brought from Veracruz and taken from ships that Cortés had ordered disarmed, but not burnt as legend has it), and launched into the lagoon. As the banks were marshy and unsafe, however, the brigantines were assembled in a dry dock almost

3 kilometers from the shore. It was necessary then to dig a canal 12 feet wide (3.60 meters) and equally deep, with sides reinforced by trunks and planks to prevent them from collapsing. The brigantines were launched in this canal. These were large vessels about a dozen meters long and two and a half meters wide with a shallow keel and one or two masts; they could carry up to twenty-five men including the oarsmen. Construction of the canal took 8,000 Indios fifty days to complete. The population around the lake, subdued by the Spanish, was given the task of constructing lodging to house Cortés's troops during the siege that was less precarious than the straw huts and would protect them from the torrential rains; 2,000 Indios completed that task in a short time.[62] These examples bring home the point that the Conquest depended on the mobilization of masses of indigenous workers; subsequently that mobilization would constitute the basis for development of the colony.

The normative and juridical framework that regulated Indian labor and personal service and the real situation on the ground, which was often very different, are exceedingly complex and the topic of in-depth studies. Nonetheless, It is important to consider these, as in the accounts of many contemporaries one of the most frequently cited causes of population decline was the exploitation – or simple appropriation – of that population's labor and energy. Beyond that general observation, however, it is difficult to identify the specific links between the level of exploitation and population decline. Did mortality increase by means of the classic biological mechanisms (greater susceptibility to disease, risk of violent death, and exposure to variations in climate and environment), or through other ones that affected fertility, family, or social cohesion, or more generally by means of a lowering of the standard of living. Everything that we can say in this regard is necessarily the fruit of conjecture.

Once the Conquest was completed, Cortés had to compensate hundreds of comrades in arms who had taken great risks and received little or nothing in return. The most efficient method turned out to be assigning the Indio lords and their peoples in *encomienda* to his most important soldiers; this way the Spaniards could extract labor and tribute in exchange for a vague promise of protection and indoctrination into the True Faith. Cortés overcame the opposition of Charles V by a mixture of delaying tactics relative to the king's ordinances and diplomatic skill. Cortés claimed that the *encomienda* was necessary to bind the Spaniards to the new possessions, that otherwise they had no source of support, that the colonists were necessary to hold the territories for the king, and that it would have been impossible to extract tribute directly from the Indios; the Crown could not use tributes in kind, nor was there currency for making money payments. The Indios, moreover, in his account, had been liberated from forced servitude, if not slavery, in the period just before the Conquest; their conditions had been much harder previously. Finally, his twenty-year experience in the islands had taught him the necessary precautions to take in order to avoid abuses.[63] The *encomienda* remained, and the Prima Audiencia committed the worst abuses in this regard, partially eliminated by the Segunda Audiencia. The first viceroy, Antonio de Mendoza, basically upheld the practice, while the *Leyes Nuevas* introduced significant limits (the *encomienda* passed to the Crown on the death of the *encomendero*) and made it notably less onerous. It is of course not so much the institution of the *encomienda* that interests us, but the labor regime that system imposed on the Indios, whether assigned to private individuals or the Crown. In this regard the introduction of the *Leyes Nuevas*, strongly reaffirmed in 1549, represented an innovation insofar as they provided greater protection for the Indios. The new laws stipulated, among other things, that the Indios were free and vassals of the Crown (art. 10); that no Indio could be made a slave, even following wars and in cases of rebellion (art. 26); that enslaved Indios had to be freed immediately (art. 27); that Indios should only transport goods for a salary (art. 28); and that they could not be made to fish for pearls against their will (art. 30).[64] The royal ordinance of 1549 reaffirmed that the Indios could not be forced into personal service as a substitute for tribute payments. These regulations, subsequently reinforced, were applied by Mendoza's successor, the viceroy Luis de Velasco, to varying degrees. In particular, a halfway measure was adopted according to which the Indios were "distributed" by an official to various jobs for limited periods of time and at set salaries. This was a sort of limited forced rental of labor, one that the demographic decline progressively undermined. The theoretical justification for this compromise relied on the widely held belief in the "natural laziness" of the Indios and the need to force them to perform services essential to the survival of the colony.[65]

Within this framework, several attendant circumstances help us to understand better the exploitation of Indian labor, to which moreover we can trace many of Motolinia's "plagues." The furious reconstruction of Mexico City atop the ruins of Tenochtitlan was accomplished with the labor of Indios from the city and surrounding area. Given the marshy nature of the region, stone (beyond that salvaged from the destruction of the temples) had to be brought long distances, requiring a huge expenditure of energy. Public works (regulation of the lake's water, roads, the Chapultepec aqueduct), administrative buildings (the *cabildo*, prison, slaughterhouse, etc.), churches and monasteries, and other public buildings were built with Indian labor, mostly not paid for.[66] According to López de Velasco, around 1570 there were ninety monasteries in the diocese of Mexico City and thirty in Tlaxcala, many of which, imposing for their large size, are still standing. Kubler has compiled an interesting statistic for the number of constructions (churches and monasteries) completed by the major mendicant orders (Franciscans, Dominicans, and Augustinians) during the first century after the Conquest: from about ten in the decade 1520–30 to about forty in each of the two following decades, to an average of about sixty for each of the decades between 1540 and 1570.[67] Subsequently the building frenzy abated, and fewer than thirty buildings were completed in the last decade of the century. Initially the Indios were obliged to provide their labor at no cost for these building projects, sometimes having also to supply their own food and even building materials.[68] The Indios were also responsible for building village churches. The grandeur of the Santo Domingo monastery in Mexico City, considered excessive, was such as to generate a memo from the Segunda Audiencia to the empress in 1531.[69] Cortés was much criticized for the huge number of workers employed on the construction of his residences in Mexico City and Cuernavaca. There is good documentation for intense building activity in Tlaxcala between 1530 and 1550 and for heavy investments in roads and bridges: thirty-three stone bridges were built in that province between 1555 and 1560.[70] Indios from Cholula and Tlaxcala provided the labor for building the new city of Puebla, begun in 1530, including laying out the plan of the city, leveling the roads and squares, and erecting the residences of the first few dozen Spanish colonists and the first public buildings.[71] Free Indian labor was essential for the construction of the new road between Mexico City and Veracruz, begun by Cortés himself and including bridges and rest stations. Among public works, the gigantic *desagüe* project for Mexico City stands out; this was an attempt to prevent the periodic flooding of the city by the lagoon (many buildings sank under their own tremendous weight) by means of a canal, excavated in part (for 6 kilometers) as a tunnel cut into the rocky sides of the valley. This huge project, begun in 1607, employed 6,000 Indios continuously for more than fifteen months. It did not resolve the problem, however, which dragged on for two more centuries, absorbing infinite resources.[72]

Another area for which Indian labor was essential was transport. We have already described the work of the Tlaxcaltecs, but all of the *entradas* throughout Meso-America, including Cortés's unfortunate expedition to Honduras, were accompanied by thousands and thousands of porters and auxiliaries. Fifteen thousand reportedly accompanied Nuño de Guzman's expedition to Jalisco.[73] After the first years, a degree of normality set in, but the demand for porters, filled naturally by Indios, continued. According to Zavala:

In New Spain, the Spaniards found an extensive, mountainous terrain where travel was difficult. Beasts of burden were unknown, and their reproduction and expansion, once they had been introduced from Europe, were not rapid enough to satisfy the demand for the transportation of goods and people. Native culture had resolved this problem by means of *tamemes*, or Indian porters, and the Spaniards continued to use them even while the laws encouraged new solutions more in keeping with humanitarian treatment and economic development. The introduction of animals and the building of roads that could accommodate caravans and carts helped to change the system, but it did not happen immediately or at the same time in all regions, especially the most remote ones. Finally, the construction and maintenance of the new roads required a large labor force and tools, incurring costs that had in one way or another to be covered.[74]

Countless laws and regulations were introduced in the course of the century which sought to regulate and moderate the use of the Indios for transport, regulations, however, that were caught between the demographic decline of the Indios on the one hand and the expanding activities of the Spaniards on the other. As the colony and the number of colonists grew, so did the needs of expanding commerce, of mining activity, of agricultural production on the farms of the colonists, of public works, and so on. All of these activities required notable supplies of energy that could only partially be met by the growing stock of animals. Given current knowledge, no one is able to estimate the quantity of indigenous labor appropriated by the Spaniards and so to determine the demographic impact. According to witnesses at the time, it was not a secondary factor in the catastrophe of the first century after the Conquest.

Slavery was surely a cause in the demographic destruction of the Indios. It was already widespread before the Spaniards arrived, and the colonists took ample advantage of the system, especially in their hunt for gold during the first part of the Conquest. In his pamphlet-letter of 1555 to Charles V, Motolinia challenges Las Casas's assertion that there had been 3 or 4 million slaves in the New World, concentrated primarily in New Spain; he maintains instead, having consulted experienced elders, that there had been at most 150,000, and perhaps not even 100,000. The brand for marking slaves arrived from Spain in May 1524, but Cortés was disinclined to use it and called a meeting, attended by Motolinia.[75] Motolinia had in fact included slavery as the eighth plague in his list of ten (see chapter 2). Many abuses were committed during Cortés's expedition to Honduras. Rodrigo de Albórnoz, a high official of the king, wrote a letter to Charles V in December 1525 on the abuses carried out when Cortés was absent. Regarding the permission given to Spaniards to "redeem" the slaves belonging to local lords (redeem in the sense of transferring them into their own service), it happened that:

The Christian demands gold of the cacique, and if he says he has none, or if he has it and gives it to him, he is required to give a hundred or two slaves besides. And if perhaps the cacique has not so many, for the sake of obeying he gives others of his vassals who are not slaves.[76]

Albórnoz added that this quantity of slaves naturally brought with it certain advantages, as they were sent to hunt for gold and silver and so increased the income of the Crown. On the other hand, the colonists who used slaves to work their land saw productivity decrease and so the Indios' ability to pay tribute.

Moreover, if great moderation and care are not exercised, the slaves will diminish daily, although the land is well peopled, because the slaves taken in the cold provinces and brought to the mines in the hot country die and diminish from the labor as well as from the heat, and the same holds true for those brought from the hot country to the cold, although not so much . . .[77]

In 1527, a vein was discovered near Mexico City. There was a small gold rush as a result, and squads of eighty to a hundred Indios, presumably slaves, were sent there, but with limited results on account of flight and death.[78] In any case, the category of slave soon ceased to have much relevance, whether because of natural decline, because recruitment, a fruit of war before the arrival of the Spaniards, dried up, or because, as Motolinia assures, the slaves were effectively liberated by the *Leyes Nuevas*. According to James Lockhart, "by the 1550s, hardly any indigenous central Mexicans were held as slaves either by Spaniards or by Indians . . . After that time, Indian slaves were a negligible factor in indigenous society. However, to the extent that . . . tlatlacotin [slaves] were assimilated to other lesser dependents and servants, their disappearance implied no major social rearrangement."[79] For the sake of thoroughness, we should add that Cook and Borah estimate the number of enslaved Indios at the time of the *Suma de Visitas* as 50,000.[80]

Among the great transformations that took place as a result of the arrival of the Spaniards, one in particular had lasting effects of a sort that are difficult to evaluate. This was the arrival of plants and animals from Europe that adapted well to the Meso-American climate. In the long run, the effects of this European "invasion" were certainly positive, as diet improved – pigs and chickens became a universal addition to the Indian family economy – and the Indios were able to use animal power for traction and transport. In other ways, the impact was negative, especially in the early years, as the expansion of livestock and the raising of crops interfered with traditional Indian agriculture. Many scholars believe that before the Conquest the population of Meso-America was in the final phase of a Malthusian cycle:

population density was high; the soil was exhausted; woods and forest had been cut. Some hold that the population had reached a limit after which a destructive cycle would have followed even without the arrival of the Spanish. These opinions are compatible with the high estimates, in some cases very high, proposed over the past fifty years for the pre-Hispanic population. After the Conquest, that demographic pressure suddenly let up, while environmental deterioration continued for other reasons. According to Peter Gerhard:

As native communities declined and even disappeared, many of the old communal lands were acquired by vast, Spanish-owned haciendas. Areas long cultivated became pastures for immense herds of cattle. Sheep and goats further denuded the barren hillsides, while old maize fields and previously untilled lands were planted to wheat and sugar cane. Terraces were less used for agriculture, and some alluvial soils were worked for the first time, with wooden plows. Forests near cities and mining camps disappeared entirely, canyons cut deeper into the plateaus. Many of the lake-filled volcanic basins dried up, some artificially drained, others through natural desiccation.[81]

With regard to the mining sites, Viceroy Mendoza warned his successor that in just a few years enormous expanses of forest had been cut and that the lumber would likely be used up before the metal was.[82] Environmental decline in the valley of México was rapid: the demand for wood created by the reconstruction of the city and to supply energy to a wealthy and growing Spanish population stripped the sides of the valley of its timber, causing heavy erosion; the equilibrium of the land in the plain was altered by the replacement of traditional agriculture with other sorts, the spread of livestock raising, new irrigation techniques, the employment of the waters to operate mills, and the attempts to defend the city from flooding. According to Charles Gibson, "none of the new techniques was disastrous in and of itself, but the combined effect over time led to an accelerated reduction of agricultural land."[83] Other studies have brought to light the profound conflict between livestock and agriculture: the huge herds of the Spanish landowners devastated the fields of the natives in spite of rules directing that they keep their distance and not cross over property lines. This tension led to constant conflict and forced the Indios over time to abandon their fields to the great haciendas, while they

themselves were transformed from peasant farmers to day laborers. "In 1594 one of the largest towns of the province [of
Tlaxcala], Hueyotlipan, was temporarily abandoned by the
Indians after the destruction of its *nopal* and fruit crops by roving
cattle."[84]

Much remains to be understood about the demographic history of
Mexico during the first century of the Conquest. Given a population reduced to less than 1.3 million at the end of the century, it is
conceivable that, over a stretch of eighty years, the pre-Conquest
population was halved three times, so an initial figure of 10 million
seems plausible. It is also certain that much of the demographic
catastrophe must be ascribed to epidemic crises – in particular
those of 1520–1, 1545–7, and 1576–80 – though there are also
signs that by mid-century the reproductive capacity of the population was seriously compromised. The particular configuration of
central Mexico, with a large, centrally located capital well connected to the rest of the country and a centralized and high-density
population (at least in the initial phases) help to explain the impact
and rapid spread of the diseases imported from Europe. The
appropriation of Indian labor and energy by the Spaniards, their
territorial dislocation, and the abandonment of traditional modes
of production likely also contributed to high mortality (as many
contemporary observers believed). Environmental changes caused
by the introduction of European population, animals, and plants
brought about changes in ways of living that, at least temporarily,
posed new risks to survival. In the second half of the century, more
attention to the protection of the Indios, by means of the *Leyes
Nuevas*, coincided with an increase in tribute pressure and a shift
of Indian labor to the agricultural, manufacturing, and mining
enterprises of the Spaniards. Meanwhile the ratio between
Spaniards and Indios was rapidly changing in favor of the former:
around 1570 there were about two Spaniards for every hundred
natives, while by the mid-seventeenth century there were more
than ten, certainly a trend with important ramifications for indigenous society.[85] Overall, however, the conditions experienced by
the Indios in Mexico were better than those in Perú, a fact recognized at the end of the century by Luis de Velasco (the son), who
had been viceroy in both Mexico and Perú. The weight of colonization – in terms of tributes, labor, and subordination to the

Spaniards – was less burdensome in Mexico. It is difficult just the same to understand the demographic consequences of this differential impact, except that in Perú it created an intense internal migration of a sort that did not transpire in Mexico.[86]

7 The Incas and many millions of subjects. A quarter-century of wars: Indios versus Indios, Spaniards versus Indios, Spaniards versus Spaniards. "Quipu" pen and ink. A viceroy who counts, measures, and acts. Epidemics: the moderns debate them, the ancients ignore them.

At the moment of the Conquest, the Andean world governed by the Incas extended from present-day Ecuador to the Chilean desert, from the Pacific to the western part of the Amazon basin. Even today, the borders between states in this vast section of the world are uncertain and the source of conflict. We can approximate in any case that the area under Incan control amounted to about 3 million square kilometers, stretching over 4,000 kilometers from north to south and several hundred kilometers from east to west. Estimating the population of greater Perú at the moment of Conquest, however, is nearly impossible, for two concurrent and overlapping reasons. The first has already been discussed relative to Mexico and holds for any calculation that involves working backward in time from what was known (the first counts made for fiscal purposes once the Conquest was complete) to an unknown situation several decades before. The second is specific to Perú. At the time of the Conquest, furious wars of succession between Huascar Capac and Atahuallpa, the sons of Huayna Capac, had devastated the country and taken a demographic toll. Many of the scholars who have embarked on this exercise in speculation, then, have focused instead on the presumed situation at the end of the reign of Huayna Capac, coming up with estimates ranging from a few million to several tens of millions. As we shall see, the more careful and documented researches today put the total in the area of 10 million. The demographic destruction of the Andean world then takes on a different aspect from that of the other population concentrations of the Americas; it both precedes and follows upon the Conquest.

Perú enjoys a geography rich in contrasts, with an arid coastal region in the west, the Andean peaks and the cold highlands at the center, and plains and tropical forests in the east. Three-quarters of the population of Perú, perhaps more, lived in the highlands at elevations between 3,000 and 4,000 meters, and in the high valleys that cut through the Andes. Nature is stingy there. The principal resources above 3,300 meters were – and still are – the raising of llamas and other cameloids and the cultivation of some minor grains (*quinoa*) and potatoes. At lower elevations, the growing of maize becomes possible. The Andean population then was accustomed to high altitudes, limited availability of local resources (generally complemented by trade), and air thin in oxygen with the attendant bioanthropological consequences. As compared to the indigenous populations living at lower altitudes, their bodily development was slow and sexual maturity delayed. The scarcity of oxygen resulted in the development of a large chest cavity in relation to weight and height and so a large aerobic and pulmonary capacity. This adaptation has given the Indios of the highlands, in the face of a hostile environment, a high level of physical efficiency as well as good resistance to the cold. Studies of present-day populations in the highlands, with ways of life not very different from those of the past, have revealed adaptation to a modest diet high in carbohydrates and typical of a society with limited agricultural resources, and good efficiency in the face of climatic stress reflected in their clothing and the building materials used for their homes. These particularities are the product more of cultural and physiological adaptation than of genetic selection. Modern studies have also revealed other characteristics of great demographic relevance. The first is the high incidence of respiratory illness, linked to the scarcity of oxygen: tuberculosis, pneumonia, bronchitis, and other minor ailments. These target especially the young and account for a high proportion of deaths. The second particularity is that gastro-intestinal infections, a principal cause of death for children in tropical zones, are less frequent among the Andean populations, as are cardiovascular diseases.[1]

These adaptive strategies are relevant to our discussion. Vulnerability in the face of respiratory illness – pathologies common to the indigenous populations both before and after contact with the Europeans – suggests that "normal" levels of survivorship were low both before and after the Conquest, and that, while the arrival of new diseases may have altered overall mortality in the short run, it probably did not change it in the long run. Secondly, given that the delicate equilibrium of survivorship was maintained by means of a complex system of physiological and cultural adaptation, the disruption of that system had dramatic consequences. That sort of disruption attended the transplanting of native population from the mountains to the coast or vice versa, as attested by a multitude of contemporary accounts of the Conquest, accounts that praise the Inca for the care that was used to transfer groups to areas with similar ecological conditions. The greatest disruptions were caused instead by wars and other disasters that destroyed the delicate balance between the meager resources of the highlands and the careful use made of them by the inhabitants.

The Incan Empire included, in addition to present-day Peru (which from 1563 corresponded more or less with the Audiencia of Lima), also Ecuador (Audiencia of Quito) and Bolivia (Audiencia of Charcas); its population was less dense than that of Mexico and considerably more dispersed. The Incas, moreover, had developed registration procedures – until a few decades ago we would have called them statistical systems; today instead we prefer information systems. Their statistical instrument was the *quipu*, which Father José de Acosta describes as follows:

memorials or registers made of cords that with different sorts of knots and different colors mean different things . . . Official deputies kept these *quipu* or memorials . . . they were required to keep track of all things like our public record keepers, and one has to give them full credit for fulfilling their duties. Since there were separate *quipu* for different topics, such as war, government, tributes, ceremonies, land, and so on.[2]

Until Acosta's time – the last third of the sixteenth century – the Indios kept their accounts and employed them in case of need or disagreement.[3] In fact, "they were accustomed to keep great quantities of these accounts and knots in specific places, just like the royal record keepers keep theirs in the archives."[4] As we shall see, the survival of the *quipu* and its use during the period of Spanish rule will be useful for our analysis. Nor, however, was the accounting and planning ability of the Spaniards inferior to that of the Incas.[5] Once the tumultuous period of the Conquest and native rebellion was over, around the 1540s, the need to establish a government with a solid base forced the administrators to undertake intensive efforts to know the colony better; among other things, it was important to establish the criteria for the assignment of the Indios to the *encomenderos* and evaluate the tribute-paying capacity of the population. Already under Pizarro there had been several inquiries aimed at understanding the geographic, economic, and demographic characteristics of the various *encomiendas*. Little has survived in the way of documentation, however, and the methodologies employed are unclear. The first systematic effort took place around 1550, when the civil wars were over, at the initiative of President La Gasca and under the direction of Archbishop Loaysa.[6] The *visitas*, or inspections, with their economic and demographic documentation, continued through the 1550s; few have been located and studied, but a summary was compiled in 1561 and has survived. Subsequently, Viceroy Francisco de Toledo carried out a general *visita* (we might say census) for the vast territory, primarily in the period 1572–5. Sixty-three ecclesiastical and lay officials were employed to oversee the delicate operation which sought to identify the *encomenderos*; the amount and composition of the tributes; the number of tribute-payers (able-bodied men aged between eighteen and fifty); and the size of the population subject to tribute, making distinctions for married, unmarried, children, and the elderly. Since the population was declining and there were constant requests to review the imposed tributes, the districts were subject to new censuses (*revisitas*) in the decades that followed. Much of this documentation has survived and constitutes a rich source of information that, albeit with a series of defects, continues up to the first years of the seventeenth century. A summary by district of two counts (dated 1561 and 1591, but lacking precise chronological references) is included in table 13. The first, that of 1561, was compiled by the secretary of the Audiencia and presumably relates to inspections made at the end of the 1550s (the document refers to Marqués de Cañete, viceroy from 1556 to 1561). It counted 397,000 tribute payers, corresponding to 1,785,000 inhabitants. We have to keep in mind that a number of categories were exempt (ethnic Incans, the Cañari tribe) and that many Indios had fled or were in hiding, or in any case were not counted (especially the *yanaconas* or servants to the Spanish families), an unknown but surely significant number.

In 1567, Juan de Matienzo, a high official who knew the country well, estimated the (potential) tribute payers at 535,000, starting with the figures for 1561 (which he reprinted) and presumably adding the Indios from the non-taxed provinces and those who had re-emerged, given that at the time of the previous count "more than 200,000 were in hiding."[7] We can imagine, then, that the population of greater Perú between the end of the 1550s and the middle of the following decade stood at 2 to 2.5 million, with a number of tribute payers between 430,000 and 530,000. More than half of the population (55 percent) was concentrated in the five center-south provinces of Cuzco, La Plata (or Charcas, today Sucre), La Paz, Arequipa, and Guamanca. Elaborating on the more secure figures of Toledo from 1572–5, Cook attributes a population of 261,000 tributaries and 1,291,000 inhabitants to the area of present-day Peru (without Ecuador and Bolivia). For greater Perú, these figures can be expanded (and rounded) to 400,000 tributaries and 1.95 million inhabitants; yet Matienzo's observations regarding the incompleteness of the counts of 1561 apply to these figures as well. The second summary is dated 1591, but this document also refers to *revisitas* made in previous years and in some cases probably to Toledo's original *visita* in the early 1570s. Assuming that thirty years passed between the two counts and that each suffered from similar underestimations, the number of tributaries would have declined by 22 percent, or at an average annual rate of −0.81 percent. It is possible, though, that the interval between the counts was shorter and so the decline more rapid.

So between 1560 and 1570, with the civil wars over and the country stabilized save for a last outpost of Incan independence (swept away in 1572 with the execution of Tupac Amaru), the indigenous population must have been between 2 and 2.5 million. But before that? Is it possible to make demographic estimates for the moment of contact, or even before? All the chronicles and testimonies speak of a demographic disaster (in chapter 2 we reported the observations of Cieza de León, made during his long travels from the Caribbean to Bolivia). But what was its scale and what were the causes and mechanisms at work? As we shall see, half a dozen authors have attempted in recent decades to give reasonable numeric estimates of the unknowable. But before reviewing those efforts, it will be useful to look at a few cases for which we have quantitative information from the "time of the Inca," and so from which we can estimate the degree of depopulation.

A well-documented example of the depopulation of a region is that of the Huanca tribe, strategically situated in the Mantaro river valley on the Lima–Cuzco axis. The breakup of the empire exposed tribal and territorial contrasts that were exploited both by Spaniards during the Conquest and by various factions during the civil wars. The Huanca tribe was traditionally loyal to the Spaniards from 1533, and allied themselves with the faction loyal to the Crown during the civil wars. This alliance translated into a continual supply of men, animals, rations, and goods of all sorts between 1533 and the defeat of Hernández Girón's rebels in 1554.[8] When Viceroy Toledo made his *visita* in 1572, the tribute-paying Indios of the region were counted. Since the scope of the *visita* was also to ascertain the change in the tribute-paying capacity of the population, the communities noted the number of tributaries at the time of Huayna Capac, presumably at the beginning of the 1520s and so half a century before. This number had been meticulously recorded by the record keepers in the knots of their *quipu*. The number of tribute payers in the three districts was as follows:[9]

	Jatunsausa	Lurinhuanca	Ananhuanca	TOTAL
Time of Huayna Capac	6,000	12,000	9,000	27,000
Visita of La Gasca (1548)	800	2,500	1,700	5,000
Visita of Toledo (1572)	1,200	3,500	2,500	7,200
% var. (Huayna C./Toledo)	−80.0	−71.8	−72.2	−73.3

The decline between 1520 and 1548 was drastic, followed by a gradual recovery afterward. Certainly these figures can give only a general indication, though one that is in keeping with opinions expressed at the time. Here is Cieza de León: "This valley is 14 leagues long and about 4 or 5 leagues wide. It was very populous, and they say with great assurance that when the Spaniards arrived there were more than 30,000 Indios here; today I doubt there are 10,000."[10]

Further to the north, in the Huánuco region inhabited by the Chupachos, a *visita* made in 1562 can also be compared with earlier *visitas* and with the time of the Inca. Those documents report that the population of tribute-payers dropped from 4,000 in 1530, to 1,200 in 1549, to 800 in 1562, a decline to one-fifth of its original size in the span of little more than thirty years.[11] We encounter a similar story in the Yucay valley, midway along the Urubamba river and about 20 kilometers northwest of Cuzco, also known as the "Valle Sacra," where there were lands belonging to the Incas and to other important lords. The surviving documents refer to about 3,000 tributaries around 1530, who then decline to 800 in 1552 and 780 in 1558. In this case the tributaries declined to about one-quarter of their original number, a disaster comparable to that of the Huanca.[12]

The disaster of the Huanca and other communities cited above was not repeated everywhere. On the western shore of the *laguna de Chucuito* (Lake Titicaca), at an elevation of over 3,800 meters, the entire region was subjected in 1567 to an accurate inspection by the royal envoy Garci Diez de San Miguel.[13] During this long inspection – it lasted several months – an important local personage appeared before Garci Diez and his scribe Francisco López:

don Martin Cari, principal *cacique* of the *parcialidad* of Anansaya, and he carried with him several knotted strands of wool that he said were the *quipu* with the count of the tribute-paying Indios in the province of Chucuito, and said moreover that this *quipu* was the last that was done in the time of the Inca, and then reading the aforementioned *quipu* and the count and swearing in the required way that these were reliable and true, he made the following declaration.[14]

The number of ethnic Aymará and Uru tributaries (the latter were fishermen considered of low social standing) from the seven villages of the district were transcribed on two sheets; those numbers can be compared with the figures from the 1567 *visita*:[15]

	Aymará	Uru	TOTAL
At the time of the Inca	16,156	4,119	20,275
1567	11,622	3,782	15,404
% var. (1567/Inca)	−28.1	−8.2	−24.0

A reduction of less than one-quarter in forty years or so is not a collapse. In the case of Chucuito, as elsewhere, a number of problems arise relative to this comparison: what exactly constituted a tributary (the definition from the Spanish period – an able-bodied adult male between eighteen and fifty – cannot be automatically applied to the time of the Inca).[16] Who was exempt? What was the level of evasion? What was the size of the tribute payer's family (from which figure the eventual population totals are calculated)? These are indispensable philological issues, but not always essential for answering the question: After the Conquest, was there catastrophe, more or less drastic decline, or stability? These distinctions do not require precise figures, provided that the sources on which we make the distinction are not themselves the product of pure fantasy or speculation. In the province of Cajamarca (in the ancient "Reino de Guzmango"), a dispute between two *encomenderos* led to an accurate *visita* of forty-three villages in the area for 1571–2 (though four of these were completed only in 1578), giving a total of 5,008 tributaries. That number can be compared with the 3,493 tributaries counted in a first *visita* of 1540 ordered by Pizarro (and the one that resulted in creation of the *encomienda* at the heart of the dispute). In this case we find a notable and surprising increase over time; that increase would have to raise considerable suspicion were it not possible to ascribe it to different levels of evasion generated by the inspection methods used (in 1540 the information was gathered from the *caciques*, in 1571–8 by means of house-to-house visits).[17] We take note of this case not so much to suggest a counter-tendency, but rather to highlight the delicate nature of these comparisons. Finally, for the province of the Yauyos, in the central part of the country, the geographic report of 1586 estimated that there were 10,000 tributaries at the time of the Conquest; that number had declined to 7,000 according to the *visita* of Toledo.[18]

Starting with the accepted 1560–70 estimates, a number of authors have sought to apply these few examples of depopulation to the whole of Perú, in order to work backward and derive the size of the pre-European population. This is indeed an arduous enterprise, as the cases are few and refer to only a few thousand tribute payers, and the figures for the time of the Inca are shrouded in mystery; these are necessarily estimates with an exceedingly fragile basis. For Rowe there were 6 million; for C. T. Smith, 12.1 million; and for Nathan Wachtel, about 10 million. Cook, working with great care and accuracy, and also with a large number of hypotheses, comes up with values between 4 and 10 million for present-day Peru; he concludes offering 9 million as the most plausible figure, which corresponds to 13 or 14 million for greater

Perú. Daniel Shea offers the lowest estimates (2 to 2.9 million) by working backward to the pre-contact period with depopulation rates observed at the end of the century. Finally, Henry Dobyns, on the basis of a wholly arbitrary rate of depopulation (linked to epidemiological collapse) of between one-twentieth and one-twenty-fifth, comes up with a range of 30 to 37.5 million.[19] Rather than choosing one estimate over another (those listed above span a ratio of 19 : 1), it may be more productive to analyze some concrete data that will help us to understand better the possible trends in the thirty or forty years before 1560.

The population of Chucuito in 1567 was counted and categorized according to gender, marital status, and several age groups; a summary of the data (Aymará and Uru combined) is listed in table 14, along with a number of relationships derived from that data. These relationships should be interpreted with great caution: age was certainly judged from appearances; the categories of married, widowed, and single imposed definitions taken from Christian Spain onto a reality that was different and more fluid in the native community; omissions were certainly frequent. Still, a number of elements stand out and are consistent with a decreasing population, if not one in headlong decline. The first is the low ratio of males to females; while a value below eighty males for every hundred females is consistent with the higher mortality of males resulting from the quarter-century of wars, it can also be a sign of male migration to the Spanish cities and elsewhere in order to avoid paying the tribute. Another significant element is the low reproductive capacity of the population, as indicated by the low percentage in the population of married individuals of reproductive age (44 percent of men and 33 percent of women) and the high percentage of unmarried men (one for every five married; the figure for women cannot be calculated, but it was surely higher given the scarcity of men). Nonetheless, families seem to have had a number of surviving offspring compatible with high mortality and a normal level of fertility within marriage (on average there are two children between zero and sixteen for every married man of reproductive age, and about 1.5 for every tribute payer). But given the relative scarcity of married individuals of reproductive age, overall fertility had to have been modest, as attested by the small percentage of young people in the total population (37 percent).

The reasons for this, based on an elementary demographic analysis, can be found in the notes.[20] Similar observations apply to the Chupachos (Huánuco) in 1562 (a low ratio between the sexes, a low proportion of married women, high levels of non-marriage), even though the proportion of young people was relatively high and so not really compatible with a population in rapid decline.

By about 1570 the Spanish had consolidated their hold on Perú: administrative and economic institutions were in place, the last Incan resistance had been definitively defeated, the children of the first conquistadors had entered into the social life of the colony, and the native population included an entire generation that had been born and grown up under Spanish rule. Greater Perú at that date numbered about 400,000 tributaries and 2 million inhabitants. David Cook has estimated the population within the borders of present-day Peru through to 1630; the values for 1570 and 1600 can be found in table 15. I have chosen the first date because it is close to the time of Toledo's *visitas* in the early 1570s, which covered almost the whole of the territory, and the second because *visitas* and *revisitas* were frequent and widespread in the late sixteenth and early seventeenth centuries. These estimates, then, are based on solid evidence. After 1600 they become shakier: the growing number of *forasteros* (Indios who avoided the tribute by emigrating from their place of origin) makes the estimates less reliable. In the country as a whole, there is a population decline between the two dates of about a third, but the coastal area (which in 1570 accounted for only 15 percent of the Peruvian population) suffered a much more rapid decline: 50 percent as compared to 30 percent for the mountains. That translates into an annual rate of decline of about 1.4 percent. This rate may be too high, given the increase in *forasteros* who were not counted (in addition to those who systematically avoided being counted, as attested by many), and so should be adjusted, as we argue below. So after a quarter century of catastrophe due to war and uprisings, followed by a decade or two of relative calm, the final third of the sixteenth century was marked by sustained decline, but not collapse.

Keeping in mind the necessary criteria of comparability and analyzing the data from Toledo's *visita* of 1572–5, gathered by Cook, and that from the *revisitas*, gathered by Vázquez de Espinosa and referring to various dates (but concentrated around 1602 according to the careful reconstruction of Cook), we can put

numero delos pueblos de tierras calidas y templadas
figurados e intitulados enla plana siguiente.
que son veinte y dos pueblos § § . las cosas
que tributavan alos §§. de mexico y son las que
se siguen

tributaron mill y seyscientas cargas de
mantas ficas y toça y bestian los §§. caçiques

mas seyscientas cargas de mantas listadas
de colorado y blanco xxx de

mas quatro cientas cargas de naguas y guypiles
todo lo qual tributavan de seys en seys meses.

y en mas tributaron una pieça de armas con un
ysodela geranesa ras con plumas ficas con un demsa
de pajaros y colores segun § estan figuradas.

mas una ysodela de ceso

mas una demsa zpa armas o manera de ala y deplu
mas omarillas ficas

mas una diadema de ceso dela hechura § esta figu
rado.

mas un apretador de ceso zpala cabeça de anchp
una mano y de grosor como deupergamino.

mas dos sortas de cuentas y collor de ceso.

mas tres pieças grandes de chalchihuitl zpiedras ficas

mas tres sortas de cuentas todas fedonditas de chal
chihuitl zpiedras ficas

mas quatro sortas de cuentas de chalchihuitl zpiedras
ficas.

mas veynte becotes de ambar claro guarnecidos con oro.

mas otros veynte becotes de cristales conun esmalte de
azul y guarnecidos con oro.

mas ochenta manojos de plumas ficas verdes §
llaman quecali.

mas quatro pieças de plumas ficas ydes como manos
dos guarnecidas con plumas omarillas ficas

mas ocho mill manojuelos de plumas tar gruesas ficas.

mas ocho mill manojuelos de plumas coloradas ficas.

mas ocho mill manojuelos de plumas ydes ficas.

mas çien ollas o cantaros deliqui sombar o ino.

mas dozientas cargas de cacao.

mas diez y seys mill pellas fedondas como pelotas de
oli ques goma de arboles y dando conlas pelotas en
el suelo saltan mucho en alto. todo lo qual
tributaron una vez enel ano.

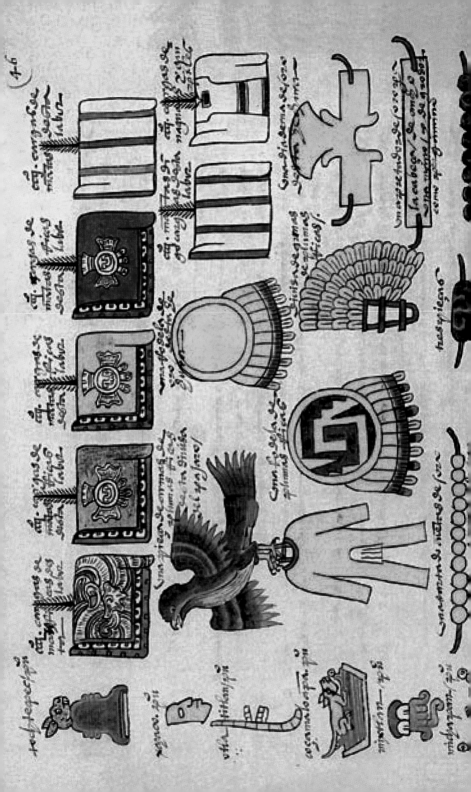

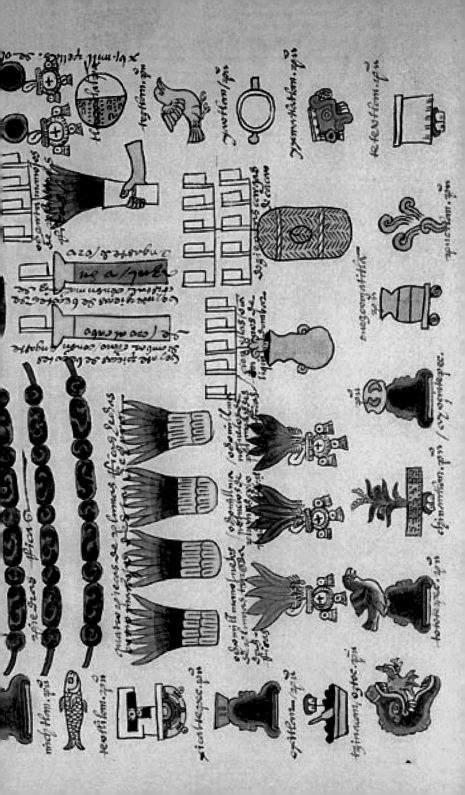

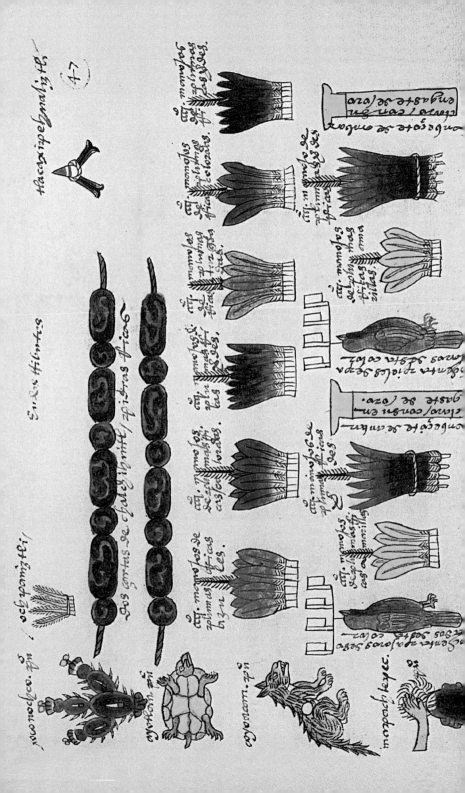

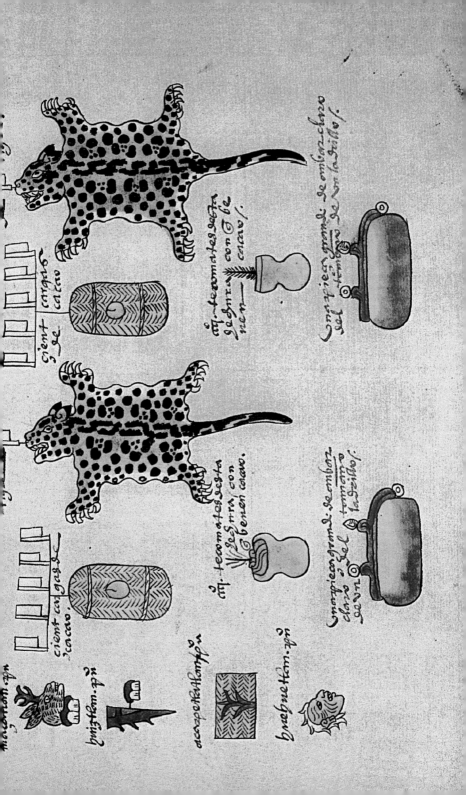

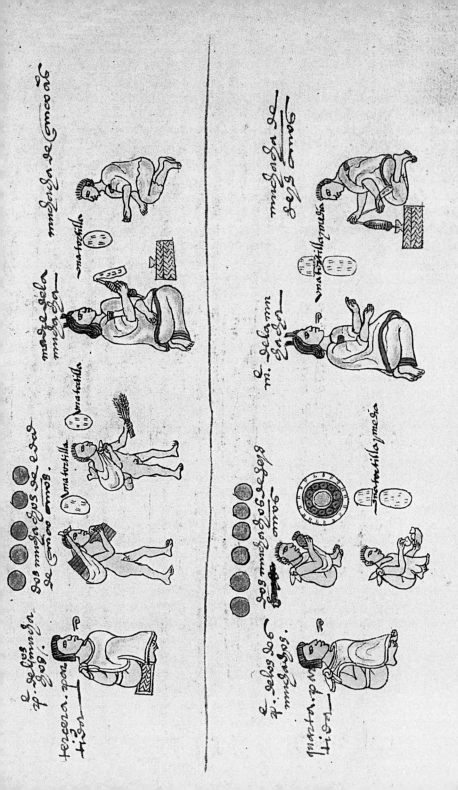

estas siete açotes pintas de azul
signi fin siete años el

madre de los muchachos
y maestro seguros contemplos

muchacho de. vij. años.
en madre le enseñava
a hilar

matluztilli 2
ración

muchacho de. vij. años
en esto engeñava
a conocer de
pescozudilla
los a tierra
en su mano

1. de los muchachos
p... maestra seguros contemplos

matluztilli
y ración

1. partida

estos dos pintas signifi
con dos años

muchacho de. viij. años
padre le enseñava
a coser menos
le castigava
en desnudo
que el acto
en la tierra

muchacho de. viij.
años la madre le
amenaza
con penas a maña
y enseñavale a hilar

2. de los muchachos
en esta seguros contemplos

matluztilli
2 ración

puas de maguey

4. partida

matluztilli
y ración

puas de maguez

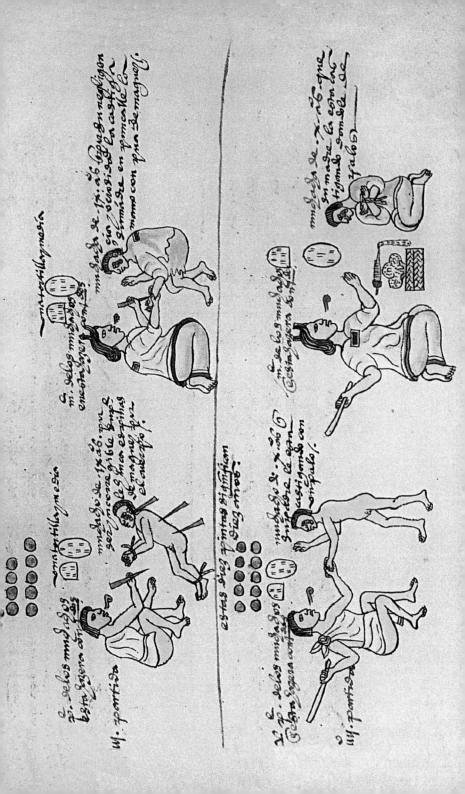

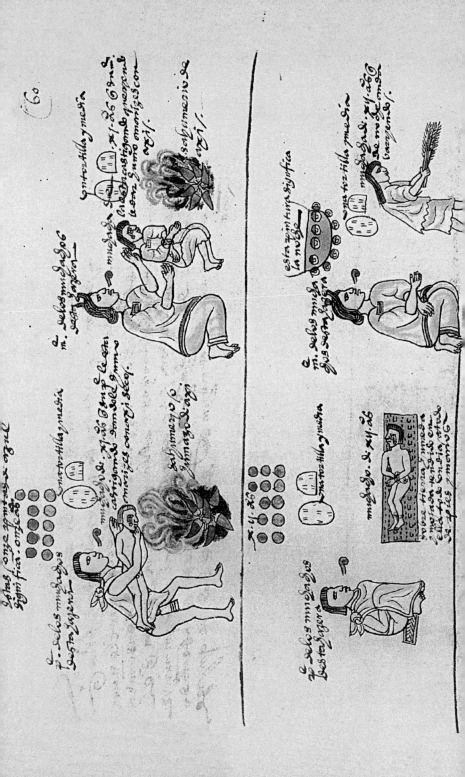

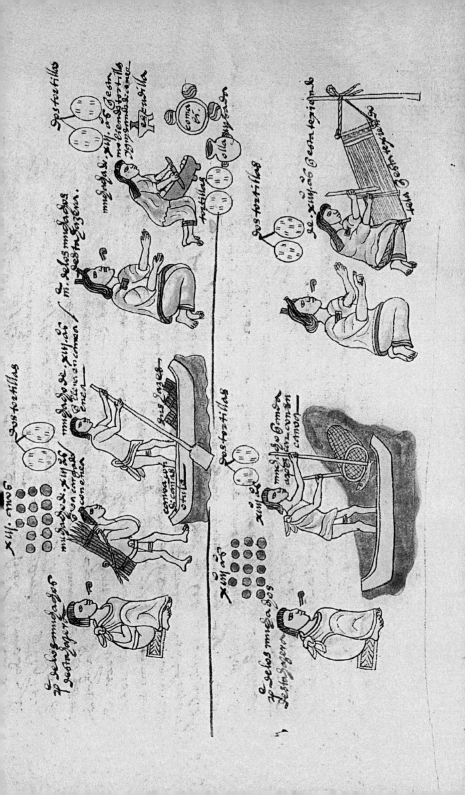

60

52

1

Homaracgr. alfaquino vico. l. Azanacaçose bazzez

alfaqui/notico Tiene selmote gado se llamasen enferma en la mesyter

alfaqui. nobico ba cargado con zanas se maguez por en mesquita pori conello Tfulazsaca Tha se señora Somoz el semana

alfaqui. promisso que no calgado se contad Des gota mezquita secozoz el Tos enformach/.

2

momcabo Ta cargado con tres granos con la Tener Los se encari enla mes qmitr

macns Tbamcaga6 con todos se lema zpo tencaz min da Embze/ Enla mezqmitr.

macnbo Tbamcagas con Tfumas Zpa enfermoe la mezqmitr

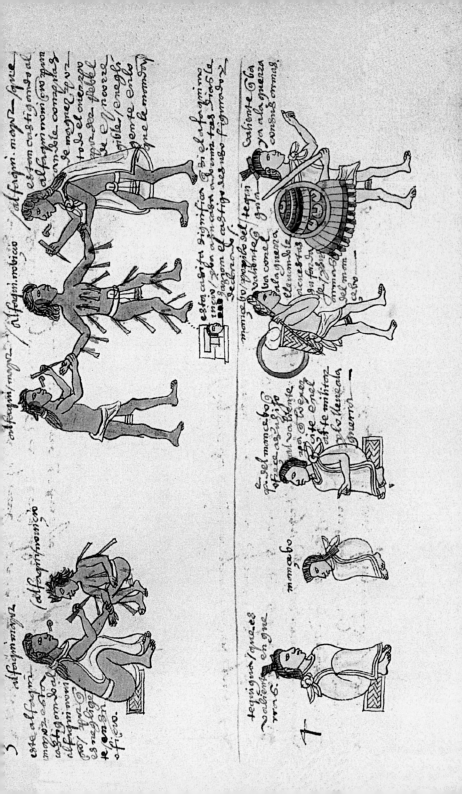

alfaquinmoyaque ‧ alfaquinmoyaque ‧ alfaquinnobico ‧ alfaquinmoyaque

alfaquinmoyaque
(alfaquinnomico)

este alfaqui
mayoz esto
castigam dos
alfaquinovic
ios hazien
do lo mesmo
es neçessa
rio en ma
teria ofi
cio.

estom castigam al
alfaquinom ço
alfaquinovicios
se mazen. por
volo el cuerpo
todo cudelas
espinas de mag
el. enovaze
fible / enel qu
gente enlo
que le mesm

esta castigo significa
que el alfaquino
enlo qual ba asicon
nuestras tres figuras
bajom el castigo es uso figurado
se denota.

mancebo pzopio del tegun
valiente gun
a la guerra
un come
ala guera
nuestras
gar fon an
ja. este
mancebo
del mom
caso

mancebo pzopio
valiente
que tra asucho
se entra enel
este mihioz
calo llaneala
guerra

mancebo
es
que ealuatente
con xeyey

teviguno / que es
valiente en que
rra 6.

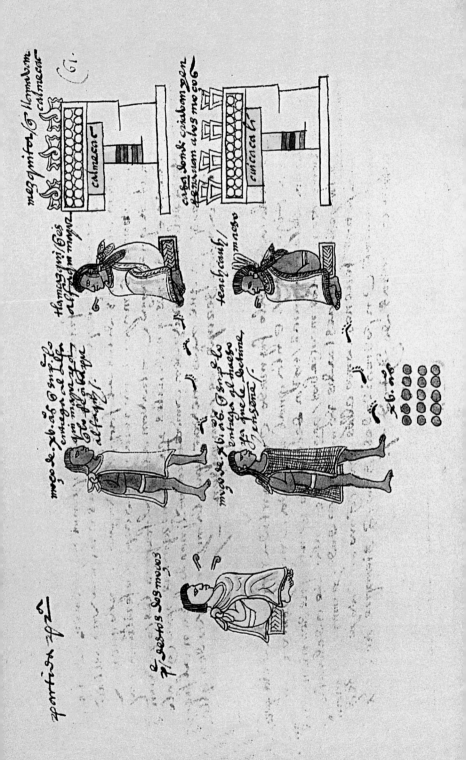

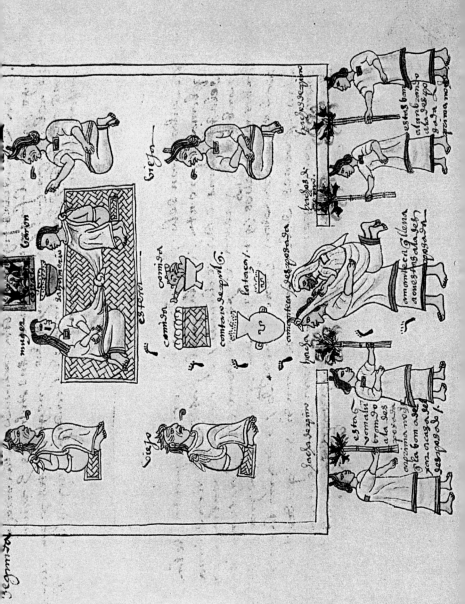

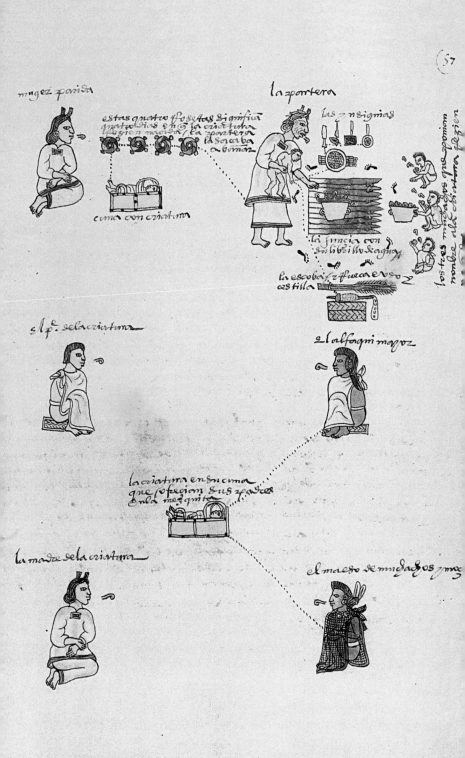

muger parida

estas quatro rrosetas significā
quatro dias en que la criatura
nasçio morda, la parterra
la sacaba
a bañar

las insignias

cama con criatura

la portera

los tres muchachos que ponen
nombre ala criatura platican

la sunçia con
su librillo dagua

la escoba y fuñea en
castilla

el p.e de la criatura

el alfaqui mayor

la criatura en encima
que profeçion sus padres
en la mesquita

la madre de la criatura

el maestro de muchachos y mas

EL DOZENO LIBRO

Tracta de como los es
pañoles conquis
taron ala ciu
dad deMe
xico.

406

pacoa, nexuchitlamachtilo: vncā
tlatlātlanj, tlaneneguj, in tlato
anj, in catle cujcatl coneoaz, in
anoço auextecaiotl, tlaoanca cuex
tecaiotl, vexotzincaiotl, anaoca
iotl, oztome caiotl, nonooalcaiotl,
coztatecaiotl, tenjcaiotl, tepetla
caiotl, chichimecaiotl, metztlan
calcaiotl, oton cujcatl, quatacuj
catl, tochcujcatl, teponazcujcatl.
Et si. eoacujcatl, atzotzocol cujcatl,
auh in anoço çanauj l cujcatl, ix
cueculechcujcatl, coco cujcatl, quap
pitzcujcatl, quatecocuj cujcatl,
auj l cujcatl. Et si. yc mjtoaia ca
nel onjcac in suchitl. Ioan vncā
qujcenqujxtiaia, in ccalpixque
mjxquj ch imācccallatquj tlatoanj
qujtlanencctia, qujtlātlattilia, in
catle conelcujs, ipan onmjtotiz,
ipan ontetlattitiz: ioan vncan qujn
tlaujzmacaia, in tlacaoan, inte
tlaujceaoa, in otomj, in quaqua
chichi, in tlatlacatecca, intlatla
cochcalca, in tevitequjnj, in tema
lacachoanj, in teviltequjnj, inte
tzacujianj, intetlallanvianj: yoan
vel oncan mocnaviaia, mopixquj
aia, tlatemachiaia, netlauhtiltica,

mochi tlaçoihuitl vel ipan tlapiuia:
ic nonqua quintecac, quincaltin cen
tetl calli quinmacac iniscoian iiama
tecahoan catca imtech pouia: nepam
toca in tenochtitlan amanteca ioan
in tlatilulco amanteca. Auh miehoan
tinjy, canquiscahuiaia mquichioaia
tlatqui vitzilobuchtli inquitoca
iotiaia teuquemitl, quetzalquemitl
quitzitzilquemitl, xiuhtotoquemitl,
ie tlatlaçicuilolli, ic tlatlatlamachilli
injemochi iniz quican icac tlaçoihuitl. yoan quichioaia miscoian
tlatqui motecuçoma: mquin maca
ia, inquintlauhtiaia icoahoan in
altepetl ipan tlatoque, ic monotzaia
moten ehoaia tecpan amanteca
itultecahoan in tlacatl. Auh mce
quintin, motenehoaia calpiscan
amanteca, itechpouia iniz quitetl
icaca icalpiscacal motecuçoma:
iehoatl quichioaig, intlein imàceh
ça tlatqui motecuçoma inipan ma
cehoaia, mitotiaia: inicoac ilhuitl
quiçaia, quitlatlattitia, quitlane
nectiaia, mçaço catlehoatl quteuiz
inipan mitotiz: cacecentlamantli
iecauia, cecentlamantli quichioaia

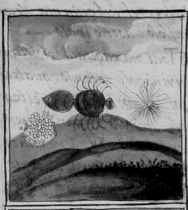

tute ceuinjqere: mochi que coa
mochi pan vetzi: velmotlatla
motla, momamaiavi intoca
qualo, vel mochi chiaoa inj
nacaio, injcpan vetzi intoca
tonqualachi: vel tlatla injiol
lo, velkneoa. Inic mopale
via: quipapachoa, ipan mo
tlatlalia: yoan iciuhca quj
chichinjtia, yoan qujtema.
yoan injec inquj octli: ince
caihiio eilhujtl, navilhujtl
jnqujcaoaz, mathicevi3. In
m tueatl: velteihiioti injto
qualac, iece innanaoati: ca
vncā contlatlalilia, incanjn
ca inanaoauh, icpati, ic
ce çanpanj: njman ieichoatl
mcooacivi3tli, axio, tlllo,
ic momatiloa: caqujcevia.
Inmtueatl: vmpā nemj in
tlatutonia, iuhqujn mjtua
tlalomjtl: in aqujn qujmj
naz, auh çan chiavaca tla
mj3, çan ixicatuz in vncā
qujmjna: auh cenca tlatla3
injiollo, injnacaio: vel tza

245

¶ Capitulo. 15. de los ata
uios, de las señoras.

Ysauan las señoras vestirse los vi
piles labrados, y texidos, de muy mu
chas maneras de labores, como va
aqui declarado, en la lengua.

Ni Motecuçoma se nos podra asconder
por mucho que haga, aunque sea ave
y aunque se meta debaxo de tierra
no se nos podra asconder de verle
avemos yde oyr avemos loque
nos dira. Yluego con aseñta em
biaron aquel principal yatodos

teca, cempoalteca, injcquimo
ichteca tlatlanjque: conjtvque
caamoie ichoatl tvtecujoane.
In injtzioac popocatzin, qujnj
xiptlatica in Motecuçomatzin:
qujshuijque. Cuix iete intiMo
tecuçoma: conjtv. Canehoatl
in namotechiuh cauh in npMo
tecuçoma. Aich njma qujlkeij
que. Nopa xiauh, tleica inti
techiztlacavia, atitechmati
amo veltitechiztlacaviz, amo
veltiea timocaiaoaz, amo vel
titech quamanaz, amo velti
techix mamatiloz, amo velti
techich chioaz, amo vel titechix
cuepaz, amo vel titechix pa
tiliz, amo vel titech tlacuepi
liz, amo vel tite chixpopoloz,
amo vel titechix mjmjctiz, a
mo vel titechix çoqujviz, amo
veltitechix çoqujmatiçaz, a
motehoatl caurca in Mote
cuçoma, amo vel technetla
tiliz, amo vel mjnaiaz, cam
paiaz, cuix totvtl, cuixpa
tlanjz, cujnoço tlallan quj
quezaz yiovi, cuix canaca
tepetl coronquj yitic calaquiz

425

Libro duodecimo

Vinjeron los Españoles que ya esta
uan en tetzcuco, y baxaron la laguna
y vinjeron por quauhtitlan hasta tla
cuba yalli se repartieron en capita
njas y se posieron en diuersas esta
cias A don Pedro de albarado le ca
po el camjno que va de tacuba de
recho al tlatilulco : el capitan do
hernando cortes se puso en coyoaca
y guardaua el camjno que va de
coyo vacan amexico. De hazia la
parte del tlatilulco se començo pri
mero la guerra en vn lugar que se
nextlatilco y llegaron peleando has
ta el lugar que se llama nonoalco
donde esta agora vna yglesia que
se llama Sanct Miguel; y los Es
pañoles se retruxeron no ganaro
nada en esta escaramuça: Tam
bien el capitan Don hernando cor
tes acometio por su parte alos me
xicanos, porel camjno que se lla
ma acachinanco: y los mexica
nos resistian los grandemente .

li, yoan mjequjntin can apiz
mjeque, apiz mjcoac, aocac
motequjtlaviaia, aocac teca
mochivaia. Auhincequjn
tin can vevexca in intechmo
tlali in cavatl, cinocenca
qujmjhioti, amononjequjn
tin icnjeque: yoan mjec tla
catl ic itlacauh injxaiac,
ichachaquachiuhque, iaca
chachaquach iuhque, cequj
tin yixcueponque, ixpopo
iotque; iquac in manca in
mtotomonjliztli, vel epoal
ilhujtl, epoal tonal inqujz
in euetlan, inneemachoc, in
iolioac; techalcopa vatzca
in totomonjliztli, yoan mjec
mjcocotutzauh: amo tal ic
cen cocotutzauh. In moma
naco Teutleco: auh in euetla
niti ipan in Panquetzalis
tli, yn can vel caxavaque
in Mexica, yntlacaoan. Auh
in ieiuhquj: njman ic vitze, va
lolinj in Españoles in vm
pa Tetzcoco: quauhtitlan

together table 16. In addition to a number of characteristic relationships, this table lists the total number of tribute payers, of children and adolescents under eighteen years of age (*muchachos*), of the elderly (*viejos*, presumably over fifty and including the infirm), and of females of all ages, for a sample of 146 out of 550 *repartimientos* located in twenty-four districts (the districts or *corregimientos* numbered fifty in all) and over half the population. The *visitas* of Toledo were made in 1571–3 (with only a few in the years that followed), while the *revisitas* in three cases out of four took place in 1602 (the others spread out over the decades on either side of that date). The average period between the two counts is twenty-nine years. During that time the population declined at an average rate of −1.25 percent per year; the number of tribute payers declined somewhat more slowly (−1.06 percent), and so the average number of persons per tribute payer declined by a fraction (from 5.16 to 4.88). The most important structural element is the relative lack of males, especially over the age of eighteen, barely seventy-six men for every hundred women in 1572 (a widespread deficit that applied to twenty-one of the twenty-four districts). This deficit is not easy to explain. It could derive from heavy losses in the many conflicts; from a higher level of evasion of men compared to women during the *visita*; or from a greater inclusion of men in Spanish households as *yanacona*.

The losses from war provide a potent reason, but perhaps not a sufficient one, as by 1573 it would have applied only to those above the age of forty-five or fifty, a segment of the population that accounted for not more than 20 percent of the total. Nonetheless, the significant increase in the percentage of the old (*viejos*) between 1573 and 1602, and the concurrent decline in the percentage of the *muchachos* (under eighteen), does suggest that the male deficit was linked to the traumatic events of the 1530s and 1540s. During the three decades in question – ones surely marked by numerous epidemics – an age structure more in keeping with the prevalent demographic regime re-established itself. Finally we should note that the ratio between the population under eighteen and women over eighteen, both in 1573 and in 1602, appears to be "normal" in a context of high mortality; this may be an indication of adequate fertility.

Assuming that the twenty-four districts are comparable for the two dates of 1573 and 1602, we can derive the interesting information described in figure 5. There exists, for example, a good correlation between the change in population size and the change in the number of tribute payers over these thirty years (figure 5a); that result is as expected, but is reassuring regarding the reliability of the counts. The simple correlation between total population and tributaries at the two dates is not as strong but still positive; on average that value ranges around the classic figure of 5 (figure 5b). There is meanwhile a strong negative correlation, both in 1573 and 1602, between the deficit of men compared to women and the relationship of population to tributaries (figures 5c and 5d). This relationship (the greater the male deficit, the larger the population in comparison to tributaries) finds at least a partial explanation in the nature of these measures. When for whatever reason (violence, flight) the able-bodied men (tributaries) are few while the other categories (young, old, women) have not suffered similar reductions, the ratio of population to tributaries is necessarily high.

Before the arrival of the Spaniards, the Peruvian populations were certainly highly mobile. Their imposing network of roads is an extraordinary testimony to their ability to move about. The Incas were in the habit of transplanting groups of colonists (*mitimaes*) into conquered areas in order to consolidate their hold on new territories. These more or less forced migrations were imposed by the Incas on top of an underlying and well-articulated system that has been described as "a system of vertical control that extended to a maximum number of ecological levels," on the part of the various ethnicities. Such was the case for example in the kingdom of the Lupaca, a group settled in the valley of Lake Titicaca (Chucuito district) that numbered about 100,000 inhabitants when the Spanish arrived. The economic and social organization of the Lupaca, at an elevation of almost 4,000 meters, depended on some basic crops (quinoa, potato) and entailed control over trade and the maintenance of reserves; groups of Lupaca, settled in the valleys sloping down toward the coast hundreds of kilometers away, grew maize and cotton, the production of which had to be integrated with that of the highlands. In other cases the original groups were much smaller and controlled small settlements stretching over the distance of a few days' walk, both at high elevations – for pasture – and at low ones for the growing of coca and cotton, the production of salt and other necessities. In either case, the particular geographic configuration of the country, inhabited from the coast up to an elevation of 4,000 meters, favored the ability to control resources not available in the single centers of settlement. The inhabitants of the secondary settlements managed to maintain their dwellings and property rights in the original central nuclei. An integrated system of this sort surely required a high level of mobility, especially "vertical" mobility between the low elevations and the mountains, between the coast and the highlands.

In the Spanish period these prerogatives were not eliminated, even if they were in part destroyed or limited by the reorganization imposed by Toledo, insofar as the "reductions" altered internal equilibria. Nonetheless, many factors contributed to maintain a high level of mobility: the foundation of Spanish cities (Lima above all) caused major movements of Indios for transportation and services; the *mita* requirements in important mining centers such as Potosí, Huancavelica, or Castrovirreina kept tens of thousands of workers in constant motion; the wars provoked continual transfers of masses of people either following the armies or fleeing their homes in order to escape violence and rapacity. At the end of the civil wars, Pedro de La Gasca could write to the Council of the Indies that the Indios "are leaving the mountains and their hideouts and returning to their villages . . . and are farming near to the roads, and they do not flee, as they used to, from Spaniards whom they see passing by, but have begun to approach them and offer to sell what they have."[21] Mobility, however, is an obstacle to every effort to count population, and, in our specific case, to the enumerations made in the course of the *visitas*.

However accurate the instructions and however conscientious the inspectors, the *visitas* nonetheless suffer from an unknown margin of approximation. Given that the enumeration of the tributaries was carried out for fiscal purposes, there was an inherent interest in avoiding being counted. Many tribute-paying Indios fled their home communities and settled in other provinces; they lost their right to land this way, but at the same time, as *forasteros*, were not subject to taxes and the *mita*. In the areas subject to the *mita* for mining work, flight was a constant problem. Moreover, from the moment the Spaniards arrived, many Indios were taken on as *yanaconas* in the colonists' homes and farms; and, while according to Toledo's instructions this group was subject to tribute, in practice they almost always avoided it. Finally, evasion, migration, and transition to domestic service must all have increased during the last decades of the sixteenth century; in part this was owing to the fact that the required tribute, established by the *visitas* of Toledo in the early 1570s, was shared by an ever smaller number of tribute payers because of population decline, and so became gradually more onerous. We can assume then that the counts made at the end of the sixteenth century and the beginning of the seventeenth make the decline appear more drastic than it really was as compared to Toledo's counts from the 1570s.

Evasion by Indios and their families subject to tribute must have been fairly common, and there is ample testimony to suggest that it was. In the by now much-cited *visita* to Chucuito, the two main *caciques*, don Martin Cari and don Martin Cusi, offered similar versions, though for different reasons. Evasion existed also at the time of the Inca, even though the Incas "tormented" evaders (Martin Cari) and made their inspections "with great rigor, killing and tormenting the Indios" (Martin Cusi); evasions certainly occurred during the Spanish *visitas*, and many Indios were hidden while the inspectors were in the villages.[22] Toledo's regulations for the province of Charcas specified: "It may occur that the principal *caciques* of the departments fail to report certain Indios and Indias of the subject *ayllu.*" Whoever discovered and denounced them would be rewarded.[23]

Migration out of the home community, however, was more significant than evasion. Sánchez-Albornoz has demonstrated the growing importance of the phenomenon for ten *repartimientos* of Upper Perú (Bolivia) between 1573 and 1683 (the enumeration of Viceroy de la Palata). In Toledo's *visita* the category of foreigner is not mentioned, as everyone had to be assigned to a community. A century later 12,138 (45 percent) of 26,696 adults were not originally from their communities of residence; and so they were *forasteros* and not subject to tribute. According to this same author, at that same date *forasteros* constituted half the population of the sixteen provinces subject to the Potosí *mita* (see map 8) plus Arequipa and Cuzco, which is to say half the country.[24] It is doubtful that this category was counted in the *visitas* following the general one carried out by Toledo. The concern of governors regarding the reduction of the number of tributaries because of migration was constant and great, and the remedies proposed were

Map 8 *Origins of* mitayos *for Potosí*

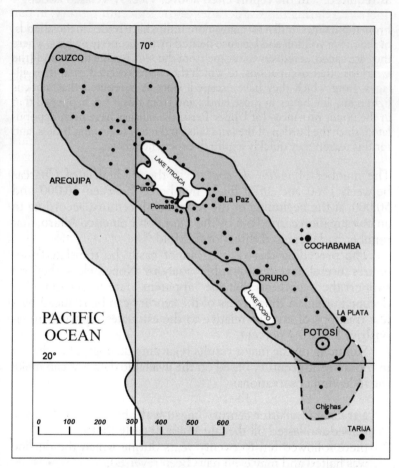

as numerous as they were inefficient.[25] In the report to his successor, the conde de Monterrey, Viceroy Luis de Velasco noted that, in the province of Chucuito, 5,000 fewer tributaries had been counted than in the previous *visita* and that a high level of flight was the main cause of the difference.[26] Many Indios left their original communities and ended up in the lands of the *encomenderos* as servants (*yanaconas de chacara*), working at farming or raising livestock, especially in the Audiencia of Charcas. Since their work was essential for supplying food to the populous city of Potosí,

Toledo himself allowed that they not be sent back to their homes as required.[27] In the report cited above, Viceroy Velasco added:

From those times until now many more Indios have settled in those lands, of their own volition and because desired by the property owners, where they are called *yanaconas* to escape from the *mita* for the mines and [the *mita*] for other occupations, to which they were assigned from their villages, from which they have escaped, since it is reputed that work is lighter and life better in those lands; and from this it has happened that in the upper provinces [of Upper Perú] the villages have been depopulated, since the burden of the *mita* falls on the few remaining Indios, and for this reason they quickly expire as experience shows.

The number of *indios de chacara* in the Audiencia of Charcas between 1560 and 1570 likely numbered between 30,000 and 50,000; at the beginning of the seventeenth century, according to an investigation carried out by the *oidor* don Francisco Alfaro, that number had increased three- or fourfold.[28]

The preceding discussions cannot easily be translated into figures useful for demographic analysis. Nonetheless they do support the hypothesis that the "apparent" rate of demographic decline in the last thirty years of the century can be reduced by a few fractions of a point relative to the estimates reported previously of 1.2 to 1.4 percent.

Summing up the major results regarding demographic change in the sixteenth century based on the available data, we can make the following observations:

1 a traumatic quarter century began with the death of Huayna Capac and lasted till the late 1540s or early 1550s;
2 there followed ten to twenty years during which the decline was halted and may even have been reversed;
3 the last third of the century saw another period of rapid decline, but not collapse;
4 the coastal areas were more vulnerable than the mountains;
5 there was a serious deficit of males, for reasons of both violence and social disruption;
6 the overall demographic vulnerability owed more to structural factors (male deficit) and high mortality than to fertility patterns;
7 levels of migration were high.

Compiled for many districts of Perú in the 1580s, the *Relaciones Geográficas* reveal to us the opinions of the second and third generations of Spaniards – and indirectly of the second and third generations of Indios after contact – about the demographic changes that had taken place. Those opinions emerge in particular from the replies to questions number 5 (number of Indios, whether increasing or decreasing compared to the past, ways of life, and languages spoken), 16 (types of settlement), and 17 (healthy versus unhealthy regions and diseases).[29] From an anthropological and sociological point of view, the descriptive value of the *Relaciones Geográficas* is considerable, though the information given relative to the past needs to be treated with great caution: the Conquest by then was a distant memory and only a few surviving Indios and Spaniards could offer direct testimony. Although in most districts opinion held that population had declined dramatically since the time of the Inca, there were atypical situations. For the province of Yauyos, Diego Brizeño, who had been *corregidor* for thirteen years, states that "it is generally believed that the decline in the number of people is not as great as is widely claimed" compared to past times; and Juan de Ulloa, *corregidor* in the province of Collaguas, affirms: "There were many fewer in the past and they continue to multiply." Just the same, most of the *Relaciones* reported a strong decline: in the province of Soras it was said that in the time of Tupac Inca Yupanqui, the Indios were "two-thirds more" than at present; while in La Paz it was "widely held that in ancient times there were more Indios"; and in Vilcas Guaman "there were many more Indios than there are today."[30]

Out of twenty-one *Relaciones*, sixteen report the number of Indios in decline, three that they are increasing, and two say nothing. The causes given for demographic change in the *Relaciones* are also interesting. "Infirmity," smallpox and other illnesses are blamed for the decline in many cases; memory of the epidemics that had stricken the country in the preceding twenty years was still fresh. Just as often, however, either together with or independently of disease, the long-prevailing state of war is cited. It is again Diego Brizeño who affirms, relative to the province of the Yauyos, that it was "over-run and disrupted and many people were taken from here at the time of the civil wars between the Spaniards, because the armies that crossed the land recruited people for service in the camps, and since these were a war-like people they willingly joined these armies and camps"; or, in the province of Guamanca (Ayacucho), the Indios "died in large numbers from the wars and have always been in decline."[31] We shall return to this argument below.

Nathan Wachtel has cataloged and summarized the responses to the twenty-one *Relaciones* relative to the numbers of Indios, their state of health, and their longevity between the time of the Inca and the period of the *Relaciones*:[32]

	Increase or improvement	Decrease or deterioration	No change	No indications	TOTAL
Number of Indios	3	16	0	2	21
State of health	2	6	1	12	21
Length of life	0	6	0	15	21

We also derive interesting information from the *Relaciones Geográficas* regarding the "reductions" of the population; originally dispersed or living in small settlements, these populations were combined into larger groups in planned organized villages, with streets laid out in orthogonal grids, a central plaza, a church, and public buildings. It was a process that impacted all of Spanish America in the course of the sixteenth century and was a constant concern of the Crown, the Council of the Indies, the viceroys, and Church, and administrative authorities.[33] That concern had at least three components: a political one – better control of a population that traditionally lived spread out over a vast and often unreachable expanse; a religious one, to insure conversions and indoctrination; and an economic one – identification of the tributaries and collection of the tribute. In Perú, Toledo sped up this process with the *visitas* of 1572–3, in relation to which he gave the inspectors specific instructions regarding the reductions of the Indios. Those instructions included the general principles that would underlie that gigantic operation. The inspectors were to identify appropriate places to concentrate the population in the minimum number of villages and trace out village plans with a gridwork of streets and blocks; these plans were to specify rules for the construction of houses, among them that of the main *cacique*, which had to include some sort of bed so that the Indios did not sleep on the ground. The Indios were not to be deprived of the fields around these villages. The villages were to be built far from the traditional temples and places of worship. Indios would be transferred to these villages and their original homes would be razed.[34] At the end of his mandate in 1581, Toledo expanded on the argument in his *Memoria* to Philip II; he complained that it was impossible to impose a Christian and "political" life on the Indios "so long as they remain settled in the steppes, in the steep valleys, and on the hills and mountains where they are spread out and hidden and able to avoid contact with the Spaniards, whom they detest." For Toledo, the *visitas* into every corner of the kingdom had "as their principal aim that of reducing and aggregating the Indios in villages located in places the inspectors, based on their direct experience, thought most advantageous relative to the climate to which the Indios were accustomed." He himself traversed much of the country during his years there: "I devoted nearly five years to the general *visita* and to the special one." Or again:

It was not possible to indoctrinate these Indios or to make them live in an orderly political way without dragging them out of their hiding places. In order to do this, we had to move them to villages and public places and lay out a gridwork of streets as in the Spanish towns, making sure that the doors [of the houses] opened on to the streets so that they could be seen and visited by the authorities and the priests. In carrying out these reductions, we always had as our objective to locate the villages in the best places of the districts and ones that had a climate similar to that from which the Indios came. Moreover, the new villages should have a sufficient number of tributaries to support one or two priests for the work of indoctrination.[35]

The transfer of population "was a colossal undertaking, involving a million and a half people. It has never been thoroughly studied, but it evidently took place, at any rate in southern Peru where the Viceroy himself was nearby to inspire action."[36] This is Hemming's conclusion, with which we can agree, though it is impossible to know with any precision how many people were involved. The *Relaciones* give various hints: Brizeño speaks of 200 villages reduced to thirty-nine; the average population then would have grown from 150 to 200 people per village before the operation to 900 to 1,000 afterward. According to an earlier source (1557), a first reduction in the province of Guamanca in the late 1540s concentrated 22,000 tributaries into 252 villages from the original 676. In the districts of Moquega and Arica on the southern coast, Juan Maldonado de Buendía describes having created twenty-two villages out of 226 settlements; and the already noted *visita* of Garci Diez de San Miguel in Chucuito confirms that 280 villages were reduced to fifty-eight on the occasion of the *visita* in the coastal areas of Sama and Moquega.[37] In the province of the Pacajes, between Lake Titicaca and La Paz, the information gathered by the investigator Juan de Ulloa – who, as often the case, was also the *corregidor* – allows us to construct the following table:[38]

Districts	Villages		Tributaries per village	
	pre-reduction	post-reduction	pre-reduction	post-reduction
Callapa	9	3	136	409
Caquingora				
Coaquiauire	23	1	65	1,500
Machaca	15	3	133	667
Tiaguanaco	10	1	80	800
Guaqui	6	1	200	1,200
Viacha	10	2	80	400
TOTAL	73	11	114	757

The operation was not always successful, and sometimes the Indios tried to return to their homes, often far from the new villages. They complained about the lack of adequate land available to them or the long distance to their old fields. They had trouble getting used to the new region or in any case considered the change to have been a negative one. It needs also to be said that first the Conquest and then the civil wars had profoundly disrupted traditional settlement patterns and caused massive flight from Spanish rule. Toledo's enterprise was also then a powerful normalization project. The reductions and the creation of a network of new Spanish towns had important consequences for the geography of settlement. It may also be the case that the process of demographic concentration had some effect on the epidemiological situation. When a disease – say smallpox or measles – was introduced into a region, it is possible that its diffusion and the proportion of the population exposed were greater after the process of reduction as compared to before. Just the same, the territory was vast and the villages far apart, so the spread of the infection depended on chance contacts. The "reduced" villages themselves were modest

in size, and an unknown but surely significant percentage of the
population continued to live dispersed in the countryside. And
even the largest cities did not have populations sufficient to maintain a disease in an endemic state. It is doubtful, then, that the
spread of the epidemics, and so also their impact, was increased by
the changes brought about by Toledo.

As compared to Mexico, where Cortés's victorious campaign was
followed by a pacification free of violent incidents, save on the
unstable northern frontier, the conquest of Perú took place on the
heels of a furious indigenous civil war, inspired widespread rebellion, and initiated a long war between Spanish factions. After the
death of Huayna Capac (which probably took place between 1525
and 1527), the struggle for succession between his sons Huascar,
raised to the throne in Cuzco and recognized by the center-southern
portion of the empire, and Atahuallpa, lord of Quito and supported
by a strong army, ended with the victory of Atahuallpa, the death of
Huascar and the extermination of his clan, and the return of the
invading army to the north. It was only then in 1532 that Francisco
Pizarro made his decisive disembarkation and pushed inland with
sixty-two cavalry and 106 infantry toward his encounter with
Atahuallpa at Cajamarca, the encounter which led to Atahuallpa's
being captured and taken prisoner. In November 1533 Pizarro's
expedition entered Cuzco, and at the beginning of the following
year the organized resistance was defeated. The very young Manco
Capac was placed on the throne in Cuzco by the Spaniards as the
Inca puppet, but soon rebelled. That insurrection spread through
the empire and culminated in the siege of Cuzco (1536–7) by the
Spaniards and their allies. Only in 1539 was the insurrection
defeated and Manco pushed back and trapped in the inaccessible
Vilcabamba valley. In 1538 a conflict exploded between the two
long-time comrades Francisco Pizarro and Diego de Almagro and
their followers; after the deaths of these two protagonists,
Francisco's brother, Gonzalo Pizarro, rebelled against the royal
authorities. The envoy of Charles V, Pedro de la Gasca, got the
better of the rebels in 1548. Nonetheless, the civil wars were not
finally over until the defeat of Hernández Girón, who led a final
rebellion against royal authority in 1553–4. So for a quarter century
the entire empire was riven and thrown into disorder by tremendous conflicts, whose consequences can be compared to those

which devastated central Europe during the Thirty Years' War. This claim may seem exaggerated given the relatively small number of Spaniards involved in the battles, the rudimentary nature of native weapons, and the vastness of the country. But it is not if we consider together all the various aspects of the devastation, as has been done in a conclusive way by Carlos Sempat Assadourian.[39] Those aspects include: (a) direct losses from the conflicts and their aftermath; (b) losses from punitive actions carried out against civilian populations that supported one side or the other in the struggles; (c) the effects of raids, the appropriation of labor, the abandoning of fields, the ruining of harvests, and the destruction of irrigation systems; (d) population displacement, flight, and migration.

A few examples taken from reliable sources will serve to give an idea of the consequences of thirty years of war. Naturally we do not know much about the native wars, but there are a few illuminating examples. The Cañari people lived in the north of the country in the region of Tumibamba; later they were allies of the Spanish. In the native wars they sided with the Cuzco faction, as a result of which the men and boys were cruelly decimated by Atahuallpa.

When a Spanish army passed through the province, since they were obliged to provide Indios to carry the Spaniards' gear and supplies, many gave their wives and children. I saw this myself when I went to join President de La Gasca, as they gave us a large number of women to carry our baggage.

This is Cieza de León speaking, fifteen years later. As a consequence of that reprisal: "Those who are alive today say that there are fifteen times more women than men."[40] Meanwhile Pizarro, who on his second voyage to Perú disembarked in the well-ordered city of Tumbez, returned four years later in 1532 to find it in ruins as a consequence of the civil war. When the forces loyal to Atahuallpa and under the command of Quisquis abandoned Cuzco and returned toward Quito:

the army still had between 12,000 and 20,000 effectives and vast quantities of camp-followers, conscripted porters and animals on the hoof. It was rounding up llamas, guinea-pigs and other food from the villages along its path, and was also burning and destroying the country it was abandoning. This was partly to prevent pursuit . . . and to diminish the value of the land being abandoned to the Spaniards.[41]

In the initial phase the Spaniards were few. Pizarro's expedition to Cajamarca numbered a little over 200 men (a third the size of the expedition of Cortés), reinforced the next year by the arrival of Almagro with another 150. Those numbers increased rapidly, however, as news spread of the fabulous riches of Perú. Nonetheless, the Spanish forces remained small, and most of the battles involved only a few hundred men; even during the civil wars of the 1540s the contending sides could count on no more than 2,000 men each. In the 1542 battle of Chupas, in which Vaca de Castro defeated the rebellious Diego de Almagro "the Younger," the two sides numbered 750 and 500 respectively. In 1547, at the battle of Guarima, the loyalist Diego Centeno fielded almost 1,000 soldiers and the rebel Gonzalo Pizarro 500. The following year, in the decisive battle of Jaquijaguana, President de la Gasca headed a force of 1,900 and Gonzalo Pizarro no more than 1,500.[42] Given these numbers, and in spite of the great experience and excellent armaments, the direct losses suffered and inflicted – even in the wars against the natives – must have been numerically small. But this is a short-sighted view. Each Spanish force – as was also the case for native forces – depended upon a large number of auxiliaries, male and female Indios enrolled under varying degrees of duress. "If one is to insist upon the great evils and harm and insults and theft, mortifications and mistreatment that were visited upon the natives . . . then one will never finish recounting it all in an ordered way."[43] Cristóbal de Molina, called "the Almagrista," was a soldier in Perú for many years and offers realistic descriptions. Starting with the encounter in Cajamarca, the Spaniards began enrolling large numbers of natives: "There were Spaniards who had as many as 200 *indios* and *indias* in their service, because of the great fear the natives felt as a result of the many deaths they had suffered."[44] When Pedro de Alvarado ventured into the interior of the country with 500 comrades and many Indios brought from Guatemala, the local natives related:

All his men came into our country to destroy us, make us prisoners, and put us in chains day and night, taking our wives and daughters and killing many of us. [He] went into the Zarapate Valley as far as the mountains and so far no one whom he took away has returned, and we think that they are all dead and that those who are still alive will never return to their land.[45]

In another passage, Molina comments on the losses the natives suffered subsequently "while in service and transporting loads, because all [Spaniards] move about with a great escort of servants, wreaking destruction on the villages they pass through." And if the natives fled from the *Camino Real* traveled by the Spaniards "hoping to avoid rendering service and so being taken away together with their wives and children, [the Spaniards] search after them here and there, waging war and calling them rebels with whom they can do as they please, and so they rob them and carry them away in chains, keeping them as if they were slaves."[46] Polo de Ondegardo also attests to the great depopulation of the region crossed by the *Camino Real*, and so the most exposed to Spanish soldiering.[47] The introduction of heavy artillery, carried long distances over mountains and valleys, required enormous manpower. Gonzalo Pizarro used 6,000 men in the expedition from Cuzco to Lima at the beginning of his rebellion.[48]

Once Pizarro was defeated, President de La Gasca found a country devastated by civil wars and pacified only at a high price; he offered a chilling testimony of the treatment of the Indios during the preceding years, reiterating the ban on their being loaded like pack animals, because:

a great multitude has died as a result, and this has been a great cruelty, because not only have they been loaded to the point of breaking under the sun and for hard marches, but they have been chained day and night; they have been put into gangs so they cannot escape, marching loaded down and chained together in gangs of fifteen or twenty, with iron collars around their necks; so it happened that one fell off a bridge and dragged the rest with him so that they all drowned. And this I heard from people who witnessed it. And as a result of these great cruelties and mortifications a large portion of the natives of this land have perished and many of them have fled, leaving their villages and homes, fleeing into the mountains, into rocky and hidden places far from the roads.[49]

This was not the lament of a compassionate friar, but the report of a steely royal official, one who did not hesitate to send the head of Gonzalo Pizarro from Cuzco to Lima so that it could be displayed in the public plaza.

We have already mentioned the drastic decline of the Huanca population between the time of Huayna Capac and Toledo's *visita*. In half a century the number of tributaries dropped to a quarter (doubts of course remain as to the comparability between the category of tributary in one regime and another, though the Spaniards based their system on that from the time of the Inca). What were the causes of this collapse? Certainly among the first to consider is their close alliance with the Spaniards. "Because of the Spanish–Huanca alliance . . . the *curacas* were obliged to supply hundreds and even thousands of men and women, as soldiers, *yanacona*, and even concubines. The majority of these never returned to their *ayllu*: they died far away or stayed on as servants in other provinces." And it was not only the Huanca who died serving the Spanish. Pedro de Cutimbo, who was governor of Chucuito, relates that 3,000 of the 10,000 Indios who took part in the siege of Cuzco perished.[50] The truth of assertions regarding the Huanca finds support in a legal proceeding begun by them in 1554 to obtain from the Crown recognition of services rendered, first to Francisco Pizarro and then to the legal governors of Perú from 1533 to 1554.[51] A document from 1558 recounts the assistance provided over a twenty-year period: a detailed list of 154 categories recorded in the *quipu* and transcribed to this document, which includes men and women provided for service, as well as the numbers and quantities of llamas, sheep, swine, poultry, fish, grain, potatoes, salt, textiles, clothing, shoes, crockery, lumber, rope, copper, and lead supplied to the Spanish. We will limit our considerations to the men and women, supplied as auxiliaries for transport and provisioning and as servants. Hundreds and sometimes thousands of these accompanied the various expeditions, and for very many of them one encounters laments about their murder, death, disappearance, flight, or assignment as servants to the Spanish – a series of reasons why they did not return to their original communities. As we have seen, the Lurinhuanca numbered 12,000 tributaries at the time of the Inca, but suffered a collapse such that by the time of La Gasca there were barely 2,500. In a period of fifteen years, from the death of Atahuallpa to the defeat of Gonzalo Pizarro, the number of Huanca Indios furnished to the Spaniards for their wars and other expeditions amounted to about 27,000.[52] Imagining that four-fifths of these were men, then on average about 1,400 able-bodied Indian males were taken from the community per year. This figure amounts to about one-eighth of that particular segment of the population (tributaries, that is able-bodied men) at the time of Huayna Capac, but over half in the final phases of the civil wars. About 7,000 of those put into service, more than a quarter, are described in the document as dead or missing.

As noted above, this document also lists the appropriation of goods during the fifteen years in question. That included 57,000 *fánegas* of maize, equivalent to 2,600 metric tons, with a nutritional value equal to the annual caloric intake of almost 700 adults.[53] But, in addition to maize, the Spaniards took quinoa, potatoes, eggs, meat, and fish; according to the account, appropriated llamas, goats, and sheep amounted to 13,172 head (878 per year). Finally the list also includes raids made by the enemy ("and then José de Acosta came through and took away a great quantity of livestock, stole many things, destroyed our houses, and robbed our babies").

These figures, taken from the memorial of the Huanca and translated into comparative and relative terms, help us to understand that the impact of the close alliance with the Spanish – in terms of human resources both employed and lost, of foodstuffs and other goods appropriated, and of attendant destruction and mayhem – was extreme and such as to bring about the demographic collapse of the community. This was, moreover, a group allied with the strongest contender and ultimately the victor both in conflicts with the Indios and in the civil wars. One can only imagine that those who supported the losers must have paid a still higher price.

More generally, first the wars of succession and then the Conquest and putting down of rebellions must have provoked many instances of famine and want in the 1530s; according to Assadourian these were "long and widespread."[54] In testimony before Vaca de Castro in 1543, the speaker confirmed that, as a result of the native rebellion:

no crops at all have been planted for three years in the district of Cajamarca and beyond because of the war, and in the rebellion the Indios themselves have burned the food that had been stored in the Inca warehouses . . . Because of the hardships brought on by the rebellion, all the children up to the age of six or seven have died of starvation, so that there does not remain a one, and similarly the old and infirm. After which, because of the great mortality brought about by the rebellion, they did not begin farming the land again for another four years.[55]

In general, the so-called *entradas* – explorations for the purpose of conquest – of the Spanish were expeditions that required complex logistics and the employment of hundreds or thousands of Indios. Many of these *entradas* ended disastrously, with huge loss of life. Those which have most attracted the attention of chroniclers and historians are the expeditions of Almagro into Chile in 1535–6 and of Gonzalo Pizzaro into the Amazonian part of the kingdom of Quito ("in search of Eldorado and the land of cinnamon"), both of which ended badly.[56] Almagro left Cuzco in July 1535 with 570 companions and many thousand Indios led by Paullu Inca; after having made it to central Chile and overcome tremendous obstacles, he returned one and a half years later having lost most of his native auxiliaries, who either died of cold and exhaustion in the mountain passes (1,500 deaths on the voyage out according to Oviedo) and on the long marches or were lost or fled. Assadourain speaks of a following of 12,000 Indios and at least 5,000 deaths in the passage over the *cordilleras*.[57] Nonetheless, he opened the way to the subsequent conquest of Chile by Valdivia. The expedition of Gonzalo Pizarro ended still more disastrously. He left from Quito in February 1541 with 210 Spaniards, 4,000 Indios, 4,000 to 5,000 pigs, 1,000 dogs, and large herds of llamas; having crossed the Andes they arrived in the Amazon jungle and were decimated by famine and fever. Forced to retreat, Pizarro made it back to Quito one and a half years later with a bedraggled group of about half the Spaniards; they had lost all of the Indios to either death or flight.[58]

There were many *entradas* throughout Spanish America; those that sought to penetrate vast and impervious regions such as the Andes were especially risky. Mercadillo, Diego de Rosas, Pedro de Candia, Pedro de Valdivia, and many others undertook expeditions that exacted a high toll in human life. Certainly these constituted a secondary element in the demographic collapse, but they are revealing of the mechanisms that prevailed in the first two or three decades of the Conquest, devastating in their consumption of human life.

As throughout the New World, European disease bears important responsibility for the native population decline. As we have seen, the *Relaciones Geográficas* attribute equal importance to disease and war – but with an important difference: by then the wars were distant memories and the country had lived in peace for three decades; diseases (old and new) and epidemics were instead the burden of all societies in past times and were striking Perú at just the time some of the *Relaciones* were being written in the late 1580s. It was natural then that great weight be given to them; weren't contagious diseases responsible for almost all deaths at the time, whether Indio, *mestizo*, African or Spanish? Unfortunately, given the scarcity of the documentation (scarcer than for other parts of Spanish America), analysis of the consequences of European epidemics in Perú can only be conjectural. And that scarcity of course compounds our uncertainty about the nature of the epidemics, uncertainty deriving from summary and contradictory descriptions of symptoms and the confusing and ambiguous labels used. We should not be deceived by the long and apparently dense lists compiled by patient scholars of epidemic episodes occurring in the vast empire after 1532. Many affected limited areas or had only a brief existence; others instead are uncertain. Moreover, contemporary to these events we can compile for any part of Europe – where we have diaries, memoirs, and administrative documents – an impressive list of epidemic incidents, diseases, and disasters, though these did not lead to demographic catastrophe.

We have already discussed in chapter 3 the supposed epidemic of smallpox in the 1520s meant to have caused the death of Huayna Capac. Those who speak of "*viruela*" – essentially Cieza de León and, less explicitly, Betanzos – did so thirty years after the fact.[59] Other diseases might have been responsible for the death of the Inca leader and some of his family members and for the high mortality of that period. Some have suggested that the illness that killed Huayna Capac could have been *verruga peruana*, or bartonellosis, an illness transmitted by sand flies and endemic in Perú that has symptoms similar to smallpox. The hypothesis according to which the epidemic of smallpox that broke out in Hispaniola in 1518, and then spread to Mexico and perhaps Guatemala, after which all traces are lost, somehow made it to Perú before the Spaniards is extremely tenuous. We have already explored the reasons why, in particular the difficulty of transmitting a "face to face" contagion over thousands of kilometers in sparsely populated territory characterized by limited mobility and widely differing climates and geography. And while we cannot exclude the possibility entirely, it seems highly unlikely. Unfortunately, current historiography nonetheless takes it as a given that the disease in question was smallpox; if we are not dealing with a case of historical falsification, then we are at least dealing with a hypothesis that by dint of repetition has taken on the status of truth, in spite of the inconsistency of the evidence. Discussion of that argument is an interesting academic exercise, but in the absence of new proofs (for example paleopathological analyses) it is destined to remain an unresolved one.[60]

The first general epidemic for which we have testimony – leaving aside small localized ones such as that of *verruga peruana* which struck the Spaniards in Coaque in 1531 – appears to be that of 1546 mentioned by Cieza de León: "While Viceroy Núñez Vela was dealing with the uprisings caused by Gonzalo Pizarro and his followers, a general pestilence struck the entire kingdom of Perú; it began first in Cuzco and then struck all the land, causing innumerable deaths." We can only guess at the nature of the epidemic, as Cieza's description of the symptoms is odd: "the disease caused headaches, and then the pain passed from the head to the left ear, and the illness was so great that the sick did not survive more than two or three days." These lines were written by Cieza as part of a description of the province of Quimbaya (Colombia) made during his travels in 1547: "now I will tell of what happened in 1546 in the province of Quimbaya."[61]

Another general epidemic broke out in 1558; we have reliable testimony for Colombia (where it presumably arrived brought by African slaves coming from Hispaniola), present-day Ecuador, and Peru. Contemporaries spoke of smallpox – making this the first smallpox epidemic after the arrival of the Spaniards – but also of measles.[62] Information is vague, however, regarding the spread, seriousness, and duration of the epidemic.

The years 1585 to 1591 were those hit hardest by epidemics that spread throughout the entire continent. It was unquestionably a period of serious demographic decline, well attested in the available documentation. Memorials, reports, and official correspondence all refer to high mortality, to the economic damage it wrought, and to the need to review the taxation levels for communities that had suffered serious reductions in numbers because of disease (and flight) and so could not make their required payments.[63] It is not surprising that much of the decline from the last third of the century took place in these years. We find references to smallpox, but also to measles, to "*dolor de costado*," and to typhus. It may be that a plurality of causes combined to generate a disaster that stretched from Cartagena to Chile, from Brazil to Paraguay. In the *Relacion Geográfica* of Abancay written in 1586 we find reference to an epidemic of *tabardete* that spread throughout the kingdom.[64] Several letters from Viceroy Conde de Villar to the king between April and July 1589 refer to an epidemic of smallpox, measles, and *romadizo* that began in Quito province and then spread to Cuenca, Loja, and Trujillo, and finally to Lima, with many deaths not only among Indios, Blacks, and Mulattoes, but also among Spaniards born in Perú and even among those born in Castille. In 1590 the epidemic appeared in Cuzco.[65] Viceroy Garcia Hurtado de Mendoza, in a letter to the king from December 1590, reports on the scarcity of the harvest and the want of food, as during the epidemic little sowing took place. The smallpox and measles epidemic had traversed much of the kingdom, and when it arrived in Lima (in November 1589) was also afflicting upper Perú. It was necessary then to adjust the tribute required of the Indios based on the number of survivors.[66] If the previous general epidemic (that of 1558) had also been smallpox, that which broke out three decades later would have found a large non-immune population (all those under thirty – between half and two-thirds of the entire population). We could expect, then, the death of a high proportion of the population (between a third and a quarter), and that would explain a great deal of the population decline of the last thirty years of the century. It may also be that the "reductions" of population into large villages made the consequences of the epidemic still worse than they would otherwise have been.

The demographic history of Perú in the first century after contact is a tortured one (as was the political and social history); it suffers from many obscure points and gaps. Given the current state of knowledge, it is difficult to assign a numeric estimate to the population during the last peaceful phase of the empire, at the time of Huayna Capac. What we do know is that the ten "plagues" Motolinia blamed for the Mexican disaster all apply equally well to Perú, and that the population at the end of the sixteenth century (less than a million and a half) was a fraction of what it had been: half in some areas, one-tenth in others, disastrous for all. A largely qualitative study of that first century supports several hypotheses.

Regarding the speed of the decline, it must have been more precipitous in the period of conflicts during the first half of the century than it was later. As for the factors of the decline, it would seem reasonable to revise the role of European epidemic diseases, providing that one is willing to abandon the theory that smallpox decimated the empire before the arrival of the Spaniards, a theory in any case based on exceedingly weak evidence. There were instead three large and generalized epidemic waves, in 1546, 1558, and 1585–91, a chronology similar to that of any European population at the time. In the second half of the century the Peruvian population was surely in crisis but not experiencing full-scale collapse. It is rather the destructive effects of war that need to be re-emphasized, both direct and indirect (oppression, want and famine, illness, flight without return), some extending over long periods and leading in particular to the selective destruction of young males.

This entire experience needs moreover to be understood in the context of the destruction of the Incan system, a system based horizontally on the reciprocity and solidarity of different ethnic groups and communities and vertically on the redistribution between the communities and the state. In Wachtel's interpretation:

the ideology which had justified the Inca system lay in ruins: in a society dominated by the Spanish, notions of reciprocity and redistribution had become meaningless. Or, more exactly, the Spanish system was made up of fragments of the former system; reciprocity still played a part in the relations between *ayllus* and *curacas*, and the latter still acted as intermediaries between the Indians and their new masters; but while reciprocity had maintained a rotation of wealth (even though fictitious or unequal) between *ayllu*, *curaca*, and Inca, Spanish rule brought about a one-way transfer of goods from Indians to Spaniards, without return.[67]

A fundamental aspect of the problem noted by Wachtel is the personal service that the Indios were obliged to provide: for the local *curacas*, for the *tambo* (the postal stations), for transportation, for the mines, and for the monasteries, all more or less forced labor. Viceroy Luis de Velasco offered a bitter synthesis at the end of the century, lamenting the intolerable exertions and mortifications associated with mining, farming, and transportation, burdens that grew ever heavier as the Indios became fewer and fewer; "and all of this falls on the backs of these miserable creatures because the Spaniards do not come here to work but rather to use them," while from Cuzco to Potosí the country is losing population. The Spaniards exchange Indios for money "as if they were animals." The ordinances meant to insure decent treatment of the Indios were a dead letter, and so it would be necessary to find "a guardian angel for the defense of each Indio." The Indios of Mexico, he opines, are fortunate, "because while they do not have a good life, they are without question . . . better treated and better paid than ours are, and they are not sent such great distances to work." And finally, "the servitude and forced labor to which we subject these poor Indios, especially that in the mines, truly militates against their decent treatment and protection."[68] Velasco, son of the second viceroy of Mexico, was a man with long experience; he had been viceroy of Mexico himself and had known Indian society all his life. Nor did the Indios escape this sort of oppression if they were assigned to the king, rather than the *encomenderos*, or were protected by the Jesuits. The Indios of Chucuito province, for example, were unable to pay their annual tribute, and found themselves 400,000 *pesos* in arrears. The Jesuits had succeeded in convincing the Crown to pay for the construction of parish and larger churches (twenty-two in all), but little had been accomplished and the churches were not much more than huts. The solution found was to use personal service from the Indios to build the churches in exchange for payment of their debt; two had already been built "better than any others in Indian villages in all Perú." This required procuring and transporting the lumber from 40 leagues away (given that there were no trees at 3,800 meters of elevation).[69]

The exaggerated amount of personal service required of the Indios aggravated the other interlinked negative effects already examined separately: wars, disease, exploration, mining, migration and climatic change, and forced resettlements. The pressure on the Indios tended to get worse as the Spanish population grew and the indigenous one declined. The rapid depopulation of the coastal regions, where the native population was concentrated in narrow valleys, has with good reason been attributed to the higher density of European settlement there, the consequent competition for limited agricultural land and water, the fragility of the environment, and the greater demand for personal service.[70] In the highlands, especially in the center and south, the depopulation as we have seen was less severe; citing Cook again, it was "not catastrophic as elsewhere. Large populations allowed the highland Indian to maintain social and economic institutions long after they were lost on the coast and in the far north. Much of the contemporary Peruvian highlands, in fact, retains a largely indigenous culture, in spite of contact with the Spanish and the wider western world for the past four-and-a-half centuries."[71]

It is not so much, then, the European microbiological invasion that we need to consider in order to understand the demographic fate of Perú, as the tragic mechanics of the Conquest itself.

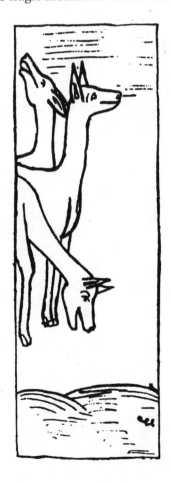

8 Colonists and "Paulists" hunting down Guaraní between the Paraná and the Uruguay. One hundred Jesuits for 100,000 Indios. Steel axes and security in exchange for Christian habits. Monogamy and reproduction stronger than crowd diseases

For over a century and a half (till the expulsion of the order in 1767) the Jesuits evangelized, governed, and organized the economic and social life of the Guaraní Indios in the immense region crossed by the Paraná and Uruguay rivers, concentrating and settling them in their thirty missions in Paraguay. It was an extraordinary experiment in a number of ways, not least of which were the demographic and social aspects. There is more than one good reason to reconsider the demographic history of the Guaraní: their social system was disrupted by the missions, but at the same time those missions protected them from raids and eventual enslavement by the "Paulists" and from serfdom in the *encomiendas* of the Spanish settlers. If the Jesuits did not protect the native population from the "invisible enemy" (microbes), they did protect them from the "visible" one (the Iberian colonists). Hence the interest in reconstructing the evolution of the Guaraní, a group whose social experience was notably different from that of the majority of the native American populations, and that for more than a century enjoyed demographic expansion rather than catastrophe.

Spanish penetration of the vast region of the Río de la Plata was overall later and less vigorous than in other parts of America. Given the relative lack of riches to exploit there – no precious metals and a lack of manpower, as the indigenous population was small and widely dispersed – attention was focused instead on Meso-America and Perú. Exploration of the region found its rationale first in the hope of finding a passage to the "Mar del Sur" (the Pacific Ocean) and subsequently in order to open (and protect from the Portuguese) a passage to Upper Perú (present-day Bolivia) and its rich mines. Following the unlucky explorations of Juan de Solís in 1516 and Sebastian Cabot in 1526, the first true settlement expedition was that of Pedro de Mendoza in 1535 that led to the ephemeral founding of Buenos Aires and of Asunción; the latter remained until the beginning of the seventeenth century the major center of colonization in the area.[1] We need to keep in mind that at the time of contact the indigenous demographic settlement – for the most part Tupí and Guaraní tribes – was not imposing. A recent "revision" estimates about 1 million inhabitants in a vast region including southern (non-Amazonian) Brazil and present-day Uruguay and Paraguay, plus another 900,000 in all of Argentina.[2] By contrast, the Spanish population numbered several thousand at the beginning of the seventeenth century. The Jesuits were authorized to begin evangelizing the Indios and in 1587 entered the Guayrá region. With the creation in 1604 of the Jesuit province of Paraguay (Paraquariae), the order's penetration of the area south of the Amazon grew more vigorous. As with Perú, we should not be confused by terminology; Paraguay province included present-day Chile (till 1625), Argentina, Uruguay, Paraguay, and about one-third each of Bolivia and Brazil, for a total of 7 million square kilometers.[3] The steel axes and wedges carried by the Jesuit fathers served as efficient credentials with the *caciques*. Moreover the fathers were well received by the local populations as they freed them from the *encomienda* system; they were directly assigned to the Crown, to which they owed tribute, though they were also temporarily freed from paying tribute to the king. These prerogatives were confirmed in 1611 by the ordinances of Alfaro, a royal official. The system was based on the creation of "reductions," or the concentration of Indios in planned villages, where religious, social, and economic organization was strictly controlled by the Jesuits. Map 9 shows the location of the Jesuit-run reductions in South America. The Crown's expectations included containment of the Portuguese, who were infiltrating from the region of Sao Paolo along the rivers, and protection of the communication link with Upper Perú. Up to the time of their expulsion, the Jesuits established ninety-eight missions in the province of Paraquariae; the thirty we examine constituted the nucleus of greatest success. Most were established along the existing and projected lines of communication.[4] The "reduced" Guaraní populations enjoyed protection from the exploitation of the colonists and, within certain limits, defense against the well-organized raids of the Paulist *bandeirantes* and other nomadic and bellicose tribes.

Map 9 *The missions of South America*

Foundation of the Jesuit reductions began officially in 1609, branching out from Asunción in three directions: north into the Itatín region inhabited by nomadic Indios; east into the Guayrá region along the banks of the Parapané river; and south toward the confluence of the Paraguay and Paraná rivers and then into Tapé. Constant raiding by the *bandeirantes*, however, led to the destruction of ten out of the twelve missions in Guayrá and forced the survivors to undertake a difficult migration southward in 1631–2. Similarly the "reduced" Indios of Itatín also moved south. By the 1640s, a stable network of missions had been established in the basin of the Paraná and on the western bank of the Uruguay. Initially there were twenty-two missions; another eight were founded between 1687 and 1707 by dividing up some of the latter when they became too large (see table 17 and map 10). Each of these was normally administered by two Jesuits under the direction of a superior. The missions lay between 26° and 30° S longitude and 54° and 57° W latitude, an area of about 100,000 square kilometers, but Jesuit control extended over a region more than twice that large, including extensive pasture and lands where *yerba mate* grew and could be gathered.[5] The straight-line distance between the northernmost (Santa Maria de Fe) and southernmost (Yapeyú) missions was about 300 kilometers, and between the westernmost (San Ignacio Guazú) and easternmost (San Angel) about 350. The "reduced" population constituted the majority of the native population in the area; it has been calculated that around 1680 there were approximately 68,000 Indios in the missions, representing 54 percent of the native population of the vast provinces of Río de la Plata including, in addition to Buenos Aires, Tucumán, and Cuyo, present-day Paraguay and Uruguay.[6]

The "reduced" population reached its maximum in 1732, at 141,000, embarking subsequently on a long and serious crisis that brought it down to less than 90,000 by the time of the decree expelling the Jesuits in 1767 (see figure 6). When the thirty missions were transferred to the civil government in 1768, the experiment ended and the population declined rapidly – from both migration and crisis – to about 40,000 by 1800.[7] Important for our purposes, from the mid-seventeenth century the missions constituted relatively stable collectivities in the sense that proselytism and the addition of other communities were over, and subsequent numeric change resulted primarily from natural growth while the mobility of the populations was limited. That stability, though, refers to periods of peace and calm since, as we shall see, in times of crisis emigration was significant. Contact with the Spaniards, moreover, was forbidden and a *mestizo* population non-existent. This was then a well identified population that we can treat with the traditional tools of demographic analysis.

Organization of the thirty missions was well documented by contemporary writers and has been the object of many studies;

Map 10 *The thirty missions of Paraguay*

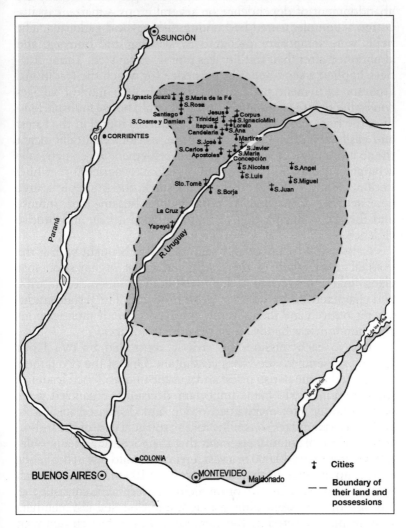

here we will touch on only a few fundamental points.[8] Reduction into stable communities – a process that took place in much of Spanish America, often under the auspices of religious orders – changed the living conditions of the Guaraní in significant ways. The Jesuits, as compared for example to the Franciscans, stand out for the changes they brought about in the native economy and rhythms of life. The greatest of these changes was certainly the abandonment of dependence on several crops – maize, cassava, cotton – complemented by hunting, fishing, and gathering. The fields were temporary, prepared by slashing and burning, and abandoned after their fertility was rapidly exhausted. Those practices implied a semi-nomadic existence for which the traditional Guaraní settlement pattern was well adapted: modest villages consisting of large communal huts that could house multiple families; the huts were easily built with materials found in the forest and easily abandoned. Transfer to the missions naturally meant the abandonment of nomadism, stable settlement in geometrically arranged villages, and conversion to sedentary agriculture, which became, along with the raising of livestock, the principle source of sustenance. Consequently work rhythms became more intense and the daily organization of time acquired a new and precise cadence.

Conversion to Christianity naturally also brought with it the gradual dismantling of the traditional social organization into clans, linked to a *cacique*, living together in common dormitories, and characterized by a degree of promiscuity.[9] The Jesuits gradually introduced and then severely enforced a strictly monogamous and mononuclear family life in separate residences.

Life in each mission was strictly controlled by two Jesuit fathers, sometimes aided by a coadjutant. One of the two fathers functioned as the parish priest and was the unquestioned leader of the community. He made important decisions, organized work and economic life, maintained order, and dispensed justice, in addition to taking responsibility for the spiritual care of the Indios. It is a source of some amazement that the governing of a population greater than 140,000 in a vast territory should rest in the hands of a group of religious that never exceeded 100 men. In truth each mission also had a *cabildo* or municipal government consisting of a dozen Indian elders with various responsibilities; the members were formally elected by the community but in fact chosen with the approval of the Jesuit father. Initially the missions sought to maintain some of the pre-existing power structure, continuing to assign the *caciques* to positions of responsibility and respect. In contrast to other communities, the *corregidor* of the *cabildo* was an Indio rather than a Spaniard. A *Libro de Ordenes* approved by the provincial superior functioned as a sort of civil and penal code for the missions and regulated the government of the communities.[10] The fathers organized instruction in the catechism, but their educational activity extended well beyond that to include literacy and music, as well as techniques of handcrafts, agriculture, and livestock raising. The daily, weekly, and annual schedule of celebrations, work, and prayer were precisely regulated. Given the strategic importance of the missions to the Crown in its competition with the Portuguese, and the need to protect themselves from raids by the *badeirantes* and hostile tribes, each mission also had a military force and created companies trained in the use of arms and coordinated by the superior of the thirty missions. As we shall see, the civil authorities of Asunción and Buenos Aires were continually calling on the missionary Guaraní to put down revolts, secure the borders, and engage in true military operations.

It was in the economic field that the Jesuits achieved notable results and where their efforts were distinguished from other reductions organized by different religious orders in other parts of the Americas that were more focused on religious and social aspects. Agriculture was organized in part along private lines, and each individual family was given enough land (theoretically) to satisfy basic needs. Nonetheless, a considerable portion of labor was devoted to communal fields, whose produce complemented family consumption, provided the necessary reserves for sowing next year's crop and for times of scarcity, and fed with its surplus a vigorous commerce both within and outside the missionary communities. The primary crops of maize, cassava, sweet potatoes, greens, fruit, and cotton combined with the raising of cattle and sheep (and wool production) to make the communities self-sufficient. Livestock raising took place in large *estancias* in the territories controlled by the villages, but the missions also culled cattle from the huge wild herds (*vaquerias*) that lived in the vast and remote expanses (*nullius*). Export consisted primarily of *yerba mate* – two Jesuits in Santa Fe and Buenos Aires functioned as agents – which makes a tea-like beverage the Río de la Plata population consumed in large quantities (and still does). The proceeds from that export provided the resources needed to pay the required tribute to the king (imposed on Indios aged between eighteen and fifty) and to buy tools, arms, ornaments, and other goods not produced at the missions. The overall enterprise was maintained by organized communal labor for the purposes of building churches, homes (initially little more than huts and later built of stone), workshops, and warehouses, for the maintenance of roads, and for the fitting out of *estancias*. Over the course of a century and a half, the structural endowment of the missions as well as the material life of the population enjoyed notable improvement, albeit experiencing ups and downs along the way.

Both the changed environment and social regulations had an impact on the demography of the Guaraní in the missions, and so it is worth spending a moment to review the important aspects of both in order to understand better the demographic evolution of the collectivity. The thirty missions (see map 10) situated in the Paraná and Uruguay valleys enjoyed a "benign and healthy climate, and while there is a distinct winter and summer, neither is harsh,"[11] so that simple cotton clothing was adequate, with the addition of a wool poncho for the occasional periods of cold in June and July. This characterization held, though, only for the sub-tropical region, and in fact a *Real Cédula* of 1706 forbade the sending of Indios to "*tierras frias*"; in Buenos Aires – with a more temperate climate – the Guaraní sent in work gangs died from the cold because of their inadequate clothing and lack of wood.[12] The ridge that divides the two river basins rarely rises above 500 meters and separates two regions of rolling hills and plains, well watered and with thick sub-tropical forests, especially along the rivers. Location of the missions took into account a series of favorable natural and physical factors, from availability of water, to quality of the soil, to access to communication, whether by river or over land.[13] These choices were not always good ones, and on several occasions costly transfers had to be undertaken. The complexity of economic life, the need for space for agricultural activity and pasturing, not to mention the impossibility of controlling collectivities that were too large, all combined to impose a numeric limit – corresponding to 1,000 families – to the demographic size of the missions. When that limit was exceeded, a new mission was founded. The famous Father Sepp left a detailed description of the founding of the mission of San Juan in 1697 with some of the inhabitants of San Miguel, which had grown to more than 6,000 people.[14] Sepp describes the criteria followed for selecting the location, distributing the land, assigning the crops, planning the village, and constructing the buildings. After 1690, seven new missions were founded by splitting off from older villages that had grown too large. In 1732 – the year of the demographic peak – only one of the thirty missions exceeded a population of 7,000.

Except for the families assigned to the *estancias*, and so living far away, the population of the missions was concentrated in the villages. These were laid out according to precise plans: a large central rectangular plaza onto which faced the church, the home of the Jesuits, and other public buildings (such as the home for widows and orphans). The Indios lived in row houses a few dozen meters long and 10 to 12 meters deep, including the porticoes that ran the length of each house front and back; the houses were laid out on wide streets that stretched out perpendicularly from the central plaza. Each building housed between six and twelve families in single family spaces about 5 to 6 meters square and opening out on to the porticoes.[15] In the later period, the buildings were made of stone, though the family spaces lacked fireplaces just the same.[16] So while the layout of the buildings recalled the traditional communal living quarters, the real innovation was the separation of nuclear families that had previously lived together. Father Diego de Torres, in the 1613 *Carta anua*, wrote: "We must eliminate the inconveniences associated with the large houses . . . for every cock his own enclosure."[17] Nonetheless, at various times the traditional tendency to communal living reasserted itself – when the population of a village grew too large or when one village was divided to create a new one – and the Jesuit fathers had to employ all their authority to combat it.[18] Separated from the residential quarters, a building equipped as a hospital was constructed to house and isolate those afflicted with contagious diseases. Rudimentary medical assistance and a locally produced pharmacopoeia – thanks in particular to the Italian and Central European fathers – were employed in an effort to limit the impact of those diseases.[19] Each mission had an adequate source of running water and rudimentary sewerage. As already discussed in chapter 3, the "reduction" policy, bringing together into compact groups Indios who had previously lived in more dispersed settlements, carried with it a number of consequences. It undoubtedly favored the spread of contagious diseases, especially smallpox, measles, and typhus, with disastrous consequences. Isolation of the sick and the assistance provided them by the communities could only slow down the contagion and limit its impact, preventing the flight of family members and death from abandonment. We shall return to this topic below, one that is central to the demographic history of the Guaraní.

The daily rhythm in the missions involved precise regulation of time spent working, resting, and praying, but these topics are not particularly relevant to our study. The semi-nomadic origins of the Guaraní made them skillful workers, but with little propensity for discipline or continuous employment. While they were excellent artisans, decorators, and musicians – well attested in all contemporary reports – they were reluctant farmers and had to be overseen and punished for their lapses. For the preparation, sowing, and harvesting of their individual fields they were given six months, though "the effective work of four weeks would have been sufficient to provide food for a year . . . as the land was very fertile."[20] Yet they used the full six months, and the greatest problem for the Jesuit fathers was to ensure, with oversight and punishment, that the natives produced enough to survive. That aim was often not met, and so the community had to supplement the meager individual harvests. Regarding maize, for example, it has been estimated that the effective yield from the individual plots was one-fifth of what was theoretically obtainable given the methods available at the time.[21] Taking into account the work on the communal fields, limited to Monday and Saturday, one can conclude that the work regime was moderate. And in spite of various attempts, the proposal that the native families add to their domestic consumption by raising animals other than chickens was abandoned.

In normal periods – those not devastated by wars, insurrections, and of course famine – diet must have been more than adequate in terms of both quantity and quality. The mission populations enjoyed a rich and varied diet of maize, cassava, sweet potatoes, beans and other legumes, squash, fruit, sugar, and honey and a level of meat consumption several times that typical of Mediterranean Europe at the time. The Guaraní were avid and immoderate consumers of beef, to the detriment of their health according to some.[22] In some missions, butchered beef was distributed every morning at a rate of 4 to 5 pounds per family; in others distribution took place two, three, or four times a week.[23] A prudent estimate puts per capita consumption at 82 kilograms per year (as compared to 13 in united Italy in the 1860s), and that only of beef.[24] The same author has calculated individual caloric intake for the final phase of the missions – not the most prosperous one, and the calculation leaves out subsidiary foods such as rice, wheat, eggs, etc. – at about 2,500 calories per day. This needs then to be considered a lower limit, though it is about equal to Brazilian consumption in 1980 and just a little below that of Uruguay and Paraguay.[25]

A good network of roads and streams connected the missions to one another and to the major centers of the Río de La Plata region, allowing mobility and limiting the isolation of this vast and sparsely populated region (one person or just over one person per square kilometer). In 1684, Father Altamirano wrote that the missions on the right bank of the Paraná extended for 40 leagues (223 kilometers), from San Ignacio to Corpus (later transferred to the left bank), and were connected by difficult roads, over which the inhabitants nonetheless traveled from one mission to another in three to four days.[26] On the other hand, a complex system of laws and rules bridled the natural mobility of the Guaraní. The road network centered on Candelaria, the most important mission, and allowed travel with oxen-driven carts that ran down to Corrientes and up to Asunción.[27] They were equipped with frequent rest stops (*tambos*) for sleeping, eating, and the resting and changing of horses.[28] The rivers provided a natural and much used avenue of communication: "One Jesuit, writing in 1715, reckoned that there were at least two thousand canoes from the reductions in use on the Paraná and almost as many on the Uruguay."[29] The great merchant ships coming from Cadiz sailed up the Paraguay to Asunción and even reached the distant port of Candelaria, 2,000 kilometers from the estuary, via the Paraná.[30] Nonetheless, there were numerous obstacles to movement. The *Leyes de Indias* forbade Spaniards, Blacks, and *mestizos* from living in the missions, a prohibition reconfirmed several times by both civil and religious authorities.[31] The Jesuits upheld these regulations with a few convenient variations: in the *pueblos de abajo* west of the Paraná and close to the roads leading to Asunción (San Ignacio Guazú, Santa Maria de Fe, Santa Rosa, and Santiago, and later also San Cosme and Itapúa) and in Candelaria there was a great traffic of travelers and merchants who were allowed to spend not more than three days in the *tambos* in order to show and trade their wares.[32] In the other missions, between the Paraná and the Uruguay and east of the Uruguay, access was denied to non-Guaraní except for special cases, and the trade for needed products was conducted with Buenos Aires by means of river traffic.[33] The overall picture that emerges is that the separation of the missions from the rest of the world was not absolute and perhaps more social and civil than physical. There were moreover, and as we shall see, many military and civil expeditions that took the Indios out of the area of the missions and so into contact with Spaniards, Africans, and *mestizos*.

Movement of the Indios in the thirty missions was notably restricted, as laid down in the Regulations of 1689.[34] They were only allowed to leave the mission for work and other activities authorized by the Jesuit father; from time to time on certain holidays a small group of singers and musicians together with a few members of the *cabildo* might accompany the father on a visit to a nearby mission. An Indio residing for at least one year in a mission was to be returned there if he left; if husband and wife found themselves in different missions, the wife and also her children were to be sent to join the husband. When an Indio arrived at a mission he was, if possible, to be sent to his resident mission or *pueblo de españoles*. During a 1715 visit to Itapúa, the governor found an Indio in prison "because he had fled his village and did not want to live with his wife."[35] The territorial distribution of the Indios, then, could not alter in response to more or less spontaneous migrations. The surviving documents suggest, however, that flight into the forest was fairly common – often without return – especially in times of want, famine, epidemic, or political-military unrest. And there were also individuals who ran away in order to escape obligations or punishments (for killing a cow, gross negligence in agricultural work, carnal sins): "There are many Indios who flee to the villages of the Spaniards. And while they do not amount to more than one in a hundred, out of 100,000 that is in any case a thousand."[36] This was a significant annual flow and one, as we shall see, confirmed by the available data. The fugitives lived a wandering life, generally working as day laborers for the Spanish.

Other rules specifically controlled the demography of the missions.[37] According to article 20 of the General Regulations, "Marriages between Indios will normally not be celebrated until the male reaches the age of seventeen and the female fifteen, providing there are not reasons that require earlier marriages, as determined by the superior." Once the required age was attained,

marriage required the consent of the Jesuit father, apparently with
no exceptions.[38] José Cardiel stated: "They all marry. Given their
limited intellect and extreme materialism, they are incapable of
celibacy."[39] The available data confirm the universality and early
age of marriage. Father Sepp in fact lowered the ages to sixteen
and fourteen.[40] Indios from other missions could not marry
without the authorization *in scriptis* of the father from their own
mission (art. 17). In spite of these precepts and regulations, the old
practice of polygamy was not dead and buried. As compensation
for their military collaboration, the *caciques* of nine reductions
demanded recognition of their right to have multiple wives.[41] The
old ways of life also resurfaced in times of crisis, when the control
exercised by the Jesuits for various reasons relaxed.[42]

Other articles (27, 29, 31) referred to the obligation of the
fathers to visit daily those who were gravely ill; funeral practices;
and the keeping of parish registers (unfortunately lost). This
precise codification and the strict order imposed on and by the
fathers inspire confidence in the demographic data to which we
refer below. Baptisms, for example, were normally celebrated once
a week in a collective ceremony, but were administered immediately after birth if there was fear for the life of the infant.

We have then fairly reliable documentation for examining Guaraní
demography from about the middle of the seventeenth century
when the missions had consolidated themselves in the Paraná and
Uruguay basins. There are references in the second half of the
century to the requirement to keep parish registers, but if they
have survived their whereabouts are unknown. We do instead have
annual figures on population size and vital events. The collection
of these data became systematic by the late seventeenth century;
they were collected in *planillas*, or tables, that reported yearly for
each mission the size of the population and the number of families;
families referred to married couples and their children, so that the
number of *familias* theoretically coincided with the number of
married couples, half men and half women. The rest of the population was divided into *pueri* and *puellae* (up to seven years of age),
adolescentes (up to the age of marriage, fifteen for girls and seventeen for boys), and *viudos* and *viudas* (or *soluti*, that is widows and
widowers), data which can be translated into age structures. The
planillas also included baptisms and marriages – both according to

the regulations normally celebrated collectively on Saturday and Sunday – as well as deaths, distinguished as *parvulos* or *adultos*. All in all the care and meticulous attention to detail of the fathers produced high quality data for the time period and the conditions under which they were collected; analysis confirms that high quality and allows the sketching out of a coherent and reliable picture of Guaraní demography. Following the expulsion of the Jesuits, data continued to be gathered by the new religious and administrative authorities, but quality and continuity deteriorates; nonetheless, one can follow the general demographic outlines through to the beginning of the nineteenth century.[43]

In figure 6 we can follow the evolution of the mission populations from 1643 to 1812, to the eve of the movements for independence. It is characterized by a long phase of growth, starting at 36,000 in 1643 and quadrupling to the historic maximum of 141,000 in 1732. There follows a precipitous decline in the 1730s, as a result of political-military turbulence and two serious mortality crises, so that the population is halved by 1740 (74,000). In the two decades that follow, and in spite of the nearby war between Spain and Portugal, recovery sees the population reach 105,000 in 1760. After that, the population declines steadily till the dissolution of the communities in the 1810s. We can also add that during the periods of growth the dominant factor was natural increase (more births than deaths), though there was also a contribution from immigration deriving from the natural attractive force of the missions and several episodes of proselytism. The period of decline was instead almost wholly owing to a process of diaspora, as natural growth, in spite of several profound mortality crises, remained positive.

Fertility, mortality, and natural growth allow us to analyze the demographic evolution of the missions. Other measures will serve to reconstruct in detail the mechanisms of growth. As a first analysis we can look at table 18, which offers a synthesis of the data by decade. These elementary data highlight several fundamental aspects of the system. The first is the high levels of fertility and mortality, with average values close to sixty per thousand. Independently of migration (conversions and flight) that was itself at times intense, demographic turnover proceeded at a furious pace; if the population had been stationary these rates would have implied a life expectancy at birth well below twenty. This rapid turnover, combined with short spacing between generations, had two important consequences, one social and the other epidemiological. On the level of society, it accelerated the process of religious and cultural change promoted by the Jesuits through the education and discipline of small children. On the level of disease, it meant the introduction every year of a large number of individuals not immunized by previous epidemics, and so vulnerable to the re-introduction from outside the community of microbes and viruses.

A second aspect is the population's capacity for natural increase. The median value of natural growth over a period of nearly a century was about 2 percent per year. This meant that the Guaraní system could rapidly fill gaps created by periods of disruption and mortality crisis. It was, then, a system similar to that of old regime populations in Europe, able to recover from the destructive effects of crisis. That ability was not characteristic of other American populations because recovery from crisis elsewhere was compromised by restrictions and obstacles to reproductive capacity posed by the social dislocation attendant on contact with the Europeans. Those restrictions and obstacles were absent among the Guaraní, as the Jesuits sought to maximize reproduction by imposing strict monogamy and universal early marriage.

The third aspect is the seriousness and frequency of mortality crises. In the period of continuous documentation, 1728–67, the years 1733–4, 1738–9, and 1764–5 were especially critical, with mortality rates between 100 and 200 per thousand and significant (though not disastrous) drops in fertility. There were also minor crises, with mortality between 80 and 100, in 1719 (the crisis started in 1718 but quantitative data are lacking for that year) and 1749. In fact, the entire seven-year period 1733–9 was one long crisis, during which epidemics of smallpox and measles, internal insurrection, the forced recruitment of Indian work gangs, and want caused very high mortality and a deficit in births, as well as a strong diaspora from the missions. José Cardiel wrote in 1747 that, in times of want, "most fled into the bush and lived in the barbarous way characteristic of their previous pagan state."[44] The entire four decades from 1728 to 1767 saw the population of the missions decline by 41,000; three-quarters of that was the result of diaspora and the rest of natural deficit.

Given the importance of immigration and diaspora to the Guaraní system, we should explore the question of mobility in the missionary period a little further. During the phase of maturation and consolidation, proselytism (and so migration into the system) was limited and sporadic.[45] Protests and petitions within the order for the assignment of more Jesuits were constant in this period. In 1712, the Jesuit Bartolomé Jimenez wrote to the king lamenting that, although many "infidels" had been successfully induced to descend "*de los montes*," they could not be converted for lack of missionaries.[46] The small number of fathers were certainly too busy with the work of governing to engage in additional missionary activities, and the "non-reduced" populations were too spread out and far away. In other cases, the converted Indios might return to their "savage state," as happened with the Indios of Tarumá (100 leagues north of the missions), who, having been incorporated into the Santa Maria de Fe mission, returned to their homeland – "466 in a single day" – during the famine of 1734.[47] According to the provincial father, Manuel Querini, in a letter to the king, ten years later they were, however, all tracked down and convinced to return.[48] In another example it was not famine but irritation and insubordination that led a group to defect and set up an independent settlement on the banks of the Iberá.[49] In other cases, as recounted for example by Father Lozano, the work of proselytism took on the character of true "raids on the infidels," though bloodless ones, by Christian Guaraní.[50] These few episodes demonstrate that natives came and went from the missions for a variety of reasons and under a range of circumstances, and that the Guaraní missions were less monolithic than they are sometimes made out to be.

In the period during which the missions flourished, European diseases – smallpox, measles, scarlet fever – had been introduced into South America for over a century. At the price of a devastating mortality, the Guaraní must have acquired an immunity similar to that of European populations. A smallpox epidemic raged along most of the Brazilian coast in 1562–5. And there is documentation of a "plague," certainly smallpox, that began in Cartagena in 1588 and spread to much of the continent; in 1590 it devastated the recent settlements of Asunción, Ciudad Real, and Villarica, spreading also to Guayrá. Fragmentary evidence frequently refers to epidemics in the region in the early seventeenth century; in

1634–6, and again in 1653–5, almost all the missions were struck by smallpox and other diseases (measles, perhaps scarlet fever and typhus). A careful analysis of religious and civil sources (the *Cartas anuas* of the missions, for example) offers a complex picture of minor and major crises, both localized and widespread, that struck the entire region, sometimes identified by name and at other times by the simple generic label of "plague." Gonzalo de Doblas was a careful observer of Guaraní society just after the expulsion of the Jesuits; he wrote: "Smallpox and measles by themselves cause horrible massacres; and this is so because, after many years free from these epidemics, when they do appear, given that there are few survivors who have experienced them, the contagion spreads rapidly and there is no one to aid the sick, as all are fleeing in hopes of not being infected."[51] Doblas touches upon several essential points for epidemiological analysis: the size of the susceptible population and of that immunized at the time of the outbreak, the interval between outbreaks, and the deadliness of the disease. Contemporary with Doblas, another observer, Diego de Alvear, wrote that "one-quarter of the population has surely died of smallpox."[52]

The epidemic diseases that struck the missions could not have become endemic. The demographic dimensions of the villages (rarely more than 5,000 people) and of the region as a whole were certainly below the minimum thresholds needed to maintain a disease (smallpox or measles) in an endemic state. In the case of measles, for example, that threshold is on the order of several hundred thousand individuals.[53] Below that threshold, an immunizing disease (smallpox, measles, scarlet fever) tends to run its course and die out for lack of a sufficient population of susceptible individuals. In order for the disease to reappear it has to be introduced again from outside the community by the arrival of infected persons. Given that fertility was very high (sixty per thousand), and so the age structure very young (*muchachas* and *muchachos*, respectively below fifteen and seventeen years of age, constituted nearly half of the total population), the reintroduced disease could soon find large numbers of non-immune individuals. Between 1690 and 1767 we find four or five widespread waves of smallpox coming every fourteen to eighteen years (1695, 1718–19, 1733–9, perhaps 1749, and 1764–5). Fifteen years after a previous epidemic, the returning smallpox infection would find all the young people under that age (about 50 percent of the population) susceptible, as well as a proportion (say 30 percent) of the older population that had succeeded in avoiding the disease the last time around – theoretically two-thirds of the total population in all. Yet if fertility had been lower, say half of that sixty per thousand (about what it was in much of Europe), the percentage of non-immune population would have been much lower, closer to two-fifths rather than two-thirds. So even if we assume equal levels of infection and lethality (mortality rate of those contracting the disease), mortality would still be considerably higher in the case of Paraguay than in Europe.

Smallpox mortality, like that of other infectious diseases, among the non-immune population was very high. We have already seen in chapter 3 that mortality from an epidemic striking a "virgin population" can reach 30 to 50 percent.[54] But even in a non-virgin population – one with a young age structure – mortality was very high, and lower only as a function of the percentage of the population that was immune. In general we can observe that, the longer the interval between epidemics and the younger the age structure, the higher will be the mortality (and the smaller the percentage of immune population), and so also the difference from the situation of a virgin population will be less. The factors then that distinguish a virgin from a non-virgin population are (a) the proportion who are immune; (b) the proportion who are infected; (c) the rate of recovery, or the proportion of those who contract the disease and survive, acquiring immunity.

About (a) we have already spoken; with intervals between epidemics of about fifteen years, the proportion immune in the missions would have been about one-third. Regarding (b), the "reduction" of the Indios into dense settlements surely increased the percentage of those infected; previously they had lived in a semi-nomadic state spread out in the countryside and had, if nothing else, the option of flight. The Jesuits sought to minimize the infection by isolating cases in hospitals separate from the community, and this may have limited the negative effect of demographic concentration. We have already reviewed (in chapter 3) some of the ingenious strategies adopted to isolate those suspected of being infected.

On (c), or the rate of recovery, we can only conjecture. It is in any case possible that the social organization imposed by the Jesuits raised the rate of recovery as compared to that of a semi-nomadic population. One risk that rendered the epidemic more deadly was in fact reduced, namely the abandonment of the sick by family members who feared catching the disease themselves. Father Diego de Boroa, referring to the epidemics of 1635–7, observed that the related high mortality was caused both by the disease and by death from cold and starvation as the sick were abandoned by their terrorized family members,[55] an observation repeated by many subsequent observers. In the missions, abandonment was considerably less frequent than in the wandering populations. The Indios confined to the hospitals were regularly cared for and fed, and it is reasonable to imagine that their rate of survival was higher than for those abandoned by family or community.[56]

Several random bits of documentation on the deadliness of smallpox lend support to these observations. In 1612 in Arauco (Chile), 153 out of 273 infected individuals died (56 percent); in 1614 in three reductions in Guayrá lethality seems instead to have been notably less (11 percent).[57] *Carta anua* XIV describes how, in 1635 in Yapeyú, smallpox killed about 30 percent of the population.[58] In 1661 about half of the population of Santa Maria fell ill – it is not clear whether from smallpox or measles – and one-quarter of that half died. In 1667 smallpox presumably killed half of the population of Corpus.[59] More than a century later (1788) two-thirds of the population of San Borja contracted smallpox, and lethality among the sick was again around 25 percent.[60]

If we examine the crisis years after 1690, we can come up with a rough measure of the impact of smallpox, keeping in mind that the "normal" level of mortality (the median values from table 18) was between forty and forty-five per thousand. Table 19 lists the mission mortality rates in crisis years. For 1695 we have data only on the Paraná missions, but according to Father Burgés there were 16,000 deaths, corresponding to a mortality rate of 200 per thousand.[61] It should also be noted that 1719 certainly witnessed the end of a crisis that began in 1718 and may have struck with more force in that year (for which there is no data). We have defined "crisis" years as those with a mortality level over 100 per thousand and "catastrophic" years as those over 250. Nine of the thirteen Paraná missions experienced crisis mortality in 1695; four of twenty-eight missions did so in 1719; twenty-one out of thirty in 1733; and, respectively, sixteen, seven, and fourteen out of thirty in 1738–9, 1749, and 1764–5. Nor was catastrophic mortality a rare event.

Although the Jesuits sought to isolate the missions both from areas outside the Paraná and Uruguay regions and from one another, that isolation was imperfect. Regulations restricting mobility were violated; travel on river and over land was not difficult; frequent employment in press gangs brought the Indios into contact with the outside world; and trade carried on normally. Once an infection was reintroduced from outside, it spread from village to village following a path determined by their contiguity. The *Carta anua* of 1661 tells of the arrival of smallpox: two infidel Indios were not admitted into Yapeyú (the southernmost mission, located on the Uruguay river) for fear that they might be infected. They took refuge from a storm in a *rancho*, where they infected other Indios who were returning to their residence at San Tomé. After getting home, the latter "stayed hidden for eight days until on Good Friday the father was alerted to the fact that there were a number of Indios with red faces; he examined them and recognized the plague that had raged in Perú and caused such a massacre."[62] Father Sepp described the 1695 smallpox in the following terms:

As the year 1695 drew to a close and the month of October began, which here is the beginning of spring, a cruel pestilence devastated Paracuaria, and in a few months the population of almost all the missions – there were twenty-four at the time – was infected by the epidemic . . . The plague was brought by Indios returning from the city of Santa Fe. That place, inhabited by Spanish traders, was the first to be struck by the plague; Córdoba, Santiago del Estero, and other cities of Paracuaria followed. Only then did it spread with great violence to our missions, where it wreaked greatest devastation among the poor Indios, easier victims than the wealthy Spaniards because the Indio makes do with simple clothing, better suited to hide his nudity than protect him from the cold.[63]

Other sources suggest that the epidemic, having started at Itapúa and Candelaria, spread to San Ignacio Guazú, Santiago, Santa Maria de Fe, Loreto, Santa Ana, San Ignacio Miní, and San Carlos, seemingly sparing the Uruguay basin.[64] According to the account of a religious arriving from Europe, the smallpox of 1718–19 was brought by passengers on English or Spanish ships who disembarked in Buenos Aires.[65]

The continuity of the statistical information over the course of the seventeenth century allows us to make a few more observations. The spread of the crisis in 1733 was total, but in other cases the situation was different and some areas remained untouched. In the crisis of 1738–9, about ten missions out of thirty, all in the Paraná region, escaped the disaster (which is to say that they experienced normal mortality equal to or below that of the preceding years). In 1749 there were seven missions with "normal" mortality and in 1764–5 just two (both in the Paraná, as were the other missions that suffered less). This is just what one would expect when the infection, not being endemic, penetrates into a region with connected settlements: a nearly simultaneous explosion of mortality, with some zones that are not stricken because of geographic remove, because protected by effective measures taken, or by pure chance.

As for any population short on resources and knowledge, the Guaraní suffered high levels of mortality that fluctuated widely in response to abrupt changes in outside factors (food, disease, violence). The Jesuits sought to moderate and stabilize these factors by organizing food production and distribution; isolating, caring for, and feeding the Indios during epidemics; and protecting the population from attack, exploitation, and raids. Presumably those efforts had positive effects, though it is impossible to measure them; moreover, those effects were heavily counterbalanced by the fact that reductions into denser settlements increased the destructive impact of smallpox, measles, and other diseases. When the social and economic system showed signs of failing, the Indios tended to return to the wilderness and to their traditional ways of life, which, developed as they were by a process of adaptation over dozens if not hundreds of generations, may have been better adapted to survival.

A simple model lets us estimate Guaraní life expectancy; the average for the entire period is 23.3 years (and the median 24.5), a level that confirms the population's vulnerability (see table 20). During the fifty years in question, life expectancy exceeded thirty years on only three occasions (1691, 1737, 1753), while on eight it dropped below fifteen and on four below ten (1733, 1738, 1739, 1764, years during which mortality neared or exceeded 150 per thousand). There were then limits of survivorship which the Guaraní could not exceed save in exceptional years (the high life expectancy in 1737 was probably the result of a selection effect after the four catastrophic years preceding). But the lower limit of life expectancy is very low as a consequence of the rapid turnover of the population, and the resulting high proportion of very young and non-immune individuals when smallpox and measles were reintroduced from outside the community. And while the Jesuits may have been well versed in the art of medicine and maintained a significant pharmacopoeia,[66] it is doubtful that their scientific ability was any more successful at lowering mortality than were similar endeavors in Europe at the time. In spite of the efforts of the Jesuits, a life expectancy of around twenty-five, in non-crisis years, is hardly surprising among an underdeveloped population like that of the Paraná and Uruguay valleys. Potential growth in non-crisis years was close to 2 percent, but that high level cannot be attributed to a survivorship which always remained precarious.

In the missions, the Indios were spared the heavy labor regime of personal service that burdened other native populations living under the *encomienda* system. Yet this privileged regime came at a price and had to be defended. The missions were constantly being asked to support the needs of the colonial administrations in Asunción and Buenos Aires. Those needs included men to build forts and ports, to patrol the frontiers, to rebuff the attacks of enemy Indios, to suppress insurrections, and for true military operations. The policy of the Jesuits was to respond where possible to these requests, selecting and outfitting the men, and organizing and leading the expeditions themselves. The colonial administrations knew they could rely on a responsible, rapid, and efficient reply to their requests and emergencies. The Jesuits in turn relied on the protection of the civil authorities from the rapacity of colonists who, because of the reductions, were denied the human resources of that sparsely populated region. The press gangs themselves at times had a significant social and demographic impact. The long distances they traveled on foot or by canoe translated into extended absences for many able-bodied men from the villages, a compromising of the community's isolation from the outside and potentially corrupting world, the abandonment of work regimes, and a threat to family stability. During repression of the uprising by the *comuneros* of Asunción against the colonial government, don Bruno Zabala led a Spanish expedition and asked, in a letter dated October 9, 1734, and sent to the vice-superior of the missions, Félix de Villagarcia, that "6,000 Indios be sent to the border along the Tebicuarí river with the best possible weapons . . . they must establish themselves there and not allow anyone to enter or leave from the province of Paraguay, closing it completely to traffic and commerce." He asked in addition that "another 6,000 Indios be positioned in reserve near the border."[67] At the end of November the Indios began their march, and they arrived at the gathering point during January 1735. We know that contingents left from twenty-five of the thirty missions: 5,459 men, who covered an average distance of 70 leagues (about 400 kilometers) over difficult trails crossing rivers and swamps. A few months later, after suppression of the uprising, the contingents headed home. Six thousand men, absent from home for at least six months, represented 25 percent of the male adult population. But over the whole period 1732–5, 5,000 to 12,000 men were mobilized for the pacification of Paraguay and, in 1735, for the third siege (of four) of Colonia (the Portuguese enclave repeatedly conquered by the Spanish). Previously, from 1724 to 1729, several thousand Indios had been continuously recruited: to fight the Antequera rebellion in Asunción (hundreds of natives died in the battle lost on the banks of the Tebicuarí river); to undertake projects in Buenos Aires; to fortify Montevideo; and to defend Santa Fe. In order to chase the Portuguese out of Colonia – a fortified encampment built on the bank of the Río de la Plata opposite Buenos Aires – 3,000 men were employed for a year in 1680 and 2,000 to 4,000 in 1702–4. The most important expeditions, such as those to Colonia, 1,500 kilometers to the south, involved travel over river and land accompanied by carriages, arms, supplies, horses, and livestock, with assistance from (or rather under the command of) one or more fathers; they could last months. Baltazar Garcia Ros, head of the Spanish army, recounts that the Indios who brought about the capitulation of Colonia on March 15, 1704, numbered 4,000 and had left their villages at the beginning of September 1703, divided into three corps. Two of the corps sailed down the Uruguay and Paraná in flotillas of forty *balsas* (a *balsa* consisted of two canoes lashed together); the third went on foot. The first two arrived at the Spanish camp in view of Colonia about a month later; the third arrived one more month after that, having traversed – for those coming from the farthest missions – almost 2,000 kilometers. They brought with them 6,000 horses, 2,000 mules, meat, legumes, maize, tobacco, and other provisions for the journeys down and back. During the siege they supplied the army by bringing to the camp 30,000 head of cattle captured in the surrounding area. Their engagement lasted eight months, during which they comported themselves with loyalty and dedication, on guard duties, in the attacks and in the trenches, and hauling artillery on their backs. Deaths to the Guaraní forces numbered 130 and injuries 200.[68] The long list of services provided by the native press gangs, carefully described in letters from the fathers to the king or to the governors, include (to name only a few of the most notable) aid to the cities of Corrientes, Santa Fe, and Montevideo, in addition of course to Asunción and Buenos Aires; expeditions against hostile tribes such as the Guaycurús and Payaguas and against the Brazilian *"mamelucos"*; defense of the distant *vaquerías* from attacks and rustling; the construction of fortifications in Buenos Aires and Montevideo; and the repression of revolts.

How burdensome was the Guaraní commitment beyond their normal life and work? And what were the demographic consequences? We will need a good answer to the first query in order to be able to hypothesize about the second. Certainly the long crisis of 1732–9 was systemic – epidemics, famine, war, flight – and the long absence of thousands of Indios from their homes contributed in a significant way. In other cases the connection was less direct: the press gangs were a constraint on growth, but not an obstacle, and with the exception of a few episodes should not have influenced the demographic dynamic of the missions in a significant way. We can estimate the number of Indios drafted into gangs for every 1,000 families for the period 1630 to 1740 (after which the data are less thorough). Only in three out of eleven decades (1700–9, 1720–9, 1730–9) do there appear to have been more than fifty Indios per year employed per 1,000 families; in all the others the level was below that. This was a burden incomparably lighter than that borne by the Indios of the Peruvian and Bolivian highlands subjected to the *mita*. We can make a quick comparison with another rural society: in post-Unification Italy, obligatory military service annually drafted on average thirty young men for every 1,000 families. The price paid by the Guaraní, then, was not excessive and certainly much less than that paid by Indios subject to personal service in other parts of the Americas.

Conversion of the Guaraní brought with it in the first place a profound change in the rules governing unions and reproduction (about which we have already spoken). The challenges the Jesuits faced were unstable unions, promiscuity, and life in the large communal houses. They recognized that the adult population could not be converted to "non-barbarian" styles of life, nor did they attempt as much in the early phases, though discussion of the canonical significance of marriage and polygamy led eventually to consultation with Pope Urban VIII.[69] It was instead via children and the young that they sought to initiate the habits of monogamy and independent nuclear families. In the Jesuit conception, family meant the nuclear family, consisting of parents and children; widows and orphans lived apart in communal houses supported by the community. That family, then, was essentially the site of reproduction, and the Jesuit fathers sought as far as possible to remove the children from the influence of their parents before they reached the (early) ages of marriage. José Cardiel was explicit:

Starting at the age of seven, they are all entered into the register of the *alcaldes*, and from that time they are all grouped together with other [adolescents] for religious and social activities up until the age of marriage. Since, if they are left with their parents, the latter are of such limited capacities that the children will grow up as little beasts and remain lazy for the whole of their lives.[70]

The new generations were brought up according to this model in preparation for an early marriage, and observing a strict separation of the sexes for community activities (education, prayer, work). The Jesuits, in at least formal agreement with the parents, arranged for marriage to take place not long after puberty and encouraged (presumably at times even imposed) the choice of partner. According to the Regulations, marriage age was set at fifteen for girls and seventeen for boys. The fathers moreover supported respect of the marital tie with repression and punishment. The mission dwellings, while still respecting the traditional preference for communal living, nonetheless included distinct spaces for each family nucleus. Early, universal, and stable marriage was the factor behind the high fertility and high growth potential of the Guaraní. Following expulsion of the Jesuits, communal living and promiscuity reappeared in that society.[71]

The available data confirm that nuptiality was very high: about four-fifths of all adult women were married, and among women of childbearing age marriage must have been just about universal. The median nuptiality rate for 1690–1767 was 13.3 per thousand (and about double when calculated only for women; see table 20). Each year, then, about 2.7 percent of all women got married, a proportion that corresponds well with the percentage of fifteen-year-olds in the female population. It supports the observations of contemporaries according to which the regulations on marriage were strictly followed (namely that all girls marry at fifteen). High nuptiality implies high fertility, and in fact the level of around sixty per thousand was about double that prevalent in Western Europe at the time. Estimates of the average number of children per woman (TFR) for the whole period yield a high median value of 7.7, significantly higher than the 6.5 estimated for Paraguay by the United Nations in the period 1950–60 (when contraceptives were still virtually unknown)[72] – further proof that the family policy of the Jesuits managed to keep fertility high. Moreover, even in the most difficult period experienced by the missions – the disastrous years of 1733–9 – TFR remained just a little below 6 (5.85 to be precise), in spite of the press gangs, famine, and epidemics, only to rebound to over 9 for the decade 1741–50. In a high-fertility regime, the wounds heal quickly.

The expulsion of the Jesuits in 1767 speeded up a process of decline that may have already been underway in the previous decades. In 1768 the population of the thirty missions was just under 90,000; by the beginning of the nineteenth century it had dropped to about 40,000. Epidemic crises followed a similar rhythm as in the past (1770–2, 1775–7, 1788, 1796–7), but discontinuity and gaps in the data, along with their deteriorating quality, make it impossible to evaluate the impact.[73] There is some evidence that even in non-crisis years mortality was higher than in the past. For example, the average mortality rate for the years 1793, 1798, 1799, and 1803 (years free of epidemic and for which there is data) was fifty-five per thousand, as compared to forty-four during the Jesuit period. In those same four years births did not outnumber deaths, while previously in normal periods there had been strong natural increase. But it was above all emigration that determined the decline. "Depredation under the new administration, poor diet, abandonment, and poverty all forced the Guaraní to leave the villages in search of better prospects for a decent quality of life and one freed of the communal system. It was an emigration directed primarily at the provinces located just outside the mission area."[74] The replacement of a carefully selected administration of high intellectual caliber dedicated to pursuing precise objectives with one little motivated (when not simply corrupt) caused social, economic, and demographic disaster. In the words again of Ernesto J. A. Maeder:

The basic missionary effort had been to guide the Guaraní of the reductions in the formation and preservation of a native society that was Christian, isolated, and protected, as far as possible, from the colonial world. Now the proposal was instead to integrate them into that colonial world that was growing up around them, by means of continuous contact, the development of individual liberty, trade, and miscegenation; and all this in a system that was in many ways contradictory, as political and religious authority no longer resided in the same person.[75]

This transition was surely inevitable, but it was one that carried with it a host of negative consequences.

How does the Guaraní experience help us better to understand colonial demography? In the first place it tells us something about the epidemiological consequences of contact. In the mature period of the mission system – more or less the century before the expulsion – the Guaraní had already experienced the devastating impact of the European diseases for a number of generations. Yet, one or two centuries after contact, the epidemics continued to be devastating *even though they were no longer operating on a virgin population*. Mortality rates for smallpox of between 150 and 200 per thousand continued to be the norm during the epidemics. We have found the following: (a) high fertility (sixty per thousand) created a very young age structure (half of the population under fifteen); (b) the new diseases were not endemic (the low population density was insufficient to "maintain" them, and they had instead to be reintroduced from the outside) and reappeared on average every fifteen years; (c) the percentage of the population susceptible to infection (for example, at the reappearance of smallpox after fifteen years) then was very high, being composed of all those born since the previous epidemic (about half the population), plus those who survived the previous epidemic but did not contract the disease; we can imagine that at least two-thirds of the population were susceptible when the disease returned; (d) finally, concentration in the reductions must have on its own increased the percentage of the susceptible population that contracted the disease, even though care for the sick and the prevention of flight should, in principle, have increased the rate of recovery. The conclusion, then, is that the impact of the epidemics in the missions should not have been less devastating than it had been in the century following contact.

The second important point is that the Jesuit policy, encouraging monogamy, early and universal marriage, and the stability of the nuclear family, kept fertility at the maximum levels sustainable by a normal population. It was that high fertility that created demographic surplus in good years and allowed the population to compensate for the losses created by the epidemic crises, and in fact to grow at a considerable rate. In comparison with other experiences following contact in the Americas, in which high mortality generated by disease combined with social destabilization that compromised fertility and reproductivity, the experience of the missions was certainly the better one. Fertility was enhanced rather than depressed and the Guaraní multiplied for nearly a century, absorbing the negative effects of two wars and four epidemics in the last four decades.

Finally, the political system erected by the Jesuits – as long as it lasted – protected the Guaraní from mixing with Whites and Blacks. Isolation prevented the demographic impoverishment associated with the transmigration (usually forced) of women into the reproductive system of the Whites, a phenomenon that in many other parts of the Americas weakened the native populations. In the social and economic realm, moreover, the missions enjoyed notable development, and that development certainly had a corresponding positive effect on Guaraní demography.

In 1563, two centuries before the expulsion and not even thirty years after the first true Spanish settlement, the *procurador general* for Río de La Plata, Antonio de León, wrote to the king that the decline of the "naturals" in all the Indies was so great as to make necessary importation of slaves from Guinea, an unworkable solution for La Plata, as the sources of supply were so far away.[76] For 200 years the theme of native population decline would be a source of concern for the colony and the colonial power, for governors and religious, *encomenderos* and merchants. It is in this general framework of crisis that one must understand and interpret the demographic history of the Guaraní in the thirty missions.

NOVENA CALLE
LLVCACVAMRA

an prouecho   enesta

O ur search for the causes of the demographic catastrophe of the Indios began in the Caribbean, continued in Mexico and the Andes, and concluded in the Río de la Plata basin. It is an itinerary that has skipped over large areas of the continent, including the cold and temperate north, the tortured center, and the Amazonian jungle. Nonetheless, taken together, the regions we have chosen accounted for the majority of the Indian population in the sixteenth century, three-quarters or even more, and offer a broad array of situations and experiences. We can, then, draw some general conclusions, not least because the post-contact history of those other areas was not vastly different from the foci of our study. In all of them population declined and power passed into the hands of Europeans, bringing about profound economic and environmental changes and radical social and institutional transformations. The population of North America, estimated at several million at the time of contact, declined to several hundred thousand by the end of the nineteenth century and came to occupy a small number of residual physical and social spaces.[1] In Central America, the Audiencia of Guatemala – including most of the Mayan world and extending as far as Panama – was less densely populated than central Mexico, but its three-quarters of a million inhabitants in 1800 were a fraction of the contact population.[2] Brazil was sparsely populated and is thought to have numbered fewer than 3 million inhabitants when Pedro Alvares Cabral arrived; at the beginning of the nineteenth century there were fewer than a million.[3] Needless to say, these conjectures regarding the populations at contact are themselves sources of considerable debate; we cite them because they demonstrate, along with a host of other proofs, that widespread disaster struck the American continent.

Centuries later, however, the comparison is a deceptive one. It does not take into account that the Indian catastrophe followed very different rhythms in different parts of the continent. In the Greater Antilles the population became extinct, but elsewhere, once a minimum was reached, the demographic curve turned upward and rose at rates that again varied. Unfortunately the final phase of the decline and the initial one of the recovery remain shadowy. Data produced in Hispanic America in the century and a half between the first decades of the seventeenth century and the last third of the eighteenth are poor and episodic, and so then is our knowledge about the period. For Mexico, the recovery took shape in the second half of the seventeenth century. Each year the Indios paid a tribute of half a *real* for the construction of cathedrals; it was collected district by district. The number of tributaries around the middle of the seventeenth century and toward the end of the century was the following:

	Mid-17th century	End of the 17th century	Variation (%)
Diocese of Mexico City	57,751	76,626	+32.7
Diocese of Puebla	62,475	74,549	+19.3
Diocese of Michoacán	12,495	19,301	+54.5
TOTAL	132,721	170,476	+28.4

The beginning of the recovery, according to José Miranda (from whom the above data is taken), dates from between 1620 and 1640.[4] The data refer to only three dioceses and account for little more than half of the population of central Mexico. Nearly a century later, the census ordered by Viceroy Revillagigedo (1790) – whose data Humboldt gathered and published – attributed a population of about 4.5 million to New Spain, of which two-fifths were Indios, at least 50 percent more than the minimum reached at the beginning of the seventeenth century.[5] But these figures tell only part of the story, insofar as they do not take into account the growth of the mixed-race population, which included various "proportions" of Indio blood and to which the "pure" Indios of course contributed; it must have numbered around 1.5 million.[6]

For the Andean population, the bottom of the downward cycle and the beginning of the recovery came later than in Mexico. Sánchez-Albornoz's data for Upper Perú (Bolivia) suggest a doubling of population between the enumeration of Viceroy duque de la Palata in 1683 and the count of 1786: from 164,000 to 335,000 inhabitants. The viceroy's count was ordered because of concern over the ongoing and serious demographic decline, one made worse by a steady stream of emigration. That decline may have continued until the turn of the century or after.[7] For the highlands of Guatemala there are no signs of consistent recovery till well into the eighteenth century.[8] In North America recovery did not begin till the late nineteenth century. In many parts of the Amazon the decline has continued to the present day.[9]

The causes of the recovery – where there was one – still need careful analysis and suggest four different paradigms. The first is extremely general and not very useful for the purposes of analysis. It suggests that human groups are endowed with self-regulatory mechanisms, so that demographic shocks are generally followed by modifications of behavior that seek to re-establish equilibrium. This may be the case, but historical experience suggests that there are human groups that do not "respond" positively to those shocks, as confirmed by the experience of the Taíno. Nor are we able to explain how or why these mechanisms might work. According to the second paradigm – one advanced by many observers at the time – the enlightened, or in any case less restrictive, policies of the Bourbons in Spanish America and of Pombal in Brazil made for a more open society and generated economic growth that together drove the recovery. This argument adapts to the different timings of the recovery as well, earlier in Mexico, later and less vigorous in Perú. Regarding population growth in the late eighteenth century, we can cite, among many others, Humboldt:

It is certain, however, that this population [of Mexico] has made the most extraordinary progress. The augmentation of tithes, of the Indian capitation, and of all the duties on consumption, the progress of agriculture and civilization, the aspect of a country covered with newly constructed houses, announce a rapid increase in every part of the kingdom.[10]

And again:

It was King Charles III especially who, by measures equally wise and energetic, became the benefactor of the Indians. He annulled the encomiendas; and he prohibited the *repartimientos*, by which the *corregidores* arbitrarily constituted themselves the creditors and consequently the masters of the industry of the natives, by furnishing them at extravagant prices with horses, mules and clothes.[11]

But this explanation has its limits, as the life of the Indios was barely touched (if at all) by these processes of development. Humboldt in fact contradicts himself a few lines further on: "The Mexican Indians, when we consider them *en masse*, offer a picture of extreme misery."[12]

A third paradigm is biological in nature, and we have already referred to it. Following the initial impact of the new viruses and the consequent high epidemiological mortality, individuals who have contracted the disease and recover acquire protective immunity against subsequent epidemic waves, and so mortality is lessened. Beyond this well-known phenomenon, there may also have been a slow process of selection according to which individuals more vulnerable to the virus were eliminated, and so did not pass on their particular genetic characteristics to subsequent generations – generations that were as a result made more resistant to infection. This is again a possible mechanism – though not proven in its specifics – but it is doubtful that its impact would have been felt before the passage of many generations, more likely a question of millennia than of centuries. During his travels in the Amazon, Charles-Marie de La Condamine observed in the mid-eighteenth century, "This illness [smallpox], in Pará, is still more deadly for the Indians of the missions who have recently come out of the forest than it is for the Indians who were born and have long lived among the Portuguese."[13]

Finally, a fourth paradigm is an eclectic one and does not rule out any of the others. It postulates that the Conquest exercised a combined biological, environmental, economic, and political shock on indigenous societies. The violence of that shock, which varied from place to place, had a range of demographic consequences that depended on the social organization, settlement patterns, and productive systems of the affected societies. So the biological shock of a new disease, for example, and the consequent mortality could be weakened by adaptation mechanisms, including knowledge of the disease, the ability to identify it and either to isolate those who fall ill or to escape from them, the mastering of fear and the ability to feed and care for the sick, and experimentation with empirical remedies. These mechanisms certainly act more quickly than selection processes and may also be more effective. In sum, just as a variety of factors was responsible for the disaster, so a variety of factors was responsible for the recovery. We return once again to Motolinia: "God struck and chastised this land . . . with ten disastrous plagues."[14] And only when the Indios found ways to defend themselves were the American populations able to take up again a path of growth.

In these final pages we should summarize the observations made over this long voyage. There was no single cause or single model for the demographic catastrophe. The attempt to force the complexity of history into a monocausal paradigm flattens a varied terrain and ignores precious clues. At the same time, we cannot simply take the position of Motolinia or Las Casas, fashioning a modern *Leyenda Negra* which mixes together the effects of a range of causal factors without attempting to estimate their prevalence, impact, and order of importance.

Based on what we can understand from the apparent consequences, the Conquest delivered a shock to the entire indigenous demographic system: survivorship, unions, reproduction, mobility, and migration. The greatest impact was naturally that of the new diseases and the high mortality that resulted, and so we have to assign them major "responsibility" for the losses of human life in the initial phases. The range of already existing pathologies was augmented as new epidemics were added to those that had undoubtedly struck the American populations (who did not in fact live in a Garden of Eden free of infections) for millennia. In some cases ordinary mortality may have increased as well. Nonetheless, and as repeatedly observed above, increased mortality was not the only issue. Europe was struck with plague over the course of two generations (the most lethal of all epidemics and one that never arrived in the Americas) and lost only a third of its population. Other new diseases – typhus, syphilis, sweating sickness – or the return or older ones – smallpox – coincided in Europe precisely with the period of the Conquest but did not compromise European demographic growth in the sixteenth century. Moreover, the "virgin population" effect – the greater impact of a disease on a population without immunity – decreased after the first impact, and subsequently the effect of "biological" novelties lessened and blended with other largely social factors that worsened the impact of mortality. To summarize a variety of different situations: in those cases where the Conquest modified the defense mechanisms of the population or compromised its normal response mechanisms to demographic shock, the disaster was made worse and in some cases was terminal. In other cases those mechanisms were more robust, because the process of Conquest was less violent or for other reasons, and the consequences of contact were less catastrophic. To be more specific, the mechanisms of defense or reaction – examined above in a range of contexts – included the accelerated formation of new unions, high fertility, spontaneous migration, and the reinforcement of community solidarity. These mechanisms were blocked or destroyed by territorial dislocation (forced migration and reductions), the restructuring of production activities, the appropriation or increased burden of labor, and intrusion into family and community organization. In other words, the Conquest compromised what we defined at the outset as the individual demographic prerogatives that are the basis for a population's equilibrium and continuity.

Is it possible to cast the different sorts of situations created by the Conquest into a series of models or typologies? It is worth a try, providing that we do not propose ones that go too far in characterizing realities that were each unique and remain in many of their aspects unknown.

The Caribbean provides us with a first model. Impact was violent and the population was already well on its way to extinction when the first devastating bout of smallpox arrived. From that experience there evolved the *Leyenda Negra* of the Conquest. A series of negative factors operated there at full force: direct murder as an accompaniment to subjugation; enslavement and forced labor; destruction and dislocation of communities; a high numeric ratio between conquistadors and natives; the appropriation of reproductive-age women. The ability of the natives to react and defend themselves was weak, given a loosely structured society and a subsistence economy; and the population disappeared from a combination of high mortality and low fertility. A frantic search for gold was the aggravating factor in this case. The destructive Caribbean model included, in addition to the Greater Antilles, the pearl-fishing islands, the mainland coast of the Castilla de Oro, and other isolated areas.

The coastal lowlands of the Gulf of Mexico and also the Pacific coast provide another model. Population decline seems to have

been much more rapid there than in the Meso-American highlands
or in the cool and temperate Andes. There are several possible
explanations for that difference. The first is that in the low hot
zones, with a greater density of microbes, the effects of the new
diseases were amplified, making them still more lethal. But that is
a vague argument and one that needs confirmation. Another possible cause is the introduction and spread of the malaria plasmodium in a favorable environment like the warm and hot one of the
gulf; in addition to heightened mortality, malaria may have caused
depopulation by means of emigration. Yet another explanation
may be the greater vulnerability of the economic systems of Pacific
coastal valleys and the destructive impact of the Europeans, who
took the best lands for themselves and appropriated the ancient
irrigation systems, when they did not simply destroy them. It was
in fact on the coast that the city of Lima was founded, and so where
the numerical impact of the Europeans was greatest, with all the
negative consequences that the colonial presence brought for
native populations.

Another typology about which we have spoken little is that of
the gradual and at times violent expulsion of native populations
from their traditional homelands, and so their relocation in less
favorable areas. This model applies to Brazil, where the sparse
Portuguese settlements (there were about 30,000 Europeans at
the end of the sixteenth century) were spread out over a vast
coastal area.[15] The colonists' need for workers and the conflicts
that were created with the native populations led to their gradually being forced into the interior. A continual demand for labor
for production and services, satisfied in part by the steady importation of slaves from Africa, inspired inland expeditions to seek
out the only resource of value to the Europeans (at least till the
discovery of gold toward the end of the seventeenth century):
men and women who could be reduced to slavery. Such was the
objective of the *bandeiras* (expeditions that left from the São
Paolo highlands toward the interior) or the *resgates* (river incur-
sions aimed at the subjugation of the riverine populations). The
effects of these raids were considerable, though not easily mea-
sured, and many religious – including Antonio Vieira, a sort of
Brazilian Bartolomé de las Casas – denounced them vigorously.
Moreover, the enslaved Indios and those pressed into service
often did not reproduce, creating still more demand; the female

element of the population became absorbed, so to speak, into the European population and so withdrawn from the native reproductive pool. This expulsion-destruction model could perhaps also apply to areas of North America.[16]

At the opposite end of the scale compared to the Caribbean model is that of the Guaraní in Paraguay, a model of demographic expansion in spite of epidemic disease. The government of the Jesuits saved the Indios from the exploitation of Paulist *bandeirantes* and Spanish colonists; the imposition of monogamy and early marriage enhanced reproductive mechanisms; and a cooperative and collective lifestyle reinforced social integration. Recurrent epidemics, periodically reintroduced from outside the community, were highly destructive, due in part to the high proportion of non-immune population produced by very high fertility. Losses, however, were compensated by rebounding fertility following each demographic shock. In normal years natural increase was strongly positive. We do not know the demographic history of the first century after contact, but we do know that the reconstitution of the communities under Jesuit rule from the first half of the seventeenth century stands out as a demographic success, at least until external factors and a change of regime following expulsion of the Jesuits ended the experiment.

There remain the experiences of the resilient, evolved, and well-structured societies of central Mexico and the Andes, the most densely populated areas of the *meseta* and the highlands. They represent two models with many points in common but also many areas of difference. They are similar in that the strong identity of the two societies was not destroyed by the Conquest and recovery mechanisms functioned in the long run. They differed in that the impact of the Conquest was greater in Perú than in Mexico. In Perú cruel civil wars and wars of conquest raged for a quarter century, while in Mexico pacification was rapid following Conquest. In Perú the appropriation of labor for personal service, production, and mining was burdensome and continuous, while in Mexico it was less so and the work regime was relatively free. In Perú tribute was heavy, while in Mexico it was relatively light and flexible. In Perú the iron rule of Toledo imposed a radical policy of population relocation on the natives, while in Mexico the network of pre-Conquest settlements remained largely unchanged. It is difficult to make demographic comparisons, not only because of the lack of documentary evidence but also because the years before the Conquest were marked in Perú by civil wars of succession. Nonetheless, population decline in Perú in the quarter century following the death of Huayna Capac seems to have been caused primarily by the various conflicts that produced, among other things, a notable shortage of men. Moreover, the demographic crisis of the last three decades of the century seems to have been less serious in Perú than in Mexico (average rates of decline of, respectively, less than 1 percent and more than 2 percent).

Even given that there are no objective documentary proofs, one gets a strong impression that the impact of the new diseases was instead less serious in the Andes than it was in Mexico. One possible explanation lies in their different geographies, settlement patterns, and climates. Factors that may have caused epidemics to be more virulent in Mexico include high population density in central Mexico and the valley of México itself, at the center of which lay the largest European settlement in the Americas; the radial system of communication that connected that settlement to the periphery; and more frequent contact with Europeans. Perú may have benefited instead from its "comb"-like geography of parallel ridges, with settlements and communication routes located in the valleys between the ridges, a configuration that could have impeded the spread of disease. It was also less densely populated and farther from Europe, and the major city (Lima) was located on the coast rather than in the center. And we might also add a lower density of parasites and pathogens at high altitudes. So it would seem that the new diseases had a less traumatic impact in Perú than in Mexico, and that fact may have balanced out the more destructive nature of the Conquest itself in Perú. Finally, the combination of the *mita* system of forced labor and the tribute system tied to residence generated large migrations of the Andean populations, with implications that are difficult to measure but which also served to differentiate the demographic regime in Perú from that in Mexico.

The different impacts of the Conquest fall between two extremes: extinction even before the arrival of European diseases, as in the case of the Taíno on the islands of Hispaniola, Cuba, and Puerto

Rico; and growth in spite of epidemics, as for the Guaraní protected by the Jesuits between the Paraná and Uruguay rivers. The catastrophe, then, was not preordained and inevitable, but rather the product of interaction between natural factors and human and social behavior.

Appendices

Appendices

Table 1 *Estimates of the American population at the moment of contact according to various authors (figures in millions)*

	Kroeber (1939)	Steward (1949)	Rosenblat (1954)	Dobyns (1966)	Denevan (1976)	Denevan (1992)
North America	0.9	1.0	1.0	11.0	4.4	3.8
Mexico	3.2	4.5	4.5	33.7	21.4	17.2
Central America	0.1	0.8	0.8	12.2	5.7	5.6
Caribbean	0.2	0.2	0.3	0.5	5.8	3.0
Andes	3.0	6.1	4.8	33.8	11.5	15.7
Rest of South America	1.0	2.9	2.0	10.1	8.5	8.6
Continent	8.4	15.5	13.4	101.3	57.3	53.9

Source: William M. Denevan, ed., *The Native Population of the Americas in 1492*, 2nd edn, Madison: University of Wisconsin Press, 1992, pp. xviii, 3.

Note: Dobyns's estimate (1966) is the average between his low (90 million) and high (112.6 million) hypotheses.

Table 2 *American populations, European populations, and migration (figures in thousands)*

Populations	In America, c. 1800 (1)	European immigration up to 1800 (2)	Ratio between population in America and immigration (3) = (1) : (2)	Population in European countries of origin, c. 1800 (4)	Immigration per 1,000 population in European countries of origin (5) = (2) : (4) × 1,000	American inhabitants per 1,000 inhabitants in European countries of origin (6) = (1) : (4) × 1,000
Canada, French	180	25	7.2	29,300	1	6
USA, white	4,306	909	4.7	10,500	87	410
Spanish America, white	2,500	800	3.1	10,600	75	236
Brazil, white	1,010	500	2.0	2,900	172	348
TOTAL	7,996	2,234	3.6	53,300	42	150

Source: Massimo Livi Bacci, "500 anni di demografia brasiliana," *Popolazione e-storia*, 2001, no. 1, pp. 17–20.

Table 3 *Slaves brought to the Americas (1500–1800) and the black American population (1800), figures in thousands*

Geographic area	Slaves brought from Africa up to 1800 (1)	Black population in America in 1800 (2)	Ratio between the black population in America and slaves transported (2) : (1)
United States	348	1,002	2.9
Spanish mainland	750	920	1.2
Brazil	2,261	1,988	0.9
Caribbean	3,889	1,692	0.4
English and Dutch islands	*2,060*	*570*	*0.3*
French islands	*1,415*	*732*	*0.5*
Spanish islands (Cuba)	*414*	*390*	*0.9*
TOTAL	7,248	5,602	0.8

Note: Estimates for the slaves brought from Africa are from Philip Curtin, *The Atlantic Slave Trade: A Census*, Madison: University of Wisconsin Press, 1969. The date of reference for Cuba is 1805 and the data are taken from Alexander von Humboldt, *Ensayo politico sobre el reyno de Nueva España*, Mexico City: Porrua, 1973, pp. 203–4; data not included in John Black's abridged English translation), both for population and slaves transported. Where necessary, Curtin's estimates have been adjusted to take into account the effective date of the estimate of the black population. For the United states the date is 1800 (second census); for the Spanish mainland, information on the black population is taken from Gonzalo Aguirre Beltrán (*La población negra de México* [1946], 3rd edn, Mexico City: Fondo de Cultura Económica, 1989, p. 234) and for the other countries from Ángel Rosenblat (*La población indigena y el mestizaje en América*, 2 vols., Buenos Aires: Editorial Nova, 1954, vol. 1, pp. 192–207), with references and dates between 1778 and 1812.

Table 4 *Infectious diseases among indigenous populations in Amazonia*

Introduced from elsewhere	Zoonotic	Endemic
Smallpox	Yellow fever	Herpes type I
Measles	Mayaro fever	Mononucleosis
Chicken pox	Oropouche fever	Cytomegalovirus
Mumps	Toxoplasmosis	Hepatitis B
Influenza A and B	Leismaniosis	Ascaris
Parainfluenza	Trichinosis	Amoebiasis
Polio	Tetanus(?)	Treponematosis
Malaria	Malaria	Syphilis (?)
Hepatitis A		
Dengue		
Common cold		
Rotavirus diarrhoea		
Diphtheria		
Scarlet fever		
Whooping cough		

Source: Francis L. Black, "Infectious Diseases and Evolution of Human Populations: The Example of South American Forest Tribes," in Alan C. Swedlund and George J. Armelagos, eds, *Disease in Populations in Transition*, New York: Bergin & Garvey, 1990.

Table 5 *Indios employed in Potosí, 1602*

Activity	Number
Repartimento Indios working in the mines	4,000
Indios mingados (contracted day laborers) working in the mines	600
Indios washing and transporting ore from the Cerro	400
Total directly employed in the mines	*5,000*
Indios gathering slag at the Cerro (including children)	1,000
Repartimento Indios working in the mills (*ingenios*)	600
Indios mingados working in the mills (*ingenios*)	40
Indios (men and women) working the ore (*beneficio*)	3,000
Indios transporting ore to the mills	250
Indios transporting metal to the city	180
Contracted Indios doing the same	1,000
Indios supplying wood to the mines	500
Indios carrying wood to the furnaces and furnace tenders	1,000
Indios transporting combustible manure (*ocha*)	500
Indios working at the mercury amalgamation process	200
Indios transporting amalgam	1,000
Indios making candles	200
Total employed in these activities	*9,470*
Indios supplying the city from far away	1,500
Others working in the valley at various occupations	30,000
Total employed in other activities	*31,500*
TOTAL	45,970

Source: AGI, Charcas 134, fo. 5, doc. 1, undated (presumably 1602).

Table 6 *Estimates for the population of Hispaniola at the moment of contact*

Author	Year	Population (in 1,000s)
1 Verlinden	1973	60
2 Amiama	1959	100
3 Rosenblatt	1954, 1976	100
4 Mira Caballos	1997	100
5 Lipschutz	1966	100/500
6 Nabel Pérez	1992	250
7 Moya Pons	1987	378
8 Cordova	1968	500
9 N. D. Cook	1998	500/750
10 Moya Pons	1971	600
11 C. N. de Moya	1976	1,000
12 Zambardino	1978	1,000
13 Denevan	1992	1,000
14 Guerra	1988	1,100
15 Denevan	1976	1,950
16 Watts	1987	3–4,000
17 Borah and Cook	1971	7,975

Sources: Noble D. Cook, *Born to Die: Disease and New World Conquest, 1492–1650*, Cambridge: Cambridge University Press, 1998, p. 23. See also: Esteban Mira Caballos, *El Indio Antillano: Repartimiento, encomienda y esclavitud (1492–1542)*, Seville: Muñoz Moya, 1997; Blas Nabel Pérez, *Las culturas que encontró Colón*, Havana: Abya-Ala, 1992; Casimiro N. De Moya, *Bosquejo histórico del descubrimiento y conquista de la isla de Santo Domingo*, Santo Domingo: Sociedad Domenicana de Bibliofilos, vol. 1, 1976.

Table 7 *Population by category and by groups of districts, Alburquerque repartimiento, 1514*

Areas	Indios de servicio	Naborías	Old	Children	Caciques	Nataynos	Total Indios	Total encomenderos	Ratio of Indios to Caciques	Ratio of Indios to Encomenderos
				Absolute values						
5 western districts	2,861	1,622	148	318	108	0	5,057	164	46.8	30.8
9 eastern districts	12,623	5,502	1,425	1,282	271	28	21,131	574	78.0	36.8
6 mining districts	10,759	4,719	1,299	1,169	233	23	18,202	484	78.1	37.6
8 non-mining districts	4,725	2,405	274	431	146	5	7,986	254	54.7	31.4
TOTAL	15,484	7,124	1,573	1,600	379	28	26,188	738	69.1	35.5
				Percentages					Indios	Encomenderos
5 western districts	56.6	32.1	2.9	6.3	2.1	0.0	100	19.3	22.2	
9 eastern districts	59.7	26.0	6.8	6.1	1.3	0.1	100	80.7	77.8	
6 mining districts	59.1	25.9	7.2	6.4	1.3	0.1	100	69.5	65.6	
8 non-mining districts	59.2	30.1	3.4	5.4	1.8	0.1	100	30.5	34.4	
TOTAL	59.1	27.2	6.0	6.1	1.5	0.1	100	100		

Source: Luis Arranz Márquez, *Repartimientos y encomiendas en la isla Española: El repartimiento de Alburquerque de 1514*, Santo Domingo: Fundación García Arévalo, 1991.

Table 8 *Men, women, and children in the Alburquerque* repartimiento *of 1514*

Province	Men	Women	Children	Male to female ratio	Child to woman ratio
Concepción	949	786	217	0.828	0.276
Puerto Plata	128	108	108	0.843	0.315
Total	1,077	894	894	0.80	0.281

Note: The data refer to the communities of *caciques* where the numbers of men and women were specified and at least one child was counted.

Table 9 *Population of New Spain according to the royal cosmographer López de Velasco, c. 1570*

Population	Diocese of México	Diocese of Tlaxcala-Puebla	Diocese of Oaxaca	Diocese of Michoacán	Captaincy General of Yucatán	Audiencia of Nueva Galicia	TOTAL
Spanish families	2,794	400	420	1,000	300	1,500	6,414
Spanish cities	9	2	4	7	4	8	34
Pueblos de indios	247	200	350	330	200	150	1,477
Indian tributaries	336,000	215,000	96,000	44,000	60,000	20,000	771,000
Confessing Indios	739,000	–	–	–	–	–	
Repartimientos de encomederos	186	66	82	25	130	54	543
Repartimientos of the king	60	60	68	69	–	50	307
Blacks	–	1,000	–	–	–	–	1,000
Monasteries	90	30	–	–	10	–	130

Source: Juan López de Velasco, *Geografía y descripción universal de las Indias*, Madrid: Atlas, 1971.

Table 10 *A table of collapse: the population of central Mexico (1519–1605) according to the estimates of Cook and Borah (in thousands)*

	Meseta	Coastal regions	Central Mexico
1519	15,300	9,900	25,200
1532	11,226	5,645	16,871
1548	4,765	1,535	6,300
1568	2,231	418	2,649
1580	1,631	260	1,891
1595	1,125	247	1,372
1605	852	217	1,069
1519 index = 100			
1519	100.0	100.0	100.0
1532	73.4	57.0	66.9
1548	31.1	15.5	25.0
1568	14.6	4.2	10.5
1580	10.7	2.6	7.5
1595	7.4	2.5	5.4
1605	5.6	2.2	4.2
% annual variation			
1519–32	−2.4	−4.3	−3.1
1532–48	−5.4	−8.1	−6.2
1548–68	−3.8	−6.5	−4.3
1568–80	−2.6	−4.0	−2.8
1580–95	−2.5	−0.3	−2.1
1595–1605	−2.8	−1.3	−2.5
Population distribution, %			
1519	60.7	39.3	100
1532	66.5	33.5	100
1548	75.6	24.4	100
1568	84.2	15.8	100
1580	86.3	13.7	100
1595	82.0	18.0	100
1605	79.7	20.3	100

Central Mexico: states of Veracruz, Oaxaca, Guerrero, Puebla, Tlaxcala, Morelos, México, Hidalgo, DF, Michoacán, Jalisco, Colima, Nayarit, parts of Zacatecas, Querétaro San Luis Potosí. From the Chichimeca frontier in the north to the Tehuantepec Isthmus in the south.

Source: Sheburne F. Cook and Woodrow Borah, *Ensayos sobre la historia de la población: México y el Caribe*, 3 vols, Madrid: Siglo Ventiuno, 1977–80, vol. 1, p. 96.

Table 11 *Tributaries from 121 "encomienda" locales, 1569–71 and 1595–9*

Region	Number of tributaries		Var. %	Classification of variation (%)	Number of localities
	1569–71	1595–9			
				Increase	19
Diocese of Mexico	72,471	38,161	−47.3	Up to −10	5
Diocese of Oaxaca	31,132	18,480	−40.6	−10 to −20	5
Diocese of Michoacán	19,945	12,838	−35.6	−20 to −30	7
Diocese of Tlaxcala	32,822	16,879	−48.6	−30 to −40	18
Province of Panuco	1,925	1,866	−3.1	−40 to −50	21
Zacatula	983	411	−58.2	−50 to −60	12
				−60 to −70	14
TOTAL	159,278	88,635	−44.4	−70 to −80	8
				−80 to −90	10
				−90 and above	2
				TOTAL	121

Source: George Kubler, "Population movements in Mexico, 1520–1600," *Hispanic American Historical Review*, 32, 1942, no. 4, pp. 615–16.

Table 12 *Population and tributaries in Mexico City, 1562*

		San Juan	Santiago Tlatelolco	TOTAL
1	Married men	9,059	5,397	14,456
2	Their wives	9,059	5,396	14,456
3	Widows and widowers	3,912	3,268	7,180
4	Children and young unmarried	19,393	13,000	32,393
5	TOTAL	41,423	27,062	68,485
5/1 = 6	Persons per family	4.57	5.01	4.74
4/1 = 7	Children and young people per couple	2.1	2.4	2.2
3/(2 + 1) × 100 = 8	Widows and widowers per 100 married persons	21.6	30.3	24.8
4/5 × 100 = 9	Children and young people per 100 inhabitants	46.8	48.0	47.3

Source: Elaboration of France V. Scholes, *Los Indios de Nueva España: Sobre el modo de tributar a su Majestad, 1561–64,* Mexico City: Porrúa, 1958. The data are transcribed from the document "Relación de la cuenta y gente que se halló en la parte de Santiago y México, 12 de marzo de 1562" (AGI, Patronato, Legajo 182, ramo 2).

Table 13 *Population, tributaries, and tribute in Perú according to the enumerations of 1561 and 1591*

District	Count of the Audiencia secretary Avendano (1561)						Census of Luis Morales (1591)			Variation (%) between 1561 and 1591	
	Population	Tributaries	Tribute (pesos)	Population per tributary	Tribute per tributary (pesos)	Tribute per inhabitant	Tributaries	Tribute (pesos)	Tribute per tributary (pesos)	Tributaries	Tribute (pesos)
City of Cuzco	267,000	78,000	377,000	3.47	4.88	1.41	74,977	380,835	5.08	-2.6	1.3
City of La Plata	232,800	46,560	178,950	5.00	3.84	0.77	31,671	191,410	6.04	-32.0	7.0
City of La Paz	150,655	30,131	150,600	5.00	5.00	1.00	27,837	177,910	6.39	-7.6	18.1
City of Arequipa	201,830	40,366	93,700	5.00	2.32	0.46	19,794	98,335	4.97	-51.0	4.9
City of Guamanca	112,520	22,504	65,914	5.00	2.93	0.59	26,054	101,435	3.89	15.8	53.9
City of Trujillo	215,000	42,000	63,800	5.12	1.52	0.30	17,597	62,100	3.53	-58.1	-2.7
City of Los Reyes	99,600	25,577	55,600	3.89	2.17	0.56	30,708	119,920	3.91	20.1	115.7
City of Guanuco	118,470	23,506	55,650	5.04	2.37	0.47	18,089	65,180	3.60	-23.0	17.1
City of Quito	240,670	49,134	64,800	5.00	1.35	0.27	24,380	79,235	3.25	-49.3	22.3
City of San Miguel	16,617	6,054	33,800	2.47	5.58	2.03	3,537	12,890	3.64	-41.6	-61.9
City of Puerto Viejo	2,297	1,377	5,452	1.67	3.96	2.37	1,253	4,610	3.68	-9.0	-15.4
City of Guayaquil	4,742	2,280	12,664	2.08	5.55	2.67	2,198	8,515	3.87	-3.6	-32.8
City of Loxa	9,495	3,647	11,004	2.60	3.02	1.16	2,849	9,260	3.25	-21.9	-15.8
City of Los Chachapoyas	58,397	16,309	27,600	3.58	1.69	0.47	7,045	21,390	3.04	-56.8	-22.5
Valley of Xauxa	17,248	5,328	12,242	3.24	2.30	0.71					
City of Zamora	11,222	6,093	19,000	1.84	3.12	1.69	685	3,765	5.50	-88.8	-80.2

Table 13 (continued)

District	Count of the Audiencia secretary Avendano (1561)						Census of Luis Morales (1591)			Variation (%) between 1561 and 1591	
	Population	Tributaries	Tribute (pesos)	Population per tributary	Tribute per tributary (pesos)	Tribute per inhabitant	Tributaries	Tribute (pesos)	Tribute per tributary (pesos)	Tributaries	Tribute (pesos)
City of Jaén (not taxed)							2,654	7,980	3.01		
City of Santiago de los Valles (not taxed)											
Province of Chucuito							17,779	80,000	4.50		
Province of Mayobamba							678	2,290	3.38		
Province of Cuenca							1,472	7,360	5.00		
TOTAL	1,758,563	396,866	1,226,776	4.43	3.09	0.70	311,257	1,434,420	4.61	−25.6	

Sources: For 1561, Juan de Matienzo, *Gobierno del Perú*, ed., Guillermo Lohmann Villena, Paris and Lima: Institut Français d'Études Andines, 1967; for 1591, "Relación de los Indios tributarios que hay al presente en estos reynos de la provincia del Perú, fecha por mandado el Señor Marqués de Cañete, la cual se hizo por Luis Morales de Figueroa, por el libro de las tasas de la visita general y por las revisitas que después se han hecho . . . fecha en el Pardo, a 1° de Noviembre de 1591," CDI, 6.

Note: The percentage variation of tributaries between 1561 and 1591 is calculated using the total districts from both enumerations.

Table 14 *Population of Chucuito, characteristics and significant features*

	Category	Males	Females	TOTAL
1	Children, 0–10	9,788	*9,789*	19,577
2	Children and adolescents, 11–16	1,827	*1,828*	3,655
3	Married men, 17–50, and their wives	11,806	*11,806*	23,612
4	Married men, 50+, and their wives	822	*822*	1,644
5	Widowers and unmarried men in their own homes, 17–50	1,252	–	1,252
6	Unmarried men, 17–50, living with their parents	1,030	–	1,030
7	Widowers and unmarried men, 50+	315	–	315
8	Widows and unmarried women, 17–45, in their own homes	–	5,642	5,642
9	Widows and unmarried women, 50+, in their own homes	–	3,506	3,506
10	Young unmarried women, 17+ living with their parents	–	*1,287*	1,287
11	Deformed, handicapped, blind	*55*	*55*	110
12	TOTAL POPULATION	26,945	34,735	61,630
13	TOTAL TRIBUTARIES	–	–	15,304
	Married men and women (17–45 or 17–50) per 100 inhabitants	43.8	34.0	38.30
	% population 0–16	43.1	33.4	37.70
	% old people (50+, 45+)	4.2	12.5	8.90
	Children (0–10) per 100 married people (17–50)	–		1.66
	Children (0–16) per 100 married people (17–50)	–		1.97
	Children (0–10) per 100 tributaries	–		1.28
	Children (0–16) per 100 tributaries	–		1.52
	Unmarried men per 100 married men	19.3		
	Males per 100 females	–		77.60

3/12 × 100
(1+2)/12 × 100
(4+7)/12; (4+9)/12
1/3 × 100
(1+2)/3 × 100
1/13 × 100
(1+2)/13 × 100
(5+6)/3 × 100

Source: Waldemar Espinoza Soriano, ed., *Visita hecha a la provincia de Chucuito por Garci Diez de San Miguel en el año 1567*, Lima: Ediciones Casa de la Cultura del Perú, 1964.

Note: The values in italics are derived by attributing half of the total to males and half to females.

Table 15 *Population and tributaries in Peru, estimates for 1570 and 1600*

Geographic area	Population			Tributaries			Persons per tributary	
	1570	1600	Annual % variation	1570	1600	Annual % variation	1570	1600
Northern coast	80,123	40,449	-2.28	20,398	9,170	-2.66	3.93	4.41
Central coast	128,820	67,710	-2.14	25,189	14,331	-1.88	5.11	4.72
Southern coast	36,587	15,394	-2.89	8,711	3,925	-2.66	4.20	3.92
Northern sierra	209,057	146,274	-1.19	42,677	26,002	-1.65	4.90	5.63
Central sierra	240,604	159,071	-1.38	41,994	29,802	-1.14	5.73	5.34
Southern sierra	595,528	423,104	-1.14	121,584	88,611	-1.05	4.90	4.77
Peru (present-day borders)	1,290,680	851,994	-1.38	260,544	171,834	-1.39	4.95	4.96

Source: Noble D. Cook, *Demographic Collapse: Indian Peru, 1520–1620*, Cambridge: Cambridge University Press, 1981, pp. 94, 118.

Table 16 *Population and its structure, c. 1573 and 1602, for 146 "encomiendas" in twenty-four districts*

	Tributaries	Muchachos	Viejos	Mujeres	Total population
Visita of Toledo (1573)	90,422	99,612	24,733	251,795	466,748
Vázquez de Espinosa (1602)	66,596	66,967	25,072	166,260	324,895
1602 (1573 = 100)	73.6	67.2	101.4	66.0	69.6
% annual variation	-1.06	-1.73	0.05	-1.43	-1.25

Indices and ratios

	Persons per tributary	Men per 100 women	Muchachos per tributary	Muchachos/ -as per woman over 18	Viejos per 100 men	Muchachos per 100 men	Men over 18 per 100 women over 18
Visita of Toledo (1573)	5.16	85.4	1.10	1.31	11.5	46.3	75.7
Vázquez de Espinosa (1602)	4.88	95.4	1.01	1.35	15.8	42.2	92.3

Source: Noble D. Cook, "Population Data for Indian Peru," *Hispanic American Historical Review*, 62, 1982, no. 1, pp. 73–120.

Table 17 *Thirty missions: distribution of the population, 1643–4, 1702, 1732, 1767, 1802*

Region	1643–4	1702	1732	1767	1802
			Population		
Paraná, right bank	6,903	20,389	33,808	23,297	8,709
Paraná, left bank	5,366	13,145	23,841	17,753	7,174
Uruguay, right bank	23,471	35,721	44,190	27,508	16,050
Uruguay, left bank	0	20,046	39,343	20,306	12,026
Paraná	12,269	33,534	57,649	41,050	15,883
Uruguay	23,471	55,767	83,533	47,814	28,076
Mesopotamia	28,837	48,866	68,031	45,261	23,224
TOTAL	35,740	89,301	141,182	88,864	43,959
			Distribution %		
Paraná, right bank	19.3	22.8	23.9	26.2	19.8
Paraná, left bank	15.0	14.7	16.9	20.0	16.3
Uruguay, right bank	65.7	40.0	31.3	31.0	36.5
Uruguay, left bank	0.0	22.4	27.9	22.9	27.4
Paraná	34.3	37.6	40.8	46.2	36.1
Uruguay	65.7	62.4	59.2	53.8	63.9
Mesopotamia	80.7	54.7	48.2	50.9	52.8
TOTAL	100.0	100.0	100.0	100.0	100.0

Source: Massimo Livi Bacci and Ernesto J. A. Maeder, "Misiones Paraquariae: La demografia di un esperimento," *Popolazione e Storia,* 4, 2004, no. 2.
Note: The totals by geographical area are calculated keeping in mind that, for 1643–4, San Nicolas and San Miguel were on the right bank of the Uruguay (rather than on the left, as they were afterward) and that Corpus was on the right bank of the Paraná (rather than on the left). See Guillermo Furlong, *Misiones y sus pueblos de Guaranies,* Buenos Aires: Ediciones Theoria, 1962, pp. 140–1, 148.

Table 18 *Fertility, mortality, and natural increase, 1690–1767 (per 1,000 inhabitants)*

Period	Number of years in the period with useable data	Fertility	Mortality	Natural increase
		Average		
1690–1767	50	59.1	56.8	2.3
1690–1732	15	64.1	45.1	19
1733–67	35	56.9	61.4	−4.5
1690–9	4	61.6	40.4	21.2
1700–9	4	72.3	47.0	25.2
1710–19	1	59.3	91.9	−32.6
1720–9	3	62.3	37.9	24.4
1730–9	10	48.8	85.1	−36.2
1740–9	10	69.5	49.8	19.7
1750–9	10	57.6	43.1	14.5
1760–7	8	51.6	63.0	−11.4
		Median		
1690–1767	50	61.3	44.2	19.1
1690–1732	15	63.2	41.2	24.6
1733–67	35	55.4	44.3	10.5
1690–9	4	62.4	38.6	24.5
1700–9	4	74.2	46.1	26.2
1710–19	1	59.3	91.9	−32.6
1720–9	3	62.9	36.7	22.3
1730–9	10	46.9	63.6	−19.7
1740–9	10	69.8	43.7	25.8
1750–9	10	60.4	42.0	20.5
1760–7	8	51.8	46.8	4.4

Source: Livi Bacci and Maeder, "Misiones Paraquariae."

Table 19 *Mortality rates (per 1,000 inhabitants) at the missions in crisis years*

Missions	1695	1719	1733	1738–39	1749	1764–65
At the missions	197.9	88.3	157.7	169.5	84.7	116.7
Median value	231.1	41.5	124.0	141.7	71.2	98.9
			Missions according to mortality level			
Normal mortality, <50	1	17	0	11	7	2
High mortality, 50–100	3	7	9	3	16	14
Crisis mortality, 100–250	4	2	18	5	6	10
Catastrophic mortality, >250	5	2	3	11	1	4
Total missions considered	13	28	30	30	30	30

Source: Mission data collected and graciously made available by Ernesto J. A. Maeder.

Note: For 1695, only Paraná missions.

Table 20 Measures of nuptiality, mortality, and fertility, 1690–1767

Period	Number of years for which there is useable data* (1)	Mortality (2)	Parvulos deaths per 100 deaths (3)	Life expectancy at birth e(0) (4)	Nuptiality (5)	Fertility (6)	Baptisms per wedding (7)	Baptisms per 1,000 married women (8)	Total fertility rate (TFR) (9)
Average 1690–1767	50	56.8	68.1	23.3	14.6	59.1	4.29	260.8	7.7
Median 1690–1767	50	44.2	68.8	24.5	13.3	61.3	4.32	264.3	7.7
Average to 1732	15	45.1	69.1	26.0	11.8	64.1	4.81	277.2	8.0
Average 1733–67	35	61.4	67.8	22.2	15.6	56.9	4.10	253.8	7.6
Median to 1732	15	41.2	66.2	27.1	12.5	63.2	4.71	270.4	7.9
Median 1733–67	35	44.3	68.9	24.3	13.9	55.4	4.10	247.0	7.5
Average 1690–9	4	40.4	73.6	27.7	7.8	61.6	3.91	254.3	7.4
1700–9	4	47.0	66.2	23.9	14.0	72.3	4.97	295.9	8.4
1710–19	1	91.9		13.2	20.3	59.3	2.92	265.8	7.8
1720–9	3	37.9	70.4	28.9	11.0	62.3	5.73	285.1	8.4
1730–9	10	85.1	66.0	19.7	16.5	48.8	3.30	231.0	6.6
1740–9	10	49.8	72.2	22.8	16.7	69.5	4.64	298.1	9.1
1750–9	10	43.1	69.4	26.2	11.3	57.6	5.24	256.9	7.8
1760–7	7	63.0	58.0	21.4	17.8	51.6	3.22	232.4	6.9

* Relative to columns 2, 4, 5, 6, and 8; for column 3 the useable years for the entire period are 30; for column 9 they are 49.

Source: Livi Bacci and Maeder, "Misiones Paraquariae."

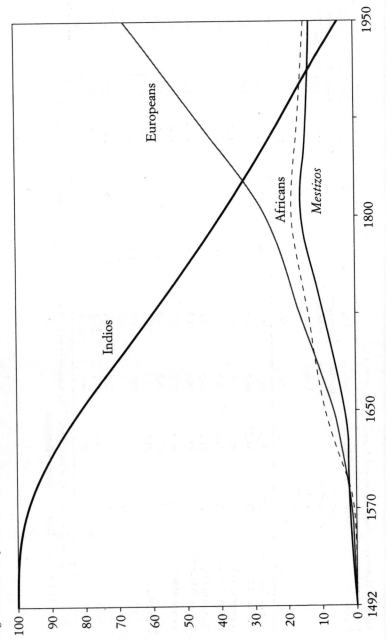

Fig. 1 *Indios, Europeans, Africans, and mestizos in America, 1500–90 (% of total population)*

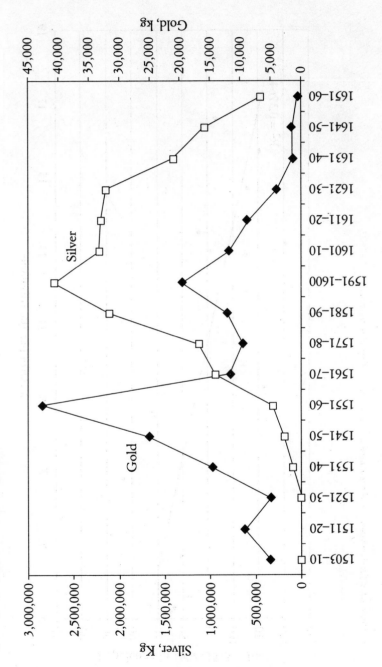

Fig. 2 Importation of precious metals in Spain, 1503–1660

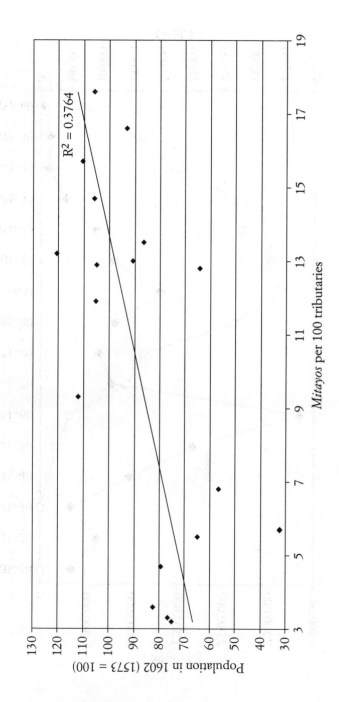

Fig. 3 Mitayos per 100 tributaries and population fluctuation in the Peruvian highlands, 1573–1602

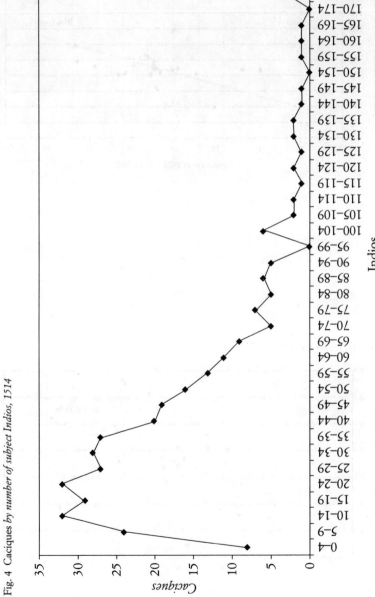

Fig. 4 Caciques by number of subject Indios, 1514

Fig. 5a *Population and tributaries, 1573 and 1602*

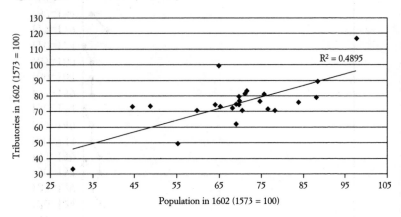

Fig. 5b *Persons per tributary, 1573 and 1602*

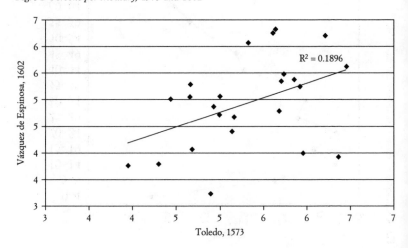

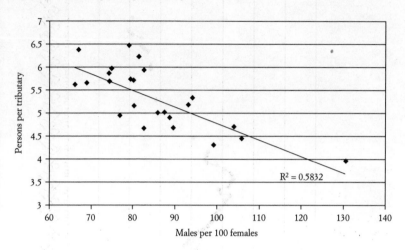

Fig. 5c *Sex ratio and persons per tributary, 1573*

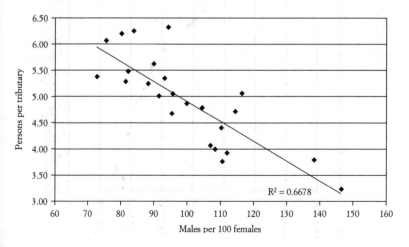

Fig. 5d *Sex ratio and persons per tributary, 1602*

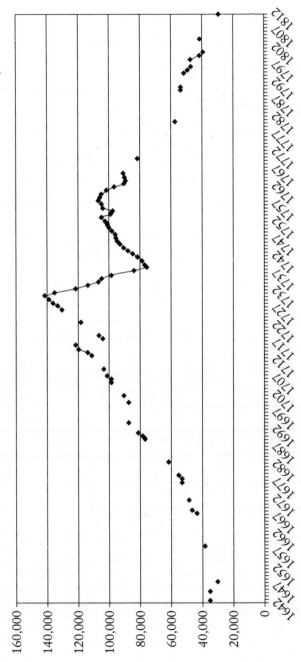

Fig. 6 *Population of the thirty missions, seventeenth to nineteenth centuries*

Notes

Abbreviations

AGI
Archivio General de Indias, Seville

CDI
Colección de documentos ineditos relativos al descubrimiento, conquista y colonización de las posesiones españolas en América y Oceania, ed. Joaquín F. Pacheco, Francisco de Cárdenas, and Luis Torres de Mendoza, 42 vols, Madrid: Real Academia de Historia, 1964–84.

CDU
Colección de documentos ineditos relativos al descubrimiento, conquista y organización de las antiguas posesiones españolas de ultramar, 2nd series, 25 vols, Madrid: Real Academia de Historia, 1885–1932.

CDD
Colección documental del descubrimiento (1470–1506), ed. Juan Pérez de Tutela, 3 vols, Madrid: Real Academia de Historia, 1994.

RCC
Reales cédulas y correspondencia de gobernadores de Santo Domingo: Colección de J. Marino Inchausteguei, 5 vols, Madrid: Colección Histórico-documental trujilloniana, vol. 1: *1516–41*, 1958.

Chapter 1 The demographic catastrophe of the Indios

1 Luigi Luca Cavalli-Sforza, Paolo Menozzi and Alberto Piazza, *The History and Geography of Human Genes*, Princeton, NJ: Princeton University Press, 1994 (abridged edn 1996).
2 Samuel E. Morison, *Admiral of the Ocean Sea: A Life of Christopher Columbus*, New York: MJF Books, 1970, p. 148.
3 Ibid., pp. 165, 226.
4 RCC, p. 133.
5 "High counter" and "low counter" were coined by Henige; see David Henige, *Numbers from Nowhere: The American Indian Contact Population Debate*, Norman: University of Oklahoma Press, 1998.
6 William M. Denevan, ed., *The Native Population of the Americas in 1492*, 2nd edn, Madison: University of Wisconsin Press, 1992, p. 3.
7 Ibid., p. xxviii.
8 Charles Darwin, *The Origin of Species* [1859], New York: Random House, 1960, p. 62.
9 Adam Smith, *The Wealth of Nations* [1776], London: J. M. Dent, 1964, vol. 1, pp. 62–3.
10 Thomas R. Malthus, *An Essay on the Principle of Population* [1798], Harmondsworth: Penguin, 1979, p. 105.
11 Bartolomé de Las Casas, *A Short Account of the Destruction of the Indies*, London: Penguin, 1992, pp. 12–13.
12 Gonzalo Fernández de Oviedo, *Historia general y natural de las Indias*, 5 vols, Madrid: Atlas, 1992, vol. 1, p. 67.
13 Ibid.
14 Andrea João Antonil, *Cultura e opulencia do Brasil por sus drogas e minas*, São Paulo: Companhia Editora Nacional, 1922, pp. 160–1.
15 Bartolomé de Las Casas, *Historia de las Indias*, 2nd edn, 2 vols, Mexico City, Fondo de Cultura Económica, 1995, vol. 2, p. 226; partial Eng. trans. (not incl. this passage), *History of the Indies*, trans. Andrée Collard, New York: Harper & Row, 1971.
16 Translator's note: Throughout the text, Perú refers to greater Perú, namely the territory of the Spanish viceroyalty, and Peru to the present-day borders. Similarly, Mexico refers more or less to present-day Mexico (or Meso-America) and México to the valley or city of México.
17 Hubert Charbonneau et al., *Naissance d'une population: Les Français établis au Canada au XVIIe siècle*, Montreal: Presses de l'Université de Montréal, 1977.
18 Philip D. Curtin, *The Atlantic Slave Trade: A Census*, Madison, University of Wisconsin Press, 1969.
19 Lorena S. Walsh, "The African American Population of the Colonial United States," in Michael H. Haines and Richard H. Steckel, eds, *A Population History of North America*, Cambridge: Cambridge University Press, 2000, pp. 203–4; Richard H. Steckel, "The African American Population of the United States," ibid., pp. 442–3.
20 Walsh, "The African American Population," p. 206.
21 Stanley L. Engerman, "A Population History of the Caribbean," in Haines and Steckel, *A Population History*, p. 509.
22 Ibid., pp. 506–9.

23 Stanley J. Stein, *Vassouras: A Brazilian Coffee County, 1850–1900*, Cambridge, MA: Harvard University Press, 1957; Emilia Viotti da Costa, *Da senzala à colonia*, São Paulo: Livraria Cienças Humanas, 1982; Stuart B. Schwartz, "A populaçao escrava na Bahia," in Iraci del Nero da Costa, ed., *Brasil: História econômica e demografica*, São Paulo, IPE/USP, 1986.

24 Thomas W. Merrick and Douglas H. Graham, *Population and Economic Development in Brazil, 1800 to the Present*, Baltimore: Johns Hopkins University Press, 1979, p. 53.

25 Schwartz, "A populaçao," p. 64.

26 Mary G. Karasch, *Slave Life in Rio de Janeiro 1808–1850*, Princeton, NJ: Princeton University Press, 1979, pp. 32–4.

27 Stuart B. Schwartz, *Sugar Plantations in the Formation of the Brazilian Society: Bahia, 1550–1835*, Cambridge: Cambridge University Press, 1985; Katia M. de Quierós Mattoso, *To Be Slave in Brazil 1550–1888*, New Brunswick, NJ: Rutgers University Press, 1986.

28 Stuart B. Schwartz, *Segredos internos: Engenhos e escravos na sociedade colonial, 1550–85*, São Paulo: C.ia de Letras, 1988, pp. 41–2.

29 Charles R. Boxer, *The Golden Age of Brazil, 1695–1750*, Berkeley and Los Angeles, University of California Press, 1964.

30 Cited in Jacob Gorender, *O escravismo colonial*, São Paulo: Atica, 1978, p. 342.

31 Las Casas, *Historia de las Indias*, vol. 1, p. 357.

32 Ángel Rosenblat, *La población indígena y el mestizaje en América*, Buenos Aires: Editorial Nova, 1954, vol. 2, p. 24.

33 Ibid.

34 Luis Arranz Márquez, *Repartimientos y encomiendas en la isla Española: El repartimiento de Alburquerque de 1514*, Santo Domingo: Fundación García Arévalo, 1991, p. 223.

35 Richard Konetzke, "El mestizaje y su importancia en el desarrollo de la poblaçión hispano-americana durante la época colonial," *Revista de Indias*, 7, 1946, no. 24, p. 236.

36 Rosenblat, *La población*, vol. 2, p. 137.

37 Gonzalo Aguirre Beltrán, *La población negra de México*, 3rd edn, Mexico City, Fondo de Cultura Económica, 1989, p. 269.

Chapter 2 Different witnesses and a common analysis of the catastrophe

1 The unpublished work of Alonso de Castro is cited by Juan Bautista Muñoz in Roberto Marte, ed., *Santo Domingo en los manuscritos de Juan Bautista Muñoz*, Santo Domingo: Fundación García Arévalo, 1981, p. 397; Gonzalo Fernández de Oviedo, *Historia general y natural de las Indias*, 5 vols, Madrid: Atlas, 1992, vol. 1, p. 66; partial Eng. trans., Jesús Carillo, ed., *Oviedo on Columbus*, Turnhout: Brepols, 2000; Juan López de Velasco, *Geografía y descripción universal de las Indias*, Madrid: Atlas, 1971, vol. 248, p. 99.

2 Sherburne F. Cook and Woodrow Borah, "The Indian Population of Central Mexico, 1531–1610," *Ibero-America*, 1960, no. 44, p. 48.

3 Noble D. Cook, *Demographic Collapse: Indian Peru, 1520–1620*, Cambridge: Cambridge University Press, 1981, p. 94.

4 See chapter 1, note 16.

5 López de Velasco, *Geografía*.

6 Antonio Vázquez de Espinosa, *Compendio y descripción de las Indias occidentales*, Madrid: Atlas, 1969; Bartolomé Bennassar, *La América española y la América portuguesa*, Madrid: Akal, 1996, pp. 194–5.

7 Fray Toribio Motolinia, *Historia de los Indios de la Nueva España*, Mexico City: Porrúa, 1973; information about Motolinia is taken from Edmundo O'Gorman's preface. Eng. trans., Francis Borgia Steck, ed. and trans., *Motolinia's History of the Indians of New Spain*, Washington, DC: Academy of American Franciscan History, 1951; the ten plagues are described in chapter 1 and the quotations taken from pp. 87–93 of the translation.

8 Motolinia, *Historia de los Indios*: "Carta de Fray Toribio de Motolinia al Emperador Carlos V," pp. 207–8.

9 The bibliography on Las Casas is vast. See, among others, Alvaro Huerga, "Vida y Obras," in Fray Bartolomé de Las Casas, *Obras completas*, Madrid: Alianza Editorial, 1998, vol. 1; Lewis Hanke, "Bartolomé de Las Casas historiador," in Bartolomé de Las Casas, *Historia de las Indias*, 2nd edn, 2 vols, Mexico City, Fondo de Cultura Económica, 1995, vol. 1.

10 Las Casas, *Historia de las Indias*, vol. 2, pp. 441–2; partial Eng. trans., *History of the Indies*, trans. Andrée Collard, New York: Harper & Row, 1971, pp. 183–4.

11 Academia de la Historia, Colección Muñoz, vol. 52, fo. 38.

12 Bartolomé de Las Casas, *A Short Account of the Destruction of the Indies*, London: Penguin, 1992.

13 Ibid., p. 12.

14 Ibid., pp. 23–4.

15 Oviedo, *Historia general*, pp. 66–7.

16 Pietro Martire d'Anghiera, *Mondo nuovo*, Milan: Alpes, 1930, p. 368.

17 José de Acosta, *Historia natural y moral de las Indias*, Madrid: Historia 16, 1986, pp. 198–9.

18 Ibid., p. 199.

19 Garcilaso de la Vega, *Royal Commentaries of the Incas, and General History of Peru*, trans. Harold V. Livermore, 2 vols, Austin: University of Texas Press, 1966, vol. 1, pp. 296–7.

20 Ibid., p. 572.

21 Ibid., p. 178.

22 Manuel Ballesteros, "Introducción", in Pedro Cieza de León, *La crónica del Perú*, Madrid: Historia 16, 1984; Eng. trans. of pt 3: *The Discovery and Conquest of Peru: Chronicles of the New World Encounter*, ed. and trans. Alexandra Parma Cook and Noble David Cook, Durham, NC: Duke University Press, 1998.

23 Cieza de León, *La crónica*, pp. 75, 361.

24 Ibid., p. 215.

25 Ibid., p. 120.

26 Ibid., p. 283.

27 Huamán Poma, *Letter to a King: A Peruvian Chief's Account of Life under the Incas and under Spanish Rule*, ed. Christopher Dilke, New York: E. P. Dutton, 1978.

28 Ibid., p. 206.

29 Ibid., p. 208.

30 Ibid., p. 209.

31 We could of course add more. Two works on Perú that pursue this line in an original way are Nathan Wachtel, *The Vision of the Vanquished: The Spanish Conquest of Peru through Indian eyes, 1530–1570*, New York: Barnes & Noble, 1977; and Carlos Sempat Assadourian, *Transiciones hacia el sistema colonial andino*, Mexico City, Colegio de México y Instituto de Estudios Peruanos, 1994.

32 *Parecer de los religiosos de Santo Domingo: Fray Pedro de Córdoba y ocho Domonicos*, CDI, 1869, vol. 1, 11, pp. 211–15.

33 For more details on the model, see Massimo Livi Bacci, "Las multiples causas de la catástrofe: consideraciones teóricas y empíricas," *Revista de Indias*, 63, 2003, no. 227.

34 Las Casas, *Historia de las Indias*, vol. 1, p. 398.

35 Miguel León Portilla, *El Reverso de la Conquista: Relaciones aztecas, mayas e incas*, Mexico City: Editorial Joaquin Mortiz, 1964, 1970.

Chapter 3 The sins of smallpox and other crowd diseases

1 The letter is signed by two of the three Hieronymite brothers who arrived in 1517, Fray Luis de Figueroa and Fray Alonso de Santo Domingo. The third, Fray Bernardino de Manzanedo, returned to Spain to present the sad case of Hispaniola to the king. *Los Padres Jerónimos, Gobernadores de las Indias, al Rey Don Carlos*, AGI, Patronato Real, 174/11. See also RCC, pp. 133–4.

2 The best historical treatment of this argument is Alfred J. Crosby, *The Columbian Exchange: Biological and Cultural Consequences of 1492*, Westport, CT: Greenwood Press, 1972.

3 Miguel León Portilla, *El Reverso de la Conquista: Relaciones aztecas, mayas e incas*, Mexico City: Editorial Joaquin Mortiz, 1964, 1970.

4 Ann L. W. Stodder and Debra L. Martin, "Health and Disease in the Southwest before and after Spanish Conquest," in John W. Verano and Douglas H. Ubelaker, eds, *Disease and Demography in the Americas*, Washington, DC: Smithsonian Institution, 1992.

5 Arthur C. Aufderheide, "Summary on Disease before and after Contact," in Verano and Ubelaker, *Disease and Demography*, p. 166.

6 Massimo Livi Bacci and Ernesto J. A. Maeder, "Misiones Paraquariae: La demografia di un esperimento," *Popolazione e Storia*, 4, 2004, no. 2.

7 Anonymous, *Cantos y crónicas del México antiguo*, ed. Miguel León-Portilla, Madrid: Dastin, 2002, p. 243. See also Carlos T. Viesca, "Hambruna y epidemia en Anáhuac (1450–54) en la época de Moctezuma Ilhuicamina," in Elsa Malvido and Enrique Florescano, eds, *Ensayos sobre la historia de las epidemias en México*, Mexico City: Instituto Mexicano del Seguro Social, 1982, vol. 1, pp. 157–65.

8 Diego de Landa, *Yucatan before and after the Conquest*, New York: Dover Publications, 1978, pp. 18–19.

9 In the lines that follow I am synthesizing that which has been well described in Jared Diamond, *Guns, Germs, and Steel*, New York: Norton, 1998, pp. 195–214.

10 We imagine that many diseases developed in Eurasia after the arrival on the American continent of the first humans, and so those diseases were not brought along by the first migrants; or in any case that the migration process

involved the selection of healthy individuals. See Francis L. Black, "Infectious Diseases and Evolution of Human Populations: The Example of South American Forest Tribes," in Alan C. Swedlund and George J. Armelagos, eds, *Diseases in Populations in Transition*, New York: Bergin & Harvey, 1990.

11 On smallpox and its epidemiology, see the classic by Cecil W. Dixon, *Smallpox*, London: Churchill, 1962.

12 The fact that Mexico City suffered an epidemic in 1779 with more than 9,000 deaths (10 percent of the population) suggests that smallpox did not survive there in an endemic state – and this for the most populous city in the Americas. See Alexander von Humboldt, *Essai politique sur le royaume de la Nouvelle-Espagne*, Paris: Antoine-Augustin Renouard, 1825–7; abridged Eng. trans., *Political Essay on the Kingdom of New Spain*, New York: Knopf, 1972.

13 Ibid.; Livi Bacci and Maeder, "Misiones Paraquariae."

14 Dixon, *Smallpox*, pp. 317–18: "Racial predisposition probably does not exist as such, but a population that has experienced the disease for some generations, even if unvaccinated, appears to have a lower mortality than one that has never experienced it before." This argument, however, is a controversial one. According to Francis L. Black, "There is no evidence of any major gap in the immune defenses of the Amerindians, but some evidence of qualitative differences in the strength of responses to specific antigens"; see Black, "Infectious Diseases," p. 72. There can, nonetheless, be a sort of social adaptation to the disease that reduces its lethality – as observed by Dixon – since the sick cease to be abandoned out of panic or else, because symptoms can be recognized, they are isolated, or again because of the application of empirical remedies and other reasons.

15 Francis Borgia Steck, ed. and trans., *Motolinia's History of the Indians of New Spain*, Washington, DC: Academy of American Franciscan History, 1951, p. 88.

16 On the question of crises and subsequent rebound, see Massimo Livi Bacci, "Mortality Crises in Historical Perspective: The European Experience," in Giovanni Andrea Cornia and Renato Paniccià, eds, *The Mortality Crisis in Transitional Economies*, New York: Oxford University Press, 2000.

17 Thomas M. Whitmore, *Disease and Death in Early Colonial Mexico: Simulating Amerindian Depopulation*, Boulder, CO: Westview Press, 1992. In his study, Whitmore employs a complex and ingenious model to interpret the depopulation of Mexico in the sixteenth century. The combination and manipulation of the model's parameters – almost all hypothetical and almost all plausible – produce a wide range of results that can be adapted to the theories of both the high counters and the low counters regarding population size at the moment of contact and subsequent decline.

18 Fray Bernardino de Sahagún, *Historia general de las cosas de Nueva España*, Mexico City: Porrúa, 1977, vol. 4, pp. 136–7.

19 The passage is taken from Francisco López de Gómara, *La Conquista de México*, Madrid: Dastin, 2001, p. 233; see also Bernal Díaz del Castillo, *Historia verdadera de la Conquista de Nueva España*, 3 vols, Mexico City, Porrúa, 1976, p. 244.

20 Robert McCaa, "Spanish and Nahuatl Views on Smallpox and Demographic Catastrophe in Mexico," *Journal of Interdisciplinary History*, 25, 1995, pp. 397–431.

21 Bernardino Vázquez de Tapia, "Relación de méritos y servicios del Conquistador Bernardino Vázquez de Tapia, vecino y regidor de esta gran

ciudad de Tenuxtitlan," in Germán Vázquez Chamorro, ed., *La Conquista de Tenochtitlan*, Madrid: Historia 16, 2002, p. 141.

22 De Landa, *Yucatan*, p. 19.
23 Noble D. Cook, *Born to Die: Disease and New World Conquest, 1492–1650*, Cambridge: Cambridge University Press, 1998, pp. 70–1.
24 Linda A. Newson, *The Cost of Conquest*, Boulder, CO: Westview Press, 1986, p. 128.
25 The theory of a single smallpox pandemic that crossed the Americas like a steam roller was proposed and strongly defended by Henry F. Dobyns, "Estimating Aboriginal Populations: An Appraisal of Techniques with a New Hemisphere Estimate," *Current Anthropology*, 7, 1966, pp. 395–449. It has subsequently been picked up by a number of other authors, including, in a tentative way, Crosby, *The Columbian Exchange*, p. 39, and, with much more conviction, Cook, *Born to Die*.
26 Pedro Cieza de León, *El señorio de los Incas*, Madrid: Historia 16, 1984, p. 194.
27 Cook, *Born to Die*, pp. 60–85.
28 Jean-Noel Biraben, "La population de l'Amérique pre-colombienne: Essai sur les méthodes," paper presented at the conference "The Peopling of the Americas," Veracruz, 1992. See also Dixon, *Smallpox*, p. 313, regarding the relationships between the spread of smallpox and climate.
29 Massimo Livi Bacci, "500 Anos de demografia brasileira: uma resenha," *Revista Brasileira de Estudos de Populaçao*, 19, 2002, no. 1, p. 144.
30 Daniel T. Reff, "Old World Diseases and their Consequences in 16th Century New Spain," paper presented at the conference "The Peopling of the Americas," Veracruz, 1992.
31 Daniel T. Reff, "Contact Shock in Northwestern New Spain," in Verano and Ubelaker, *Disease and Demography*, pp. 265–76.
32 Cook, *Born to Die*, p. 43.
33 Crosby, *The Columbian Exchange*, p. 46.
34 On the epidemiology of smallpox, measles, and other communicable diseases, see the classic by Roy M. Anderson and Robert M. May, "Population Biology of Infectious Diseases," pt I, *Nature*, vol. 280, August 2, 1979, pp. 361–7; pt II, vol. 280, August 9, 1979, pp. 455–61.
35 Huguette Chaunu and Pierre Chaunu, *Séville et l'Atlantique*, Paris: SEVPEN, 1956, vol. 6/2, p. 496. On length of voyage, see ibid., p. 320.
36 Magnus Mörner, "La emigración española al Nuevo Mundo antes del 1810: Un informe del estado de la investigación," *Anuario de Estudios Americanos*, 32, 1975.
37 Massimo Livi Bacci, *The Population of Europe*, Oxford: Blackwell, 2000, pp. 87–8.
38 *Censo de Castilla de 1591*, vol. 1, Instituto Nacional de Estadistica, 1984.
39 Lorenzo Del Panta, *Le epidemie nella storia demografica italiana*, Turin: Loescher, 1980, pp. 63–73.
40 Daniel E. Shea, "A Defense of Small Population Estimates for the Central Andes in 1520," in William M. Denevan, ed., *The Native Population of the Americas in 1492*, 2nd edn, Madison: University of Wisconsin Press, 1992, p. 161.
41 John Hemming, *The Conquest of the Incas*, New York: Harcourt, Brace, Jovanovich, 1970, pp. 393–7.

42 Guillermo Furlong, *José Cardiel, S.J. y su Carta-Relación* [1747], Buenos Aires: Libreria del Plata, 1953, p. 188.
43 Antonio Sepp, *Il sacro esperimento del Paraguay*, Verona: Edizione della Cassa di Risparmio di Verona, 1990, p. 179.
44 Hans Zinnser, *Rats, Lice and History*, Boston: Little, Brown, 1935, ch. 14.

Chapter 4 Deeds and misdeeds of gold and silver

 1 Bartolomé de Las Casas, *Historia de las Indias*, 2nd edn, 2 vols, Mexico City: Fondo de Cultura Económica, 1995, vol. 1, p. 258. On the attempt to tax the Taíno, see Luis Arranz Márquez, *Repartimientos y encomiendas en la isla Española: El repartimiento de Alburquerque de 1514*, Santo Domingo: Fundación García Arévalo, 1991, pp. 30–8, 60–4. The bell would have contained about 3 to 4 pesos of gold (12.5 to 16.7 grams).
 2 Pierre Vilar, *A History of Gold and Money, 1450–1920*, London: NLB, 1976, p. 126, where the phrase is erroneously attributed to Brother Domingo de Santo Tomás.
 3 David A. Brading and Henry E. Cross, "Colonial Silver Mining: Mexico and Peru," *Hispanic American Historical Review*, 52, 1972, no. 4, p. 568.
 4 Earl Hamilton, *American Treasure and the Price Revolution in Spain, 1501–1650*, Cambridge, MA: Harvard University Press, 1934, table 4.
 5 Vilar, *History of Gold*, p. 110.
 6 Ibid., p. 115.
 7 For estimates of gold productivity in various periods and regions of the Americas, see Massimo Livi Bacci, "Return to Hispaniola: Reassessing a Demographic Catastrophe," *Hispanic American Historical Review*, 83, 2003, no. 1, pp. 15–20.
 8 Zemira Díaz López, *Oro, sociedad, economía: El sistema colonial en la Gobernación de Popayán, 1533–1733*, Santa Fé de Bogotá: Banco de la República, 1994, p. 178.
 9 Ibid., p. 183.
10 Gonzalo Fernández de Oviedo, *Historia general y natural de las Indias*, 5 vols, Madrid: Atlas, 1992, vol. 1, pp. 159–61; Bartolomé de Las Casas, *Apologética historia sumaria*, 3 vols, Madrid: Alianza Editorial, 1992, vol. 1, pp. 313–15, 319–20.
11 Oviedo, *Historia general*, p. 162.
12 Ibid.
13 Las Casas, *Historia de las Indias*, vol. 2, pp. 336–7.
14 "Carta que escribieron los Padres de la Orden de Santo Domingo a Mosior de Xèvres, 4 de Juni de 1516," in Roberto Marte, ed., *Santo Domingo en los manuscritos de Juan Bautista Muñoz*, Santo Domingo: Fundación García Arévalo, 1980, p. 253.
15 See, in order, CDI, 10, pp. 109ff.; CDI, 1, p. 309; CDI, 1, p. 36.
16 "Carta que escribió el licenciado Alonso de Zuazo al ministro flamengo Xevres en 22 de Enero de 1518," in Emilio Rodríguez Demorizi, *Los Dominicos y las encomiendas de indios en la isla Española*, Santo Domingo: Edición del Caribe, 1971, p. 253.
17 Las Casas, *Historia de las Indias*, vol. 2, p. 356.

18 The gold prospectors were called *faisquieros*, after *faisca*, the glimmer of gold seen in the water of the streams. A classic on the gold rush in Brazil is Charles R. Boxer, *The Golden Age of Brazil, 1695–1750*, Berkeley: University of California Press, 1964. See also Universitade Federal de Ouro Preto, *Governo do estado de Minas Gerais*, Belo Horizonte, 1981.

19 Luis Capoche, *Relación general de la Villa Imperial de Potosí*, Madrid: Atlas, 1959, p. 77.

20 Cited in Lewis Hanke, "Estudio Preliminar," in Capoche, *Relación general*, p. 25.

21 Antonio de la Calancha, *Crónica moralizadora*, cited in Ricardo Rodríguez Molas, *Mitayos, ingenios y proprietarios en Potosí, 1633*, Buenos Aires: Instituto de Estudios Antropológicos, 1986, p. 181.

22 Capoche, *Relación general*, p. 75.

23 Antonio Vázquez de Espinosa, *Compendio y descripción de las Indias occidentales*, Madrid: Atlas, 1969, p. 411.

24 Ibid.

25 Gwendolyn B. Cobb, "Supply and Transportation for the Potosí Mines, 1545–1640," *Hispanic American Historical Review*, 29, 1949, no. 1, pp. 31–2.

26 Jeffrey A. Cole, *The Potosí Mita, 1573–1700*, Stanford, CA: Stanford University Press, 1985, p. 3. In addition to Cole's book and the *Relación* of Capoche, the discussion that follows of the *mita* and Potosí draws on another classic text: Enrique Tandeter, *Coacción y Mercado: La minería de la plata en el Potosí colonial*, Madrid: Siglo Ventiuno, 1992.

27 Vilar, *History of Gold*, p. 122.

28 Guillermo Lohmann Villena, *Las minas de Huancavelica en los siglos XVI y XVII*, Seville: CSIC, 1949, p. 96.

29 Cole, *The Potosí Mita*, pp. 9, 13, 72.

30 *Curaca* has the same meaning as *cacique* or *cacica* (a Taíno word), namely "local chief."

31 Capoche, *Relación general*, p. 135.

32 See document no. 82, *Carta anua* of Rodrigo de Cabredo to Padre Generale Aquaviva (28 April 1603), in *Monumenta Peruana*, Rome: Mon. Hist. Societatis Jesu, 1986, vol. 8, pp. 317–39.

33 Rodríguez Molas, *Mitayos*, p. 185.

34 Cited in Noble D. Cook, *Demographic Collapse in Spanish Peru, 1520–1620*, Cambridge: Cambridge University Press, 1982, p. 242.

35 In the year Capoche was writing, 567 *mitayos* failed to show for various reasons (death, flight, etc.); Capoche, *Relación general*, p. 145.

36 Cook, *Demographic Collapse*, p. 237; Lewis Hanke, "La Villa Imperial de Potosí," *Revista Shell*, 1962, no. 42, p. 8.

37 Pedro Cieza de León, *La crónica del Perú*, Madrid: Historia 16, 1984, p. 376.

38 Capoche, *Relación general*, pp. 179–80.

39 Cole, *The Potosí Mita*, p. 29.

40 Cook, *Demographic Collapse*, p. 94.

41 José de Acosta, *Historia natural y moral de las Indias*, Madrid: Historia 16, 1986, pp. 236–7.

42 Cole, *The Potosí Mita*, pp. 23–4.

43 Capoche, *Relación general*, p. 159.

44 Francisco López de Caravantes, *Noticia general del Perú*, Madrid: Atlas, 1987, vol. 4, p. 84.

45 Tandeter, *Coacción y mercado*, p. 57.
46 Juan de Matienzo, *Gobierno del Perú* [1567], Paris and Lima: Institut Français d'Études Andines, 1967, p. 33.
47 López de Caravantes, *Noticia general*, p. 129.
48 See Cole, *The Potosí Mita*, pp. 35–45; Tandeter, *Coacción y mercado*, pp. 42–5.
49 Tandeter, *Coacción y mercado*, pp. 42–3.
50 López de Caravantes, *Noticia general*, p. 85.
51 Rodríguez Molas, *Mitayos*, p. 187.
52 AGI, Charcas, 134.
53 Cole, *The Potosí Mita*, p. 41.
54 The quota dropped to 1,600 in 1604; Lohmann Villena, *Las minas de Huancavelica*, p. 97.
55 AGI, Lima, 271.
56 Ibid.
57 On mining activity in Mexico, see Peter J. Bakewell, "La minería en la Hispanoamérica colonial," in Leslie Bethell, ed., *Historia de América Latina*, vol. 3, Barcelona: Editorial Crítica, 1990; Francisco R. Calderón, *Historia económica de la Nueva España en tiempo de los Austrias*, Mexico City: Fondo de Cultura Económica, 1988; Peter J. Bakewell, *Silver Mining and Society in Colonial Mexico: Zacatecas, 1546–1700*, Cambridge: Cambridge University Press, 1971.
58 Alexander von Humboldt, *Political Essay on the Kingdom of New Spain*, New York: Knopf, 1972, p. 43.
59 Ibid., p. 44.
60 Brading and Cross, "Colonial Silver Mining," p. 557.

Chapter 5 One hundred thousand or 10 million Taíno?

1 Bartolomé de Las Casas, *Historia de las Indias*, 2nd edn, 2 vols, Mexico City: Fondo de Cultura Económica, 1995, vol. 1, pp. 259–60.
2 Ibid.
3 Ángel Rosenblat, *La población indígena y el mestizaje en América*, 1: *La población indígena, 1492–1950*, Buenos Aires: Editorial Nova, 1954.
4 Las Casas, *Historia de las Indias*, vol. 1, p. 272.
5 Ibid., pp. 279–83.
6 Ibid., p. 357.
7 This attempt at synthesis is based on contemporary chronicles and recent historical work. For the first: Hernán Colón, *Historia del Almirante* [1571], Madrid: Historia 16, 1984; Las Casas, *Historia de las Indias*; Antonio de Herrera, *Historia general de los hechos de los castellanos en las islas y tierrafirme del mar Océano* [1601–15], 10 vols, Asunción: Editorial Guarania, 1944–7; Pedro Martyr de Angleria, *Décadas del Nuevo Mundo* [1530], Buenos Aires: Editorial Bajel, 1944; Gonzalo Fernández de Oviedo, *Historia general y natural de las Indias* [1551–5], 5 vols, Madrid: Atlas, 1992. For recent histories, see: Luis Arranz Márquez, *Repartimientos y encomiendas en la isla Española: El repartimiento de Alburquerque de 1514*, Santo Domingo: Fundación García Arévalo, 1991; Frank Moya Pons, *Después de Colón: Trabajo, sociedad y política en la economía del oro*, Madrid: Alianza Editorial,

1987; Juan Pérez de Tudela, *Las armadas de Indias y los orígenes de la política de colonización*, Madrid: CSIC, 1956; Carl O. Sauer, *The Early Spanish Main*, Berkeley: University of California Press, 1966; Lesley B. Simpson, *The Encomienda in New Spain*, Berkeley: University of California Press, 1966. For the demographic aspects, see Massimo Livi Bacci, "Return to Hispaniola: Reassessing a Demographic Catastrophe," *Hispanic American Historical Review*, 83, 2003, no. 1, pp. 3–51.

  8 Roberto Marte, ed., *Santo Domingo en los manuscritos de Juan Bautista Muñoz*, Santo Domingo: Fundación García Arévalo, 1981.

  9 Sherburne F. Cook and Woodrow Borah, *Essays in Population History: Mexico and the Caribbean*, Berkeley: University of California Press, 1971, vol. 1, ch. 7; Francisco Guerra, "The Earliest American Epidemic: The Influenza of 1493," *Social Science History*, 12, 1988, no. 3; Sauer, *The Early Spanish Main*.

10 Arranz Márquez, *Repartimientos y encomiendas*, pp. 45–58.

11 Ángel Rosenblat, "The Population of Hispaniola at the Time of Columbus," in William M. Denevan, ed., *The Native Population of the Americas in 1492*, 2nd edn, Madison: University of Wisconsin Press, 1992; David Henige, "On the Contact Population of Hispaniola: History as High Mathematics," *Hispanic American Historical Review*, 58, 1978, no. 2.

12 Bartolomé de Las Casas, *Apologética historia sumaria*, 3 vols, Madrid: Alianza Editorial, 1992; Las Casas, *Historia de las Indias*; Oviedo, *Historia general*.

13 Las Casas, *Apologética*, vol. 1, p. 331; Oviedo, *Historia general*, vol. 1, p. 230.

14 Las Casas, *Historia de las Indias*, vol. 2, p. 483; for a discussion of the characteristics of the mounds, see Livi Bacci, "Return," p. 10, n. 9.

15 CDI, 1, pp. 366–8.

16 Oviedo, *Historia general*, vol. 1, pp. 230–1.

17 Ibid., p. 278.

18 David Watts, *The West Indies: Patterns of Development, Culture and Environmental Change since 1492*, Cambridge: Cambridge University Press, 1971; Bernard Nietschmann, *Between Land and Water*, New York and London: Seminar Press, 1973, p. 241.

19 Arranz Márquez, *Repartimientos y encomiendas*, pp. 30–8, 60–4.

20 Ibid., p. 62.

21 Earl Hamilton, *American Treasure and the Price Revolution in Spain, 1501–1650*, Cambridge, MA: Harvard University Press, 1934, table 4.

22 For a discussion of gold productivity, see Livi Bacci, "Return," pp. 11–20.

23 José Joaquín de Rocha, "Memoria histórica de Capitanía de Minas Gerais," *Revista do Archivo Publico Mineiro*, 2, 1897, no. 3.

24 Samuel Eliot Morison, *Admiral of the Ocean Sea: A Life of Christopher Columbus*, 2 vols, Boston: Little, Brown, 1942, vol. 1, p. 374; Las Casas, *Historia de las Indias*, vol. 1, p. 264.

25 Morison, *Admiral*, vol. 1, p. 376; Las Casas, *Historia de las Indias*, vol. 1, p. 266.

26 Las Casas, *Historia de las Indias*, vol. 1, p. 267.

27 Ibid., p. 275.

28 Las Casas, *Apologética*, vol. 1, pp. 292–327.

29 Colón, *Historia del Almirante*, p. 199.

30 Las Casas, *Historia de las Indias*, vol. 1, p. 287; Pietro Martire d'Anghiera, *La scoperta del Nuovo Mondo negli scritti di Pietro Martire d'Anghiera* [1530], Rome: Istituto Poligrafico e Zecca dello Stato, 1988, p. 293.

31 Irving Rouse, *The Tainos: Rise & Decline of the People who Greeted Columbus*, New Haven, CT: Yale University Press, 1992, p. 15; Oviedo, *Historia general*; Francisco López de Gómara, *Historia de la conquista de México* [1552], 2 vols, Mexico City: Editorial Pedro Robredo, 1943; Girolamo Benzoni, *La historia del Mondo Nuovo* [1565], Milan: Giordano, 1965; Jesse W. Fewkes, "The Aborigines of Porto Rico and Neighbouring Islands," in *25th Annual Report, Bureau of American Ethnology, 1903–04*, Washington, DC: Government Printing Office, 1907; Frank Moya Pons, "The Tainos of Hispaniola," *Caribbean Review*, 13, 1984, no. 4.

32 Sauer, *The Early Spanish Main*, p. 67; Rouse, *The Tainos*, p. 215.

33 José Alcina Franch, "La cultura taína como sociedad en transición entre los niveles tribal y de jefaturas," in *La cultura taína*, Madrid: Turner, 1989.

34 Oviedo, *Historia general*; Las Casas, *Apologética*; Fewkes, "The Aborigenes;" Irving Rouse, "The Arawak," in Julian H. Steward, ed., *Handbook of South American Indians*, Washington, DC: Smithsonian Institution, 1948, vol. 4; Rouse, *The Tainos*; Arranz Márquez, *Repartimientos y encomiendas*; Marcio Veloz Maggiolo, *La Isla de Santo Domingo ante de Colon*, Banco Central de la Republica Dominicana, 1993.

35 Las Casas, *Apologética*, vol. 2, p. 524.

36 Las Casas, *Historia de las Indias*, vol. 1, p. 259.

37 Ibid., p. 274.

38 Chanca, in Juan Pérez de Tudela, ed., *Colección documental del descubrimiento (1470–1506)*, Madrid: Real Academia de Historia, 1994.

39 Colón, *Historia del Almirante*, p. 120; Morison, *Admiral*, p. 260.

40 CDD, 1, p. 514.

41 Las Casas, *Historia de las Indias*, vol. 3, p. 301; Las Casas, *Obras escogidas*, Madrid: Atlas, 1958, p. 15.

42 Las Casas, *Historia de las Indias*, vol. 3, p. 123; CDI, 23, p. 314; CDI, 1, pp. 366–8; Esteban Mira Caballos, *El Indio Antillano: Repartimiento, encomienda y esclavitud (1492–1542)*, Seville: Muñoz Moya, 1997, p. 144.

43 Veloz Maggiolo, *La Isla de Santo Domingo*, p. 112.

44 Las Casas, *Historia de las Indias*, vol. 1, p. 365.

45 Ibid., pp. 346, 371; Marte, *Santo Domingo*, p. 188; Arranz Márquez, *Repartimientos y encomiendas*, p. 122.

46 CDI, 37, p. 293; Marte, *Santo Domingo*, pp. 396–7; Oviedo, *Historia general*, vol. 1, pp. 66–7; Juan López de Velasco, *Geografía y descripción universal de las Indias*, Madrid: Atlas, 1971.

47 Bartolomé de Las Casas, *A Short Account of the Destruction of the Indies*, London: Penguin, 1992, p. 25.

48 Rouse, *The Tainos*, p. 161.

49 Ibid., pp. 170–1.

50 Mira Caballos, *Indio Antillano*, pp. 165, 177, 172.

51 Ibid., pp. 46, 209; Watts, *The West Indies*.

52 CDI, 1, pp. 50–236; Emilio Rodríguez Demorizi, *Los Dominicos y las encomiendas de indios en la isla Española*, Santo Domingo: Editora del Caribe, 1971, pp. 732–48.

53 Rodríguez Demorizi, *Los Dominicos*, p. 92.

54 It is worthwhile recalling the meaning of the terms used in the *repartimiento*. *Cacique* is the head of the village or clan. *Nitayno* is an important person, a minor chief and often a relative of the *cacique*. The *indios de servicio* were

adults above a certain age (officially fourteen) and able to work. They were assigned to agricultural work, the raising of livestock, and gold mining. Juridically they were not slaves, and they had to be instructed in the true faith. The Blacks brought from Africa were instead slaves, as were the captured enemy Indios (for the most part Carib Indios). The *niños* were children under fourteen years of age. *Viejos* constituted an indeterminate category, including those unable to work because of age, illness, or some other reason. It should be added that, in Taíno society, age was an imprecise concept. The *naboría de casa* was a domestic servant assigned to the master and his family, and who lived in the houses of the Spaniards. The *allegados* was an ill-defined category that probably included Indios not tied to a specific *cacique* and so "temporarily" assigned to an *encomendero*. The *encomendero* was a Spaniard to whom were assigned the Indios belonging to a certain clan or *cacique* as forced laborers or for personal and domestic service. The *encomendero* was responsible for protecting the Indios and instructing them in matters of faith.

55 For further details, see Arranz Márquez, *Repartimientos y encomiendas*; Livi Bacci, "Return."
56 Rodríguez Demorizi, *Los Dominicos*, p. 251.
57 Oviedo, *Historia general*, vol. 1, p. 67.
58 CDI, 1, p. 309.
59 CDU, 2, pp. 1–127.
60 Arranz Márquez, *Repartimientos y encomiendas*, p. 239.
61 CDD, p. 867.
62 Las Casas, *Historia de las Indias*, vol. 1, p. 458; Martire d'Anghiera, *La scoperta del Nuovo Mondo*; Arranz Márquez, *Repartimientos y encomiendas*, p. 28; CDI, 10, p. 114.
63 Noble D. Cook, "Disease and Depopulation of Hispaniola, 1492–1518," *Colonial Latin American Review*, 2, 1993, nn. 1–2; Noble D. Cook, *Born to Die: Disease and New World Conquest, 1492–1650*, Cambridge: Cambridge University Press, 1998; Francisco Guerra, "La epidemia americana de influenza en 1493," *Revista de Indias*, 45, 1986, no. 176; Francisco Guerra, "The Earliest American Epidemic: The Influenza of 1493," *Social Science History*, 12, 1988, no. 3; Francisco Guerra, *Epidemiología americana y Filipina, 1492–1898*, Madrid: Ministerio de Sanidad y Consumo, 1999.
64 Guerra, *Epidemiología*, pp. 114–26.
65 Noble D. Cook, "Una primera epidemia americana de viruela en 1493?," *Revista de Indias*, 63, 2003, no. 227.
66 CDD, p. 867.
67 Las Casas, *Historia de las Indias*, vol. 1, p. 420; Martire d'Anghiera, *La scoperta del Nuovo Mondo*, p. 275.
68 Las Casas, *Historia de las Indias*, vol. 2, p. 226.
69 RCC, p. 131.
70 Las Casas, *Apologética*, vol. 1, pp. 361–3; Oviedo, *Historia general*, vol. 1, pp. 53–5.
71 Arranz Márquez, *Repartimientos y encomiendas*, pp. 226–8.
72 CDU, 5, pp. 43–52; Marte, *Santo Domingo*, p. 45; CDU, 9, pp. 22–3; Marte, *Santo Domingo*, p. 191; CDI, 11, pp. 298–321.
73 If instead the *repartimiento* considered *niños* to be children under an age lower than fourteen, then the implicit rate of increase would not be quite so

low: at ten years, r = −2.1 percent; at twelve, r = −2.8 percent; as compared to −3.5 percent if the age is fourteen.

74 Las Casas, *Historia de las Indias*, vol. 2, pp. 482–9; Marte, *Santo Domingo*, pp. 115–19.

75 López de Velasco, *Geografía*, p. 97.

76 These data taken from Watts, *The West Indies*.

77 Oviedo, *Historia general*, vol. 2, p. 30.

78 Ibid., p. 38.

79 CDI, 1, *Relación de la Isla Española al Rey Felipe II*.

80 Oviedo, *Historia general*, vol. 2, p. 38.

81 Watts, *The West Indies*, ch. 3.

Chapter 6 The modern dispute over the population of Meso-America

1 Hernán Cortés, *Letters from Mexico*, trans. A.R. Pagden, New York: Grossman, 1971, pp. 102–3. In 1591, according to the Censo de Castilla, the province of Seville numbered 114,618 *vecinos* and the city itself 26,181; the province of Córdoba numbered 46,209 *vecinos* and the city 10,910; see Instituto Nacional de Estadistica, *Censo de Castilla de 1591*, Madrid, 1986, pp. 506, 518, 718.

2 Cortés, *Letters*, pp. 103–4.

3 Ibid., pp. 104–5.

4 Bernal Díaz del Castillo, *Historia verdadera de la Conquista della Nueva España*, Mexico City: Porrúa, 1976, p. 172.

5 William T. Sanders, "The Population of the Central Mexican Symbiotic Region, the Basin of Mexico and the Teotihuacán Valley in the Sixteenth Century," in William M. Denevan, ed., *The Native Population of the Americas in 1492*, 2nd edn, Madison: University of Wisconsin Press, 1992, p. 130.

6 Many scholars use a "restricted" definition that refers to central Mexico or that part of Meso-America bordered on the north by the "Chichimeca frontier" – an approximate line beyond which population was scarce and composed predominantly of nomads and warriors with little in the way of settlements – and on the south by the isthmus of Tehuantepec, and so not including the Yucatán and the Mayan populations. And while inclusion of the northern part does not affect the calculation much, as there was little population there, the Mayan area was demographically significant. The estimates are taken from Denevan, *The Native Population*, pp. xxi–xxii, xxviii, 3, 77–83. More generally on the history of the population of Mexico, in addition to those works cited in note 13 of this chapter, see the classic work of Nicolás Sánchez-Albornoz, *La población de América Latina desde los tiempos precolombinos al año 2025*, Madrid: Alianza Editorial, 1994; Gonzalo Aguirre Beltrán, *La población negra de México: Estudio etnohistorico*, 3rd edn, Mexico City: Fondo de Cultura Económica, 1989; Robert McCaa, "El poblamiento de México: Desde sus orígenes a la revolución," in José Gómez de León Cruces and Cecilia Rabell Romero, eds, *La población de México: Estudio etnohistorico*, Mexico City: Fondo de Cultura Económica, 2001; Cecilia Rabell Romero, "El descenso de la población indígena durante el siglo XVI y las cuentas del gran capitán," in *El poblamiento de México: Una visión histórico-demográfica*, 2: *El México colonial*, Mexico City: Consejo Nacional de Población, 1993.

7 Classic work on the pre-Hispanic tributary system was undertaken by Alonso de Zorita, member of the Mexican Audiencia from 1556 to 1566. See Alonso de Zorita, *Relación de la Nueva España*, Mexico City: Conaculta, 1999, vol. 1, pp. 391–413. There is also a good synthesis in Woodrow Borah and Sherburne F. Cook, *The Aboriginal Population of Central Mexico on the Eve of the Spanish Conquest*, Berkeley and Los Angeles: University of California Press, 1963, pp. 6–21.

8 Lesley B. Simpson, *The Encomienda in New Spain*, Berkeley: University of California Press, 1966, ch. 5.

9 For the evolution of the tribute in the first half of the sixteenth century, see Woodrow Borah and Sherburne F. Cook, *The Population of Central Mexico in 1548: An Analysis of the Suma de Visitas de Pueblos*, Berkeley: University of California Press, 1960; Woodrow Borah and Sherburne F. Cook, *The Indian Population of Central Mexico, 1531–1610*, Berkeley: University of California Press, 1960; Bernard H. Slicher van Bath, "The Calculation of the Population of New Spain, especially for the Period before 1570," *Boletín de Estudios Latinoamericanos y del Caribe*, no. 24, June 1978.

10 Slicher van Bath, "The Calculation of the Population," p. 72.

11 Ibid., p. 71; Cook and Borah, *The Indian Population*, pp. 40–6.

12 Juan López de Velasco, *Geografía y descripción universal de las Indias*, Madrid: Atlas, 1971.

13 In fact, the first work to appear was that of Sherburne F. Cook and Lesley B. Simpson, *The Population of Central Mexico in the Sixteenth Century*, Berkeley: University of California Press, 1948, in which the authors assigned a population of 11 million to central Mexico. There followed Cook and Borah, *The Indian Population*; Cook and Borah, *The Population of Central Mexico*; Borah and Cook, *The Aboriginal Population*; and, finally, Sherburne F. Cook and Woodrow Borah, *Essays in Population History: Mexico and the Caribbean*, 3 vols, Berkeley: University of California Press, 1971–9.

14 Cook and Borah, *The Population of Central Mexico*, pp. 37–49.

15 Borah and Cook, *The Aboriginal Population*, pp. 45–71.

16 The original codex of the *Matrícula de Tributos* is in the Museo Nacional de Antropología in Mexico City. A version of the *Matrícula* was copied into the Mendoza codex prepared by Viceroy Mendoza for Charles V and sent to Spain on a ship that was captured by the French. It can now be found in Oxford's Bodleian Library.

17 Borah and Cook, *The Aboriginal Population*, p. 125.

18 Cook and Borah, *The Indian Population*, pp. 40–8.

19 Sanders, "The Population," pp. 96–7.

20 Cook and Borah, *The Indian Population*, p. 48.

21 "Suma de vistas de pueblos por orden alfabético", MS 2800, Biblioteca Nacional, Madrid, transcr. and pubd by Francisco del Paso y Troncoso, *Papeles de Nueva España*, 2nd series, Madrid: Rivadeneyra, 1905, vol. 1.

22 Cook and Borah, *The Population of Central Mexico*, pp. 67–103.

23 Sanders, "The Population," pp. 92–101; Slicher van Bath, *The Calculation of the Population*.

24 France V. Scholes, *Sobre el modo de tributar de los Indios de Nueva España a su Majestad, 1561–64*, Mexico City: Porrúa, 1958.

25 Ibid., p. 30.

26 "Carta del virrey don Luis de Velasco a su Majestad, México, 29 de abri de 1562" [AGI, Patronato, legajo 182, ramo 2]; "Relación que se envió a España de lo que parece podrían tributar y al presente tributan las siete cabeceras aquí contenidas, que están en la Real Corona" [ibid.]. Both documents are published in Scholes, *Sobre el modo*, pp. 24–8, 73–6.

27 Sanders, "The Population," pp. 122–8.

28 Sherburne F. Cook and Woodrow Borah, "Categorías civiles y grupos de edad," in Cook and Borah, *Essays*, vol. 1, pp. 239–41.

29 In a stable population with a growth rate of zero and a life expectancy of about twenty-four years (model West; see Ansley Coale and Paul Demeny, *Model Life Tables and Stable Populations*, Princeton, NJ: Princeton University Press, 1966), the ratio between young people aged zero to eighteen and half of the adult population aged twenty to fifty (imagining that this latter figure approximates the total number of married couples) is about 1.9 (though in fact the number of married couples is probably less, given that the number of unmarried and widowed aged twenty to fifty surely outnumbered those married aged fifty and above; this latter age group in any case amounted to less than one-third that of the twenty to fifty group). So 1.9 constitutes a minimum, and values of 1.3 to 1.6, as calculated by Cook and Borah, surely indicate a population in decline.

30 "Relación de la cuenta y gente que se halló en la parte de Santiago y México,12 de marzo de 1562" [AGI, Patronato, legajo 182, ramo 2], in Scholes, *Sobre el modo*, pp. 76–9.

31 See note 29; it should be added that a figure of 47 percent of young people is consistent with a ratio of children to married couples of 2.3.

32 On the *Relaciones geográficas*, see the introduction in René Acuña, ed., *Relaciones geográficas del siglo XVI: Guatemala*, Mexico City: Universidad Nacional Autónoma de México, 1982.

33 The questionnaire is reproduced in Paso y Troncoso, *Papeles de Nueva España*, vol. 4, pp. 1–7.

34 Juan Bautista de Pomar, "Relación de Texcoco," in *Relaciones de Texcoco y de la Nueva España*, Mexico City: Chavez-Hayhoe, 1941, p. 50.

35 René Acuña, ed., *Relaciones geográficas del siglo XVI: Tlaxcala*, Mexico City: Universidad Nacional Autónoma de México, 1984, vol. 2, pp. 230–1.

36 Ibid., vol. 1, p. 76.

37 Ibid., vol. 2, p. 314: "Carta de los licenciados Espinosa e Zuazo a su Cesarea Majestad (30.III.1528)." See also Roberto Marte, ed., *Santo Domingo en los manuscritos de Juan Bautista Muñoz*, Santo Domingo: Fundación García Arévalo, 1981, pp. 279–80.

38 Corinne S. Wood, "New Evidence for Late Introduction of Malaria into the New World," *Current Anthropology*, 16, 1975, no.1, p. 94; Francisco Guerra, *Epidemiología americana y filipina, 1492–1898*, Madrid: Ministerio de Sanidad y Consumo, 1999, pp. 100–1; Henry R. Carter, "Place of Origin of Malaria: America?," 1923, http://etext.lib.virginia.edu/etcbin/fever-browse?id=01107002.

39 On epidemics in Mexico and all of the Americas, see Guerra, *Epidemiología*, which offers a detailed historical account and important introductory essays. A classic and much-cited source is Fray Jerónimo de Mendieta, *Historia eclesiástica Indiana*, Mexico City: Porrúa, 1993, in particular ch. 36 of the fourth book, pp. 513–19. Among present-day authors, see the essays contained in

Elsa Malvido and Enrique Florescano, eds, *Ensayos sobre la historia de las epidemias en México*, 2 vols, Mexico City: Instituto Mexicano del Seguro Social, 1982. Epidemiological chronologies can be found in Charles Gibson, *Los Aztecas bajo el dominio español*, Madrid: Siglo Ventiuno, 1967, pp. 460–1; Peter Gerhard, *A Guide to the Historical Geography of New Spain*, Cambridge: Cambridge University Press, 1972, p. 23; and Hanns Prem, "Brotes de enfermedad en la zona central de México," in Noble D. Cook and George Lovell, eds, *Juicios secretos de Dios*, Quito: Abya-Yala, 2000.

40 Prem, "Brotes," p. 84.

41 On the 1520–1 smallpox epidemic, see chapter 3 of this volume and also the work of Robert McCaa, "Spanish and Nahuatl Views on Smallpox and Demographic Catastrophe in Mexico," *Journal of Interdisciplinary History*, 25, 1995, no. 3, and Noble D. Cook, *Born to Die: Disease and New World Conquest, 1492–1650*, Cambridge: Cambridge University Press, 1998.

42 Fray Bernardino de Sahagún, *Historia general de las cosas de Nueva España*, Mexico City: Porrúa, 1977, vol. 4, p. 137.

43 Cortés, *Letters*, p. 164.

44 José Luis Martínez, *Hernán Cortés*, Mexico City: Fondo de Cultura Económica, 1990, pp. 297–303.

45 Díaz del Castillo, *Historia verdadera*, p. 370.

46 Francis Borgia Steck, ed. and trans., *Motolinia's History of the Indians of New Spain*, Washington, DC: Academy of American Franciscan History, 1951, p. 88.

47 Cited in Germán Somolinos d'Ardois, "Las epidemias en México durante el siglo XVI," in Malvido and Florescano, eds, *Ensayos*, p. 208.

48 Mendieta, *Historia eclesiástica*, p. 515.

49 Somolinos d'Ardois, "Las epidemias."

50 Enrique Otte, *Cartas privadas de emigrantes a Indias, 1540–1616*, Mexico City: Fondo de Cultura Económica, 1995, letter 72, "Juan López de Soria a la Condesa de Ribadavia (30.XI.1576)."

51 Francisco del Paso y Troncoso, *Epistolario de Nueva España*, Mexico City: Editorial Pedro Robredo, 1940, vol. 12, documents 690, 691, 692.

52 M. J. Cuevas, SJ, *Historia de la Iglesia en México*, 5 vols, Mexico City: Imprenta del Colégio Salesiano, 1926, vol. 2, pp. 500–1, cited in Daniel T. Reff, "Old World Diseases and their Consequences in 16th-Century New Spain," paper delivered at the conference "The Peopling of the Americas," Veracruz, 1992.

53 Prem, "Brotes," p. 81.

54 Mendieta, *Historia eclesiástica*, p. 515.

55 France V. Scholes, *Moderación de las doctrinas de la Real Corona administradas por las órdenes mendicantes, 1623*, Mexico City: Porrúa, 1959, p. 16.

56 James Lockhart, *The Nahuas after the Conquest*, Stanford, CA: Stanford University Press, 1992, ch. 2; Gerhard, *A Guide*, pp. 4–5.

57 Gerhard, *A Guide*, p. 27.

58 Lockhart, *The Nahuas*, ch. 2.

59 Gerhard, *A Guide*, p. 27.

60 Scholes, *Moderación*, pp. 22–3.

61 Silvio Zavala, *El servicio personal de los Indios en la Nueva España, 1521–50*, Mexico City: Colégio de México, 1984, vol. 1, pp. 512–13.

62 Martínez, *Hernán Cortés*, pp. 293–4; Hugh Thomas, *Montezuma, Cortés, and the Fall of Old Mexico*, New York: Simon & Schuster, 1993; Juan Miralles, *Hernán Cortés*, Barcelona: Tusquets, 2003, pp. 284–5.

63 Simpson, *The Encomienda*, ch. 5.

64 Ibid., pp. 147–50.

65 For a synthesis of the evolution of the *encomienda* and labor systems, see, in addition to the work of Simpson, Zavala, *El servicio personal*, pp. 19–42.

66 Zavala, *El servicio personal*, pp. 279–92.

67 Cited in Sherburne F. Cook and Woodrow Borah, *El pasado de México*, Mexico City: Fondo de Cultura Económica, 1989, p. 254.

68 Zavala, *El servicio personal*, p. 498.

69 Ibid., p. 499; "Carta de Fray Francisco de Mayorga al Obispo de Santo Domingo, Presidente del Audiencia de México," in Paso y Troncoso, *Epistolario de Nueva España*, vol. 3, pp. 120–2. This was a protest against the practice of imposing on Indios the obligation to carry stone to Mexico City for the building projects of Cortés.

70 Charles Gibson, *Tlaxcala in the Sixteenth Century*, Stanford, CA: Stanford University Press, 1967, pp. 123–30, 135.

71 Simpson, *The Encomienda*, ch. 7; "Carta al Emperador del licenciado Salmerón (9.II.1533)," in Paso y Troncoso, *Epistolario de Nueva España*, vol. 3, pp. 19–21. Salmerón describes his efforts to convince the notables of Tlaxcala and Cholula to send more Indios to work in Puebla.

72 On the *desagüe* works, see Alexander von Humboldt, *Essai politique sur le Royaume de la Nouvelle-Espagne*, Paris: Antoine-Augustin Renouard, 1825–7, book 3, ch. 8; Gibson, *Los Aztecas*, p. 9.

73 Zavala, *El servicio personal*, p. 128.

74 Ibid., p. 121.

75 Motolinia's *Historia de los Indios* includes the "Carta de Fray Toribio de Motolinia al Emperador Carlos V."

76 Rodrigo de Albórnoz, "Contador de Nueva España, a Carlos V (15.XII.1525)," reproduced in Lesley B. Simpson, *The Encomienda in New Spain*, Berkeley: University of California Press, 1966, p. 209.

77 Ibid., p. 210.

78 Zavala, *El servicio personal*, p. 183.

79 Lockhart, *The Nahuas*, p. 111.

80 Cook and Borah, *The Population of Central Mexico*, p. 114.

81 Gerhard, *A Guide*, p. 3.

82 Francisco R. Calderón, *Historia económica indígena de la Nueva España en tiempo de los Autrias*, Mexico City: Fondo de Cultura Económica, 1988, p. 353.

83 Gibson, *Los Aztecas*, p. 10.

84 Gibson, *Tlaxcala*, p. 153.

85 Cook and Borah, *El pasado*, p. 238.

86 Carlos Sempat Assadourian, "La despoblación indígena en Perú y en Nueva España durante el siglo XVI y la formación de la economía colonial," *Historia Mexicana*, 38, 1989, no. 3.

Chapter 7 The Incas and many millions of subjects

1 Michael A. Little and Paul T. Baker, "Environmental Adaptations and Perspectives," in Paul T. Baker and Michael A. Little, eds, *Man in the Andes: A Multidisciplinary Study of High-Altitude Quechua*, Stroudsberg, PA: Dowden, Hutchinson & Ross, 1976.

2 José de Acosta, *Historia natural y moral de las Indias*, Madrid: Historia 16, 1986, p. 402.

3 Ibid.

4 Pedro Gutierrez de Santa Clara, *Crónicas del Perú, 3: Quinquenarios, o Historia de las guerras civiles del Perú*, Madrid, Atlas: 1963.

5 In the paragraph that follows, for demographic sources and investigations I have followed Noble D. Cook, "Population Data for Indian Peru: Sixteenth and Seventeenth Centuries," *Hispanic American Historical Review*, 62, 1982, no. 1, pp. 73–120.

6 "Instrucción que el Marqués Francisco Pizarro dió a Diego Verdejo para la visita que había de hacer desde Chicama hasta Tucoma (4.VI.1540)," in *Gobernantes del Perú*, Madrid: Juan Pueyo, 1921, vol. 1, pp. 19–25. "You will visit all the villages and take note of the Indios in each of those, being sure to check all of the houses in which they live." See also Pedro de La Gasca's letter to the Council of the Indies dated January 28, 1549: "In these days I have given orders to all the people of these regions in order that all the inspectors leave and carry out their inspections," ibid., p. 151.

7 Juan de Matienzo, *Gobierno del Perú* [1567], ed. Guillermo Lohmann Villena, Paris and Lima: Institut Français d'Études Andines, 1967, p. 110.

8 Waldemar Espinoza Soriano, *La destrucción del impero de los Incas*, 4th edn, Lima: Amaru Editores, 1986.

9 Ibid., p. 178; Carlos Sempat Assadourian, *Transiciones hacia el sistema colonial andino*, Mexico City: Colegio de México y Instituto de Estudios Peruanos, 1994, p. 47.

10 Pedro Cieza de León, *La crónica del Perú*, Madrid: Historia 16, 1984, p. 318.

11 John V. Murra, ed., *Visita de la provincia de León de Huánuco en 1562*, Huánuco: Universidad Nacional Hermilio Valdizán, 1967; Nathan Wachtel, *The Vision of the Vanquished: The Spanish Conquest of Peru through Indian Eyes, 1530–1570*, New York: Barnes & Noble, 1977, pp. 89, 101–4.

12 Wachtel, *The Vision of the Vanquished*, pp. 90, 109–14.

13 Waldemar Espinoza Soriano, ed., *Visita hecha a la provincia de Chucuito por Garci Diez de San Miguel en el año 1567*, Lima: Ediciones Casa de la Cultura del Perú, 1964.

14 Ibid., p. 64.

15 Ibid., p. 206.

16 On the problem of the definition of the tributary, see Noble D. Cook, *Demographic Collapse: Indian Peru, 1520–1620*, Cambridge: Cambridge University Press, 1981, p. 45.

17 Pilar Remy, "El documento," in *Las visitas a Cajamarca 1571–72/1578*, Lima: Instituto de Estudios Peruanos, 1992, vol. 1, pp. 37–46, 59–60.

18 Marco Jiménez de la Espada, ed., *Relaciones geográficas de Indias: Perú*, 2 vols, Madrid: Atlas, 1965, vol. 1, p. 155.

19 William M. Denevan, *The Native Population of the Americas in 1492*, 2nd edn, Madison: University of Wisconsin Press, 1992, p. xxviii, n.; C. T. Smith,

"Depopulation of the Central Andes in the 16th Century," *Current Anthropology*, 11, 1970, p. 459; Henry F. Dobyns, "Estimating Aboriginal American Population: An Appraisal of Techniques with a New Hemispheric Estimate," *Current Anthropology*, 7, 1966, pp. 395–416; Cook, *Demographic Collapse*, pp. 41–54, 109–14; Wachtel, *Vision of the Vanquished*, p. 90; Daniel E. Shea, "A Defense of Small Population Estimates for the Central Andes in 1520," in Denevan, *The Native Population*, p. 174.

20 See the discussions in notes 29 and 31 of chapter 6.

21 Letter of July 17, 1549, in *Gobernantes del Perú*, vol. X, p. 210.

22 Espinoza Soriano, *Visita hecha a la provincia de Chucuito*, p. 169; many other witnesses speak of evasions, ibid., pp. 151, 154, 160, 163.

23 *Gobernantes del Perú*, vol. 8, p. 372.

24 Nicolás Sánchez-Albornoz, *Indios y tributarios en el Alto Perú*, Lima: Instituto de Estudios Peruanos, 1978, pp. 29, 49; Nicolás Sánchez-Albornoz, *La ciudad de Arequipa, 1573–1645: Condición, migración y trabajo indígeno*, Arequipa: Universidad de San Agustín, 2003. According to the investigation of Felipe de Bolívar, around 1640, 49.8 percent of the men in the dioceses of Cuzco, Chuquisaca (Charcas), and La Paz were recent immigrants or their descendants; see Carlos Sempat Assadourian, "La crisis demográfica del siglo XVI y la transición del Tawantinsuyu al sistema mercantil colonial," in Nicolás Sánchez-Albornoz, *Población y mano de obra en América Latina*, Madrid: Alianza Editorial, 1985, p. 76.

25 Francisco López de Caravantes, *Noticia general del Perú*, Madrid: Atlas, 1987, vol. 4, pp. 296–7.

26 "Relación del Sr Virrey Luis de Velasco al Sr Conde de Monterrey sobre el estado del Perú," in *Colección de las memorias o relaciones que escribieron los Virreyes del Perú*, ed. Ricardo Beltrán y Rózpide, vol. 1, Madrid: Imprenta del Asílo de Huérfanos, 1921, pp. 119–20. See also the letter from the *caciques* of Chucuito to Philip II of September 2, 1597, in which they lament those who flee to escape the *mita*, the consequent increased fiscal pressure on the Indios who remain in the villages, and the excessive demands of the *alguaciles* controllers, in *Monumenta Peruana*, Rome: Mon. Hist. Societatis Jesu, 1974, vol. 6, pp. 443–51.

27 *Gobernantes del Perú*, vol. 8, pp. 253–4, 350.

28 Assadourian, "La crisis demográfica," p. 76; *Colección de las memorias*, p. 166: a number equal to 25,000, presumably referring to families.

29 For the *Relaciones geográficas*, see chapter 6, note 32; for the instructions and questions that made up the questionnaire, see "Instrucción y memoria de las relaciones que se han de hacer para la descripción de las Indias," in René Acuña, ed., *Relaciones geográficas del siglo XVI*, vol. 2: *Guatemala*, Mexico City: Universidad Nacional Autónoma de México, 1984–9, pp. 15–21.

30 Jiménez de la Espada, *Relaciones geográficas*, esp. vol. 1, pp. 155, 204, 221; vol. 2, pp. 328, 344.

31 Ibid., vol. 1, pp. 155–6, 221.

32 Wachtel, *Vision of the Vanquished*, p. 97.

33 Francisco de Solano, *Normas y leyes de la ciudad hispano-americana, 1492–1600*, Madrid: CSIC, 1996. See also Matienzo, *Gobierno del Perú*, pp. 49–50. According to Matienzo there were meant to be 500 tributaries in each reduced village.

34 "Puntos de la Instrucción que dió el Virrey Don Francisco de Toledo . . .," in López de Caravantes, *Noticia general*, vol. 4, pp. 288–9. For Toledo's *Memoria* to Philip II: *Colección de las memorias*, p. 83.
35 *Colección de las memorias*, p. 88.
36 John Hemming, *The Conquest of the Incas*, New York: Harcourt, Brace, Jovanovich, 1970, p. 395.
37 Ibid.; Espinoza Soriano, *Visita hecha a la provincia de Chucuito*, p. 223.
38 Jiménez de la Espada, *Relaciones geográficas*, vol. 2, pp. 334–7.
39 Assadourian, *Transiciones*; Assadourian, "La crisis demográfica."
40 Cieza de León, *La crónica*, pp. 208–9.
41 Hemming, *Conquest of the Incas*, p. 164; "Carta del Licenciado Vaca de Castro al Emperador Don Carlos, 24 novembre 1542," in *Gobernantes del Perú*, vol. 1, p. 58.
42 Augustin de Zarate, *Historia del descubrimiento y conquista de la provincia del Perú*, Madrid: Atlas, 1947, pp. 564, 566–7; see also "Carta del licenciado La Gasca a los Oficiales de la Casa de Contratación de Sevilla, 25 aprile 1548," in *Gobernantes del Perú*, vol. 1; James Lockhart, *Spanish Peru 1532–1560: A Social History*, 2nd edn, Madison: University of Wisconsin Press, 1992, p. 233.
43 Cieza de León, cited in Espinoza Soriano, *La destrucción*, p. 176.
44 Cristóbal de Molina, *Relación de muchas cosas acaecidas en el Perú*, Madrid: Atlas, 1968, p. 62.
45 Ibid., p. 65.
46 Ibid., p. 66.
47 Polo de Ondegardo, cited in Assadourian, *Transiciones*, p. 27.
48 Lockhart, *Spanish Peru*, p. 233.
49 "Carta del licenciado La Gasca al Consejo de Indias (28.I.1549)," in *Gobernantes del Perú*, vol. 1, p. 153.
50 Espinoza Soriano, *La destrucción*, p. 179; Espinoza Soriano, *Visita hecha a la provincia de Chucuito*, p. 170.
51 Waldemar Espinoza Soriano, "Los Huancas, aliados de la Conquista," *Anales Científicos de la Universidad del Centro del Perú*, no. 1, Huancayo, 1971. For a detailed analysis of the document and relative conclusions, see Assadourian, *Transiciones*, pp. 40–60.
52 According to our calculations, 27,014 were enrolled and 7,056 disappeared or died.
53 A *fánega* was equal to 58 liters; translated into weight, that is about 46 kilograms of maize. We have assumed that the caloric equivalent of 300 kilograms of maize corresponds to the nutritional needs of an adult male.
54 Assadourian, *Transiciones*, p. 60.
55 Ibid.
56 Frederick A. Kirkpatrick, *The Spanish Conquistadores*, Cleveland and New York: Meridian Books, 1967, chs. 14 and 19.
57 Assadourian, *Transiciones*, p. 56.
58 Kirkpatrick, *The Spanish Conquistadores*, pp. 231–7.
59 Pedro Cieza de León, *El señorio de los Incas*, Madrid: Historia 16, 1984, p. 194: "They say that a great pestilence of smallpox came, so contagious that more than 200,000 people died throughout the province, as it was general; and he [Huayna Capac] became sick."
60 This debate has been enriched recently by the papers presented at the "Epidemics and Demographic Disaster in Colonial Latin America" session at

the annual congress of the American Historical Association, held in Washington in January 2004, and in particular by the papers of James B. Kirakofe ("A Case of Mistaken Identity! Leprosy, Measles or Smallpox? Old World Names for a New World Disease: Bartonellosis") and Robert McCaa, Aleta Nimlos, and Teodoro Hampe-Martinez ("The Death of Huayna Capac Re-examined"), and the commentary on the session by Noble D. Cook.

61 Cieza de León, *La crónica*, pp. 138–9. Pedro de La Gasca may have referred to this epidemic in his letter of January 1549 to the Council of the Indies: "a disease of catarrh and chest pains that spread among them [the Indios] and the Spaniards," in *Gobernantes de Perú*, vol. 1, p. 152.

62 D. F. Montesinos, *Anales del Perú*, 2 vols, Madrid, 1906, vol. 1, p. 254. Juan B. Lastres, *Historia de la medicina peruana*, 2: *La medicina en el Virreinato*, Lima: Imprenta Santa Maria, 1951, p. 76. For Colombia, see Juan A. Villamarín and Judith E. Villamarín, "Epidemias y despoblación en la Sabana de Bogotá, 1536–1810," in Noble D. Cook and George Lovell, eds, *Juicios Secretos de Diós*, Quito: Abya-Yala, 1999, p. 146; for Ecuador, Linda A. Newsom, "Epidemias del Viejo Mundo en Ecuador," ibid., p. 127.

63 See, among other testimonies, the authoritative one of Viceroy don Luis de Velasco and the Audiencia of Lima which, with reference to the "general infirmity and deaths of the Indios" of the past few years, notes that the population has suffered a rapid decline and so it has been necessary to carry out new *visitas* to ascertain the number of tributaries who have survived. See Silvio Zavala, *El servicio personal de los Indios en la Nueva España, 1521–50*, Mexico City: Colégio de México, 1984, vol. 1, p. 209.

64 Lastres, *Historia de la medicina*, p. 77; "Descripción de la tierra del Corregimiento de Abancay," in Jiménez de la Espada, *Relaciones geográficas*, vol. 2, p. 18.

65 Letters of Conde de Villar to His Majesty from Lima on April 19, May 11, and June 13 and 16, 1589, in *Gobernantes del Perú*, vol. 3; Lastres, *Historia de la medicina*, p. 76.

66 Zavala, *El servicio personal*, p. 177.

67 Wachtel, *Vision of the Vanquished*, pp. 118–19. On the imposition of tribute, see Carlos Sempat Assadourian, "La politica del Virrey Toledo sobre el tributo indio: el caso de Chucuito," in Javier Flores Espinoza and Rafael Varón Gabai, eds, *El hombre en los Andes*, Lima: Pontificia Universidad Católica del Perú, 2002, vol. 2, pp. 741–66.

68 Zavala, *El servicio personal*, p. 207.

69 *Monumenta Peruana*, vol. 2, pp. 765–9, "Carta anua" of Rodrigo Cabredo to Father General Acquaviva (March 1, 1602).

70 Cook, *Demographic Collapse*, p. 247.

71 Ibid.

Chapter 8 Colonists and "Paulists" hunting down Guaraní

1 Frederick A. Kirkpatrick, *The Spanish Conquistadores*, Cleveland and New York: Meridian Books, 1967, pp. 329–33.

2 William M. Denevan, ed., *The Native Population of the Americas in 1492*, 2nd edn, Madison: University of Wisconsin Press, 1992, p. xxxviii.

3 David J. Owens, "A Historical Geography of the Indian Missions in the Jesuit Province of Paraguay, 1609–1768," PhD diss., University of Kansas, 1977, p. 16.
4 Ibid., p. 170.
5 Ibid., p. 4.
6 Rafael Carbonell de Masy, *Estrategias de desarrollo rural en los pueblos Guaraníes (1609–1767)*, Barcelona: Antoni Bosch, 1992, p. 95.
7 Ernesto J. A. Maeder and Alfredo S.C. Bolsi, "La población Guaraní de la provincia de misiones en la época post-Jesuítica (1768–1810)," *Folia Histórica del Nordeste*, suppl. to no. 54, 1982, p. 72.
8 There is good documentation and many contemporary and modern-day studies of the political, social, and economic organization of the missions. Of particular importance are the writings of José Cardiel, *Las misiones del Paraguay*, Madrid: Historia 16, 1989; Guillermo Furlong, *José Cardiel, S. J. y su Carta-Relación*, Buenos Aires: Libreria del Plata, 1953; Pierre F. J. de Charlevoix, *Histoire du Paraguay* [1756], 3 vols, Paris: Didot, 1956; Martin Dobrizhoffer, SJ, *Historia de los Abipones*, 3 vols, Resistencia: Universidad Nacional del Nordeste, 1967, 1968, 1970; José M. Peramás, *La República de Platón y los Guaraníes*, Buenos Aires: Emecé, 1946. See also in particular Alberto Armani, *Città di Dio e Città del Sole*, Rome: Studium, 1977; Francesco Barberani, "Le riduzioni dei Guaraní: un'alternativa al sistema coloniale," in Antonio Sepp, *Il sacro esperimento del Paraguay*, Verona: Edizione della Cassa di Risparmio di Verona, 1990; Philip Caraman, *The Lost Paradise: An Account of the Jesuits in Paraguay 1607–1768*, London: Sidgwick & Jackson, 1975; Carbonell de Masy, *Estrategias de desarrollo*; Guillermo Furlong, *Misiones y sus pueblos de Guaraníes*, Buenos Aires: Ediciones Theoria, 1962; Pablo Hernández, *Organización social de las doctrinas Guaraníes de la Compañia de Jesus*, 2 vols, Barcelona: Gustavo Gili, 1913; Ernesto J. A. Maeder, *Aproximación a las misiones Guaraníticas*, Buenos Aires: Ediciones de la Universidad Católica, 1996; Magnus Mörner, *The Political and Economic Activities of the Jesuits in the la Plata Region*, Stockholm: Library and Institute of Ibero American Studies, 1953; Owens, *A Historical Geography*.
9 Hernández, *Organización*, vol. 1, pp. 87–8.
10 Armani, *Città di Dio*, p. 115.
11 Gonzalo de Doblas, "Memoria sobre misiones," in Pedro de Angelis, *Colleción de obras y documentos relativos a la historia antigua y moderna de las provincias del Río de la Plata*, 8 vols, Buenos Aires: Editorial Plus Ultra, 1970, vol. 3, pp. 24–5.
12 Pablo Pastells, *Historia de la Compañia de Jesús en la Provincia del Paraguay*, 8 vols, Madrid: Victoriano Suárez, 1933, vol. 5, pp. 107, 148. The other volumes, to which we shall occasionally make reference are: vol. 1, Madrid: Victoriano Suárez, 1912; vol. 2, 1915; vol. 3, 1918; vol. 4, 1923; vol. 6 (with F. Mateos), Madrid: CSIC, 1946; vol. 7 (with F. Mateos), 1953; vol. 8 (with F. Mateos), 1959.
13 Francesco Barbarani, "Organizzazione del territorio e sviluppo urbanistico nelle missioni gesuitiche del Paraguay (1609–1641)," in Giovanna Rosso Del Brenna, ed., *La costruzione di un nuovo mondo*, Genoa: Sagep Editrice, 1994; Carbonell de Masy, *Estrategias de desarrollo*, pp. 301–2; Furlong, *Misiones*, p. 187.

14 Sepp, *Il sacro esperimento*, pp. 195ff.
15 Furlong, *Misiones*, p. 289.
16 Hernández, *Organización*, vol. 1, p. 102.
17 J. M. Blanco, *Historia documentada de la vida y gloriosa muerte de los Padres Roque Gonzales de la Cruz, Alonso Rodríguez, y Juan del Castillo de la Compañia de Jesús*, Buenos Aires: Mártires del Caaró y Yjuhi, 1929, p. 108.
18 Hernández, *Organización*, vol. 1, pp. 101–2.
19 Armani, *Città di Dio*, pp. 153–5.
20 Cardiel, *Las misiones*, p. 103.
21 Carbonell de Masy, *Estrategias de desarrollo*, p. 103.
22 Dobrizhoffer, *Historia*, vol. 1, pp. 321–5; Sepp, *Il sacro esperimento*, pp. 173–4.
23 Cardiel, *Las misiones*, p. 72.
24 Carbonell de Masy, *Estrategias de desarrollo*, p. 106.
25 Ibid., p. 107.
26 Pastells, *Historia*, vol. 4, p. 92.
27 Caraman, *The Lost Paradise*, p. 139.
28 Furlong, *Misiones*, p. 292.
29 Caraman, *The Lost Paradise*, p. 139.
30 Dobrizhoffer, *Historia*, vol. 1, p. 301.
31 Mörner, *The Political and Economic Activities*.
32 Furlong, *Misiones*, p. 294.
33 Peramás, *La República*, p. 139.
34 Archivum Romanum Societatis Iesu, Paraquariae 12, Rome, fos. 168–76; Hernández, *Organización*, vol. 1, pp. 592–8.
35 Pastells, *Historia*, vol. 6, p. 12.
36 Cardiel, *Las misiones*, p. 93; Branislava Súznik and Miguel Chase-Sardi, *Los indios del Paraguay*, Madrid: Editorial Mapfre, 1995.
37 Archivum Romanum Societatis Iesu, Paraquariae 12.
38 Hernández, *Organización*, vol. 1, pp. 197–8; Peramás, *La República*, p. 63.
39 Cardiel, *Las misiones*, p. 121.
40 Sepp, *Il sacro esperimento*, p. 124; Furlong, *Misiones*, p. 288.
41 Súznik and Chase-Sardi, *Los indios*, pp. 96–7.
42 Hernández, *Organización*, vol. 1, p. 90; vol. 2, pp. 34–6.
43 For a more in-depth study of the demography of the missions, including a presentation of the sources, criticism and evaluation of the data, illustration of the estimates for fertility and mortality measures, and the methods used to obtain them, see Massimo Livi Bacci and Ernesto J. A. Maeder, "Misiones Paraquariae: La demografia di un esperimento," *Popolazione e Storia*, 4, 2004, no. 2. See also Ernesto J. A. Maeder and Alfredo S. C. Bolsi, "La población de las misiones Guaraníes entre 1702–1767," *Estudios Paraguayos*, 1974, no. 2; and, by the same authors, "Evolución y características de la población Guaraní de las misiones jesuíticas, 1671–1767," *Historiografía*, 1976, no. 2, and "La población Guaraní de las misiones Jesuíticas: Evolución y características (1671–1767)," *Cuadernos de Geohistoria Regional*, 1980, no. 4.
44 Furlong, *José Cardiel*, p. 140.
45 Súznik and Chase-Sardi, *Los indios*, p. 140.
46 Pastells, *Historia*, vol. 5, p. 327.

47 Pierre F. J. de Charlevoix, *Historia del Paraguay*, 6 vols, Madrid: Victoriano Suárez, 1913, vol. 4, p. 216.
48 Guillermo Furlong, *Manuel Querini S.J. y sus "Informes al Rey" 1747–1750*, Buenos Aires: Theoria, 1969, pp. 113–14; Pastells, *Historia*, vol. 5, p. 689.
49 Ernesto J. A. Maeder, "Un pueblo de disertores Guaraníes del Iberá en 1736," *Folia Histórica*, 1974, no. 1; Súznik and Chase-Sardi, *Los indios*, p. 95.
50 Hernández, *Organización*, vol. 1, pp. 397–8.
51 Doblas, "Memoria," p. 29.
52 Diego de Alvear, "Relación geográfica e histórica del territorio de las Misiones," in Angelis, *Colección*, vol. 3, p. 707.
53 Roy M. Anderson, "Directly Transmitted Viral and Bacterial Infections of Man," in Anderson, ed., *The Population Dynamics of Infectious Diseases*, New York: Chapman & Hall, 1982.
54 Cecil W. Dixon, *Smallpox*, London: Churchill, 1962; Russell Thornton, Jonathan Warren, and Tim Miller, "Depopulation in the Southeast after 1492," in John W. Verano and Douglas H. Ubelaker, eds, *Disease and Demography in the Americas*, Washington, DC: Smithsonian Institution, 1992.
55 Owens, *A Historical Geography*, p. 240.
56 Sepp, *Il sacro esperimento*, p. 179.
57 Carlos Leonhardt, ed., *Cartas anuas de la Provincia del Paraguay, Chile y Tucumán de la Compañia de Jesús (1615–37)*, 2 vols, Buenos Aires: Iglesia, 1927–9, vol. 1, p. 452, vol. 2, p. 701.
58 Ibid., vol. 1, p. 215.
59 Pastells, *Historia*, vol. 4, p. 56.
60 Maeder and Bolsi, "La población Guaraní," p. 75.
61 Patells, *Historia*, vol. 5, p. 52.
62 *Manuscritos da Coleção de Angelis*, 4: *Jesuitas e bandeirantes no Uruguai (1611–1758)*, Rio de Janeiro: Biblioteca Nacional, 1970, p. 204.
63 Sepp, *Il sacro esperimento*, p. 175.
64 Maeder and Bolsi, "Evolución y características," p. 127.
65 Archivio Congregazione Propaganda Fide (APF), Rome, America Meridionale 2, fo. 32.
66 Caraman, *The Lost Paradise*, pp. 144–5.
67 Pedro Lozano, *Historia de las revoluciones de la provincia del Paraguay (1721–35)*, 1: *Antequera*; 2: *Los Comuneros*, Buenos Aires: Cabaut, 1905, vol. 2, p. 357.
68 D. Muriel, *Historia del Paraguay desde 1747 hasta 1767*, Madrid: Victoriano Suárez, 1918; Furlong, *Misiones*, p. 393; Pastells, *Historia*, vol. 5, p. 62.
69 Peramás, *La República*, p. 65.
70 Furlong, *José Cardiel*, p. 172.
71 Doblas, "Memoria," pp. 33–4.
72 United Nations, *World Population Prospects: The 2002 Revision*, New York, 2003.
73 Maeder and Bolsi, "La población Guaraní," p. 75.
74 Ibid., p. 78.
75 Maeder, *Aproximación*, p. 117.
76 Pastells, *Historia*, p. 276.

Epilog

1 Douglas H. Ubelaker, "Patterns of Disease in Early North American Population," in Michael H. Haines and Richard H. Steckel, eds, *A Population History of North America*, Cambridge: Cambridge University Press, 2000, pp. 53–4; Russell Thornton, "Population History of Native North Americans," ibid., pp. 13, 32.

2 George Lovell and Christopher H. Lutz, "Perfil etnodemográfico de la Audiencia de Guatemala," *Revista de Indias*, 63, 2003, no. 227, p. 163.

3 John Hemming, *Red Gold: The Conquest of Brazilian Indians*, Cambridge: Cambridge University Press, 1978.

4 José Miranda, "La población indigena de México en el siglo XVII," *Historia Mexicana*, 12, 1962, no. 2.

5 Alexander von Humboldt, *Political Essay on the Kingdom of New Spain*, New York: Knopf, 1972, p. 33. According to Humboldt, it was generally held that there were many omissions, so he proposed an alternative estimate of 5.2 million: ibid.

6 In addition to Humboldt, see Gonzalo Aguirre Beltrán, *La población negra de México*, 3rd edn, Mexico City: Fondo de Cultura Económico, 1989, p. 228.

7 Nicolás Sánchez-Albornoz, *La población de América Latina: Desde los tiempos precolombinos al año 2025*, 3rd edn, Madrid: Alianza Editorial, 1994, pp. 97, 105–6; Sánchez-Albornoz, "Migración rural en los Andes, Sipesipe (Cochabamba), 1645," *Revista de Historia Económica*, 1, 1983, no.1.

8 George Lovell, *Conquest and Survival in Colonial Guatemala*, Montreal and Kingston: McGill–Queens University Press, 1992, p. 145.

9 Thornton, "Population History," pp. 24, 32.

10 Humboldt, *Political Essay*, p. 34.

11 Ibid., p. 64.

12 Ibid., p. 65.

13 Charles-Marie de La Condamine, *Voyage sur l'Amazone*, Paris: Maspero, 1981, p. 119.

14 Francis Borgia Steck, ed. and trans., *Motolinia's History of the Indians of New Spain*, Washington, DC: Academy of American Franciscan History, 1951, p. 87.

15 H. B. Johnson, "Portuguese Settlement, 1500–1580," in Leslie Bethell, ed., *Colonial Brazil*, Cambridge: Cambridge University Press, 1987, p. 31; M. Luiza Marcílio, "La población del Brasil colonial," in Leslie Bethell, ed., *Historia de América Latina*, Barcelona: Crítica, 1990, vol. 4, p. 46.

16 John Hemming, "Indian and Frontier," in Bethell, ed., *Colonial Brazil*; Massimo Livi Bacci, "500 anni di demografia brasiliana: una rassegna," *Popolazione e Storia*, 1, 2001, pp. 15–16.

Chronology

1509	Diego, son of Christopher Columbus, arrives as viceroy, but real power is held by the royal officials
1510–12	Dominicans denounce cruel treatment of the Taíno; preaching of Fray Antonio de Montesinos; creation of the Audiencia of Santo Domingo; *Leyes de Burgos*
1513	Vasco Núñez Balboa crosses the isthmus of Panama and arrives at the Pacific coast
1514	The Alburquerque *repartimiento* of Hispaniola counts only 26,000 surviving Indios; thousands of natives seized from the Bahamas die off quickly
1516	Ferdinand, the Catholic, dies; regency of Cardinal Cisneros; influence of Las Casas
1516–19	Three Hieronymite brothers entrusted with government of Hispaniola; smallpox on the island; Taínos reduced to a few thousand
1517–18	First expeditions of Juan de Grijalba and Hernández de Córdoba exploring the coasts of Yucatán and Mexico
1519	Beginning of the reign of Charles V
1519–30	Emigration of Spaniards from Santo Domingo; depopulation of the island and the end of gold production; arrival of slaves from Africa and development of the sugar-cane plantations; Santo Domingo remains an important port and administrative center
1519–20	Expedition of Hernán Cortés from Cuba to Mexico with 600 men and sixteen horses; Cortés advances into the highlands, battles with the Tlaxcaltecs, and forms an alliance with them; Cortés enters into Tenochtitlan; imprisonment and death of Montezuma; expulsion of the Spaniards from the city (*noche triste*); smallpox epidemic
1521	Siege of Tenochtitlan and its fall, August 13
1522–4	Central Mexico is rapidly subdued; Cortés leaves for Honduras; expeditions of Pedro de Alvarado to Guatemala and Cristóbal de Olid to Honduras
1524	Creation of the Council of the Indies, highest political and juridical institution

1524–5	Francisco Pizarro explores the Pacific coast as far as the island of San Juan; death of Huayna Capac and beginning of the conflict between his successors, Huascar and Atahuallpa; arrival in Mexico of the twelve Franciscan friars
1528–30	Misgovernment of the Prima Audiencia in Mexico
1530	Departure of Pizarro from Panama on his third and decisive voyage
1532	November 15: Pizarro with 230 men penetrates into the Incan Empire at Tumbez; encounter at Cajamarca and imprisonment of Atahuallpa (who had defeated Huascar)
1530–5	Government of the Segunda Audiencia in Mexico; arrival of the first viceroy, Antonio de Mendoza
1533	Gold and silver ransom for Atahuallpa; its melting down and distribution among Pizarro's men; execution of Atahuallpa; Pizarro enters Cuzco; coronation of Manco Capac as an Incan puppet
1535	Pizarro founds Los Reyes (Lima); expedition of Diego de Almagro to Chile
1536	Incan rebellion; Spaniards under siege in Cuzco; foundation in Mexico of the College of Santa Cruz in Tlatelolco for the formation of erudite Indios
1537–9	Incan rebellion continues
1538	Pizarro–Almagro conflict; battle of Las Salinas and execution of Almagro
1540	Pizarro killed by followers of Almagro
1542–3	Issuance of the *Leyes Nuevas*; opposition from the colonial *encomenderos* to the limiting of their privileges
1544	Rebellion of Gonzalo Pizarro against the forces loyal to the king; Núñez Vela becomes the first viceroy of Perú; assassination of Manco Capac
1545–6	Silver discovered in Potosí; outbreak of an epidemic, possibly typhus, in Mexico
1548	Gonzalo Pizarro is defeated by the king's envoy, Pedro de la Gasca, and is executed

1549	*Encomenderos* are prohibited from demanding personal service from the Indios in place of the required tribute
1550	Debate between Juan Ginés de Sepúlveda and Bartolomé de las Casas at Valladolid
1551	First council at Lima
1551–64	Government of the second viceroy of New Spain, Luis de Velasco
1552	Publication in Seville of the *Brevísima relación de la destruición de las Indias* by Bartolomé de las Casas
1553–4	Last civil conflict in Perú; uprising and defeat of Hernández Girón
1554	Bartolomé de Medina introduces the mercury amalgamation process in the mines of Pachuca in Mexico
1555	First council in Mexico
1556	Abdication of Charles V; coronation of Philip II
1557	Beginning of the transformation of the tribute system in New Spain, from one that was community based to a uniform poll tax with a reduction in exemptions
1559	Discovery of mercury in Huancavelica; creation of the Audiencia of Charcas (Upper Perú)
1563	Creation of the Audiencia of Quito
1565–70	Attempts to subdue the Incas who have taken refuge in the district of Vilcabamba
1569	Arrival of Francisco de Toledo, fifth viceroy of Perú (he will govern till 1581)
1570	A commission in Lima authorizes forced labor in the mines (*mita*); Toledo begins his *Visita general* (completed in 1573)
1571–3	Forced transfer of the Indios to planned villages
1572	War in Vilcabamba and execution of Tupac Amaru
1574	Toledo reorganizes the mining work; agreement with the owners; authorization of forced labor for the Indios (*mita*); publication of *Geografía y descripción universal de las Indias* by López de Velasco

1576–80	Serious epidemic in Mexico
1579–84	*Relaciones Geográficas*, large study ordered by the Council of the Indies
1586	Serious general epidemic in Perú
1587	Jesuits begin proselytization in Guayrá
1593–1605	New programs of reductions and congregations in Mexico
1604	Creation of the Jesuit Province of Paraguay (present-day Uruguay, Paraguay, Chile, Argentina, plus portions of Bolivia and Brazil)
1609	Founding of the missions begins
1611	The *Ordenanzas de Alfaro* instruct that the Indios pay a tribute directly to the Crown, from which they are temporarily exempted, and so are spared the *encomienda* system
1628	Vázquez de Espinosa publishes his *Compendio y descripción de las Indias occidentales*
1631–2	Raids by Paulist *bandeirantes* force the Jesuits to organize a migration of the Guaraní to the south
1640	(and subsequent years) The missions are established definitively in the Paraná and Uruguay valleys
1641	The mission Guaraní defeat a Paulist expedition in the battle of Mboreré
1645	Official authorization by the viceroy of the use of firearms by the mission Guaraní
1680	Thousands of Guaraní used in the siege of Colonia do Sacramento (present-day Uruguay) to dislodge the Portuguese
1702–4	Guaraní used once again in Colonia do Sacramento
1722–3	First revolt of the *comuneros* of Asunción; the Guaraní aid the royal troops
1732–5	Between 5,000 and 12,000 Guaraní used in the "pacification" of Asunción following the second revolt of the *comuneros*; siege and conquest of Colonia do Sacramento

1756–7   War *de limites*; Guaraní oppose the dismemberment of the missions following the accord between Spain and Portugal regarding the boundary line; battle of Caaybaté and the death on the battlefield of 1,311 Guaraní

1767   Decree for the expulsion of the Jesuits from Spain and its possessions

1768   The Jesuits embark for Europe from Buenos Aires; the missions are taken over by government officials and secular clergy

1768–1815 Progressive decline and dispersion of the mission populations

Glossary

alcalde municipal authority, president of the *cabildo* with judicial functions

alguacil local authority with police functions

apiris Indio employed transporting ore outside the mine (Quechua)

arroba unit of measure equal to 11.5 kilograms

audiencia executive authority with judicial functions; the Mexico City Audiencia had jurisdiction over all of New Spain, those of Quito, Lima, and Charcas over the former Incan Empire.

ayllu group that recognized a common descent, a village (Quechua)

azogue mercury, used in the amalgamation process to extract silver

azoguero entrepreneurs in the silver mines in Perú

balsa raft

bandeira expedition organized for exploration and slave raiding (Brazil)

batea large wooden bowl used to pan gold (Taíno)

batey ball game (Taíno)

boçales slaves born in Africa (Brazil)

bohío circular hut with a conical roof in the Caribbean; by extension a native dwelling (Taíno)

cabecera head village

cabildo municipal council

cacique head of a clan or village, a leader (Taíno)

calpixque stewards (Nahuatl)

cascabel bell

cassava edible root, also called yucca or manioca (Taíno)
chacara field
chía plant with oily seeds (Nahuatl)
choco symptoms of silicosis
chuño dried potatoes, staple food of the Indios of the Andean
   highlands (Quechua)
coa pointed stick for digging and sowing (Taíno)
cocolitzle high mortality, epidemic (Nahuatl)
conuco cultivated field
corregidor Spanish royal administrator of a district with judicial
   functions
corregimiento judicial district of the *corregidor*
crioulos African slaves born in Brazil (Brazil)
cuadrilla squad, group
cuatequil forced labor, work gang (Nahuatl)
curaca head of a clan or village, a leader, like a *cacique* (Quechua)

demora work period at the mines (six, eight, or ten months)
desagüe draining canal

encomendero feudal lord, holder of an *encomienda*, that is jurisdiction over a native population, including the right to receive
   tribute
encomienda land and population assigned to a feudal lord who
   receives tribute
entrada expedition for exploration and conquest
estancia large holding, ranch, or plantation

faisqueiro gold prospector (Brazil)
fánega unit of measure equal to 55.5 liters
forastero non-native Indio in a district, not subject to tribute and
   not holding any property rights (Perú)

guayabo fruit tree (Taíno)

huautli type of beet (Nahuatl)
hutía small mammal resembling a guinea pig

indios de mese Indios available for service for a period of one
   month (Potosí)

indios de plaza Indios available for service for a short period (Potosí)

indios mingados mining Indios hired as wage laborers

legua league, equal to 5.57 kilometers

Leyenda Negra "Black Legend" of the real or presumed atrocities committed by the conquistadors

Leyes de Burgos set of norms regulating the treatment of Indios issued at Burgos in 1512

Leyes Nuevas set of norms issued in 1542 that revised the *Leyes de Burgos* to improve the situation of the Indios and limit the *encomienda*

macehuales lower class (Nahuatl)

maguey agave; *maguey* is a source of fiber and used to make *pulque*, an alcoholic beverage (Nahuatl)

mal de bubas a form of syphilis, mild for the natives, serious for the Spaniards

mal de niguas form of scabies

mayeques lower class in the service of a noble, not subject to tribute (Nahuatl)

mita forced labor, work gangs, with a system of rotation (Quechua)

mita gruesca all those engaged in forced labor, even if not on rotation

mitayo Indian forced laborer, engaged in the *mita*

mitimaes colonies established by the Inca in recently conquered territories; presidios (Quechua)

montón small mound of earth used for growing cassava in the Caribbean

naboría servant in the home of a *cacique* or Spanish lord, detached from the community (Taíno)

Nahuatl language prevalent in central Mexico

natural originating in a place

nitayno important person (Taíno)

nopal type of edible cactus

oidor member of an *audiencia* who hears cases

originario an Indio resident in his place of origin (as opposed to a *forastero*) (Perú)

paperas mumps
parcialidad part of a village or community
puna Peruvian highlands and Bolivian steppes

quinoa grain cultivated at high altitudes
quinto quota of founded gold claimed by the Crown
quipu colored cords with knots for registration and counting
(Quechua)

reducción congregation of outlying Indios in planned villages
repartimiento assigning of Indios to Spanish lords, *encomenderos*
revisita new *visita* with inspection, counts, census
romadizio respiratory infection

sarampión measles
senzala large rectangular house for slaves with separate quarters
for men and women (Brazil)

tabardete exanthematic disease, typhus
tambo road-side postal station and warehouse in the Incan
Empire
tamemes porter (Nahuatl)

vaqueria large spaces for raising of feral cattle
vecino resident family; family head; often coincident with
tributary
verruga peruana Carrion's Disease or bartonellosis, transmitted
by sand flies
visita inspection with count or census of houses, families, and
tributaries for fiscal purposes

yanacona servant in Spanish homes or farms, often exempt from
tribute (Perú)
yerba mate bush whose dried leaves are used to make a popular
beverage (Paraguay, Uruguay, Argentina)

zemi Taíno divinity in Hispaniola (Taíno)

Note on Illustrations

The black and white illustrations at the beginning and end of each chapter are taken from Guamán Poma de Ayala, *El primer Nueva corónica y buen gobierno*, ed. John V. Murra and Rolena Adorno, Mexico City: Siglo ventiuno, 1992. The original can be found in the Royal Library in Copenhagen, GKS 2232, 4°. The work was sent by the author to Spain in 1615 or 1616 as part of an appeal to Philip III. The identity of the author and above all his origins and biography remain vague. It was first published in facsimile in 1936. The manuscript includes 398 sketches which represent personages from the Incan dynasties, agricultural work, the stages of life, the events of the Conquest, colonial personages (viceroys, officials, prelates, lords, simple Indios), episodes of the oppression of the Indios at the hands of the Spaniards, and the author's voyages in Perú. Each sketch has numerous captions. The illustrations at the beginnings of the chapters are: preface: "The author walking"; chapter 1: "Columbus's fleet"; chapter 2: "*Encomendero* carried on a litter"; chapter 3: "Punishment"; chapter 4: "City of Huancavelica and the mercury mines"; chapter 5: "Boy hunting"; chapter 6: "Antonio de Mendoza, first viceroy of Mexico"; chapter 7: "Atahuallpa, Pizarro, and Benalcazar at Cajamarca"; chapter 8: "The city of Paraguay"; epilog: "Baby crawling."

The insert between pages 40 and 41 includes the twelve months of the year and the cycles of agricultural labor: the agricultural techniques, tools, and plants and animals are those of the pre-Conquest Incan world. Note in particular the irrigation system depicted in the month of November.

The first eight pages of color reproductions between pages 168 and 169 are taken from the so-called Florentine Codex, the original of which can be found at the Biblioteca Mediceo-Laurenziana in Florence (MS Mediceo-Palatino 218–20). They constitute a part of the work of Fray Bernardino de Sahagún, *Historia general de las cosas de Nueva España* (facsimile edn, Florence: Giunti, 1996). Sahagún, born in 1499 or 1500 in Sahagún, Spain, died in Mexico City in 1590. He was a Franciscan and arrived in Mexico in 1529; from 1539 he was part of the College of Santa Cruz de Tlatelolco, where he taught young Mexican nobles. For decades he gathered ethnographic and historical information and material transcribed from interviews with native informants; transcription of the manuscript took place in 1576–7. The work is divided into twelve books. The first eleven deal with religion and the society of the ancient Aztecs; the last deals with the events of the Conquest and includes a series of pictograms by Mexican artists. The first six books deal with the gods and their origins, ceremonies, philosophy, and religion; the seventh with the sun, moon, and stars; the eighth with kings and lords; the ninth with merchants; the tenth and the eleventh with the people and their lives. The text, arranged in two columns, is in Castilian and Nahuatl. One can see there scenes of maize farming, various sorts of houses, and some examples of fabrics, while the last page includes a number of individuals stricken with smallpox.

The later pages of color reproductions between pages 168 and 169 are taken from the Mendoza Codex, the original of which is held at Oxford's Bodleian Library (facsimile edn: Berkeley: University of California Press, 1992). Reproduced in it, among other things, is the so-called *Matricula de Tributos*, a codex on sixteen sheets of native paper, kept in the Museo Nacional de Antropología in Mexico City. The *Matricula* includes pictograms which give the names of provinces subject to tribute, before the arrival of the Spaniards, and the type and amount of tribute required. The codex was compiled following the orders of the first viceroy, Mendoza, for Charles V, but never made it to Spain because the ship on which it traveled was captured by French pirates. It was compiled in 1541 by local artists under the supervision of religious and contains accounts of the conquests of the Aztec kings, the tributes paid by the subjugated peoples, and a series of illustrations relating to daily life, rituals, and practices from birth to death. The first series of figures relates to tributes owed by villages, including fabrics and cloaks, feathers, jaguar pelts, warriors' outfits, precious stones, and cacao. The second series includes images of family life: education of children, advice, punishments, services, and other activities.

Index

Page references for the tables and figures are in *italics*